Proceedings of the

Third Joint Ada® Europe/Ada TEC Conference

®Ada is a registered trademark of the
Ada Joint Program Office - US Government

Proceedings of the Third Joint Ada Europe/Ada TEC Conference

Brussels, 26 - 28 June 1984

Industrial Implications of Ada and
Ada Programming Support Environment

Edited by J. Teller
Siemens AG, Munich
West Germany

Published on behalf of
the Commission of the European Communities by

CAMBRIDGE UNIVERSITY PRESS

Cambridge
London   New York   New Rochelle
Melbourne   Sydney

Published by the Press Syndicate of the University of Cambridge
The Pitt Building, Trumpington Street, Cambridge CB2 1RP
32 East 57th Street, New York, NY 10022, USA
10 Stamford Road, Oakleigh, Melbourne 3166, Australia

© ECSC, EEC, EAEC, Brussels and Luxembourg 1984

First published 1984

Printed in Great Britain at the University Press, Cambridge

Library of Congress catalogue card number: 84 - 45680

British Library cataloguing in publication data
Joint ADA Europe/ADA TEC Conference
  (3rd : 1984 : Brussels)
  The 3rd Joint ADA Europe/ADA TEC Conference,
  Brussels, 26-28 June 1984 : industrial
  implications of ADA and ADA programming
  support environment : proceedings.
  1. Industry - Data processing
  I. Title   II. Teller, J.
  338'.06   HD45.2

ISBN 0 521 30102 5

LEGAL NOTICE

Neither the Commission of the European Communities
nor any person acting on behalf of the Commission
is responsible for the use which might be made of
the following information

Contents

Foreword ix

PART I   ADA - INDUSTRIAL EXPERIENCES

Implementation reports
- The European Ada Compiler Project   E. Morel   3
- The DDC Ada Compiler System   E. Meiling   6
- The Karlsruhe Ada System   G. Persch   7

Evaluation of Commercially Available Retargetable and Rehostable Ada Systems   A. Ardo & L. Philipson   9

The Introduction of Ada in the Aerospace Industry   B. Labreuille & M. Heitz   19

Ada as a Programming Language for a Telematic Services Project   O. Maurel C. Bonnet   31

The Ada "Program Library": its Meaning and its Implementation in an Existing Generic Environment in Industry   K. Ripkin   43

Discrete Event Modelling in Ada: Implementation and Application   V.A. Downes & R. Tellaeche Bosch   53

Contents

PART II ADA - PROGRAMMING SUPPORT ENVIRONMENTS

A Minimal APSE	J.K. Romanski	67
A Revised STONEMAN for Distributed APSE	J.P. Goodwin	77
Co-operating CHILL and Ada Compiler Systems	E. Meiling & S.U. Palm	91
APSE Tools - Rolm's Experience	J.K. Elliott D.M. Klein & J.S. Williams	103
Toward an Interactive Development Environment for Ada	A.G. Duncan	113

PART III ADA - ASPECTS OF IMPLEMENATATION

Ada and Reliability	J.C.D. Nissen	119
Converting to Ada Packages	B.A. Wichman & J.G.J. Meijerink	131
Towards a Systematic and Safe Programmation of Exception Handling in Ada	M. Bidoit M.-C. Gaudel & G. Guiho	141
Guidelines for the Design of Large Molecular Scientific Libraries in Ada	G.T. Symm & J. Kok	153
Numeric Types in Ada - Some of Their Less Obvious Features	R.P. Wehrum	165
Interfacing Ada to FORTRAN	C.G. van der Laan	179

Contents

PART IV ADA - EDUCATION NEEDS

The Dependence of Ada Education on the Support Environment	I.H. Richmond	193
Some Educational Principles Relating to the Teaching and Use of Ada	M. Mac an Airchinnigh	201
A Training Concept for the Cost-Effective Development of Reliable Software Using the Programming Language Ada	H. Hummel M. Nast & E. Uthke	211
Needs in Ada Education: Experiences and Observations	M.B. Feldman	227

PART V ADA AND SOFTWARE ENGINEERING METHODOLOGY

A MASCOT Approach Using Ada	A.P. Hill & J.K. Slape	241
Limits on the Use of Ada for Specifications	I.C. Pyle	251
ASPHODEL - an Ada Compatible Specification and Design Language	A.D. Hill	261
Experience with an Object Oriented Method of Software Design	S.B. Mickel	271
Formal Specification Techniques for Parallel and Distributed Systems	Ada Europe WG on Formal Methods for Specification and Development (Read by H. Barringer)	281
AdaKOM - Electronic Mail and Conferencing Facility for the Ada Community	A. Patel & M.W. Rogers	297

Contents viii

The 1985 "Ada in Use" Conference   M.W. Rogers   301

List of Ada Europe Officers and Working Groups   304

Conference Registrations and Attendees   305

Foreword

This was the third conference in a series that continues to attract capacity audiences of around 200, whether "free" or fee paying. It was organised by the officers of Ada-Europe and the Commission of the European Communities Information Technology and Telecommunications Task Force (ITTTF), in collaboration with AdaTEC, the relevant ACM/SIGPLAN Technical Committee across the Atlantic.

Attendance at the first venue outside of the Commission Conference Centre was widely representative of Industry, Academia and Public Administrations, with no less than 16 countries represented - of which one half were encouragingly beyond the borders of the European Economic Community.

Apart from 3 days intensive conference, the usual additional meetings made for a week with no less than 20 meetings taking place - ranging from small intense working groups on very specific issues to the Group of ISO Language Experts under the guidance of Robert F. Mathis, Director of AJPO; to many Ada Europe meetings where Observers were heavy on the ground.

Geared at preparing the software industry for the introduction of Ada into industrial practices, the conference met under the theme "Industrial Implications of Ada and Programming Support Environments". Of the wide range of papers submitted under the facets of this directional theme, about 30 were selected for presentation in a number of plenaries and parallel sessions, to enable attendees to follow a line of interest with maximum follow through.

Foreword

Papers submitted afterwards for publishing are grouped into a number of topics, reflecting the selection available:

Ada - Industrial Experiences
Ada - Programming Support Environments
Ada - Aspects of Implementations
Ada - Educational Needs
Ada - Software Engineering Methodology

Industrial experiences range from Implementors reporting on their work from a marketing point of view, to aspects of introducing Ada within an Industry, and those features that could be of major significance. The APSE section deals with co-hosting other languages, tools, what an APSE, MAPSE etc. should be, and how it could be distributed.

Implementation aspects report on some of the finer detail of Ada features, and how their use can enhance safe, reliable, cost effective software production, while not ignoring some possible pitfalls!
Ada Education is an area that is not ignored either, with a set of papers on real life experiences, and concepts that could be used to teach Ada and Software Engineering more effectively.

Lastly, the impact of Ada on Industrial Software Methodology is examined from a number of angles - e.g. as a specification, design language.

Emphasis throughout is on

- the exploitation of innovative features of the language,
- ease of transition and reuse of existing libraries of software,
- conceptual basis on how these aspects of Ada may be taught and utilised and how broader issues of Software Engineering may thus be promulgated.

Ada's quality of being highly method-oriented is in the centre of contributions proposing the use of Ada for the Industrial Context.

Foreword

These proceedings provide the State-of-the-art practitioner with the latest update to the current status of the introduction of Ada into industry in Europe and the US. They highlight the insights that Ada has motivated in Software Engineering in recent times.

Combined with new support activities under the Communities Multiannual Dataprocessing Programme extension approved by the Member States Council on 28 February 1984, and the recent elevation of AdaTEC to the status of a SIG (Special Interest Group of ACM), to SIGAda for the next meeting in Paris in May 1985, the future of Ada seems healthily secure. With a spate of announcements for validation at the conference, the number of validated compilers will double by year end, for far more generally available hardware, and then the use of Ada and Ada-based Software Engineering will gather rapid momentum.

K. Ripken, Chairman, Ada Europe
J. Teller, Editor, Proceedings
M. Rogers, CEC

PART I. ADA - INDUSTRIAL EXPERIENCES

IMPLEMENTATION REPORT
THE EUROPEAN ADA COMPILER PROJECT
E. MOREL
ALSYS

1. Introduction

The European Ada Root Compiler has been especially designed and implemented to be highly portable and adaptable to a wide set of machines ranging from micro-computers (e.g. 8086 based) to large machines. The qualities of the design have already been proved by porting the root to three different hosts, and retargeting it for four different architectures (including two main frames and two micro-processors).

Moreover, the EACP effort has been to produce a root for production quality Ada compilers as opposed to prototype Ada compilers developed by other companies. At all stages of the design and implementation, all solutions leading to an unacceptable loss of efficiency have been systematically rejected. Quality of object code has been a major concern and, although a good quality is achieved by the "normal" compilation process, it has led to the introduction of two optional phases of optimizations. Additionally, the level of the intermediate code generated by the Root has been carefully studied: the P_code-like approach has been rejected as it is not optimizable and its levl is too low; the DIANA-like approach has been rejected because its too high level implies an unnecessary burden on all code generators. Finally, the EACP Root can accept large programs and this is shown by the fact that it can bootstrap itself, i.e. compile a program of more than 100 000 lines with hundreds of modules.

The Root is organized as a multipass process which transforms the Ada source:

- into a high level intermediate representation, during the Analyzer phase,
- then into a low level intermediate representation suitable for

code generators or interceptors, during the Expander phase. The Analyzer is mainly concerned with the static semantic, while the Expander produces an image of the source program where all the dynamic semantic is explicit.

Analyzer

The Analyzer performs all the syntactic and the semantic analysis on the source program and produces as output:
- the Abstract Intermediate Language (or AIL) which is a DIANA-like structured tree, and
- the High Level Symbol Table (or HLST) which is a collection of information describing the properties of all the objects (implicit or explicit) referenced by the program.

Expander

The Expander transforms the AIL + HLST representation into a more detailed representation of the source program. Its outputs are:
- the Code Generator Intermediate Language (or CGIL) which is a tree-structured representation, and
- the Code Generator Symbol Table (or CGST) which is a compact representation of the properties associated to all the objects referenced in the CGIL.

The CGIL representation of a program expresses the complete semantic of the program and provides an executable representation of the source: all the operations and data hidden at the source level but necessary for the execution are made explicit. For example, all calls to Run-Time routines for synchronization of tasks expressed; type descriptors appear as objects in the CGST and are referenced as normal objects whenever needed in the CGIL. Additionally, all operations for data access (use of a display, of a static link, of a dope, and so on) are explicit. This allows the code generators to be drastically simpler and smaller than in the approach starting from a DIANA-like tree since the work done once in the Root avoids performing a much more important amount of work normally devoted to all code generators.

2. Status

The EACP Root is fully written in Ada and contains about 100 000 Ada lines of code. Validation of the Root against ACVC 1.4 is going on. The Root is currently operational on VAX/VMS, Bull DPS7 and Siemens 7760. Transportation of the Root on Multics is planned.

The Root is currently used within ALSYS to produce self-hosted Ada compilers for 68000/UNIX and 8086/CPM based machines. Validation of such compilers is planned for the end of 1984 (for the 68000) and the beginning of 1985 (for the 8086).

A licence of the source code of the Root can be obtained from ALSYS, and several major US computer manufacturers are currently negotiating contracts with ALSYS to acquire such licences to produce Ada compilers for their own product lines.

IMPLEMENTATION REPORT
THE DDC ADA COMPILER SYSTEM
E. MEILING
DANSK DATAMATIK CENTRE
LUNDTOFTEVEJ 1C, DK-2800 LYNGBY, DENMARK

Dansk Datamatik Centre has developed a portable Ada compiler and various support tools. The DDC Ada Compiler System has been implemented for a number of host and target computers and operating systems. Further, the basic components are available to OEM customers who would want to develop new code generators and/or integrate the compiler into new host environments.

The compiler itself is a further development of a compiler constructed by DDC as a part of the Portable Ada Programming System (PAPS) project. The compiler was developed with portability as a major design parameter. The initial versions were for 16-bit minicomputers, but the compiler has been ported to 16-bit minis as well as to 32-bit computers. Hence the portability has been proven.

The DDC Ada compiler system is available for VAX/VMS end-users from 31 July 1984. For OEM retargeting/rehosting the front end and all interface specifications are available now. Certification is expected in July 1984 on ACVC test suite release 1.4 leading to validation in the third quarter of 1984. The compiler and the support tools were demonstrated during the Ada Europe/Ada TEC conference in Brussels, June 1984. The available VAX/VMS end-user components are:

- compiler, linker, run-time system
- program library manager
- program library utilities
- Ada-related editor version
- symbolic debugger (available fourth quarter of 1984)

Besides the VAX/VMS Ada compiler, the following compiler versions are under development: Olivetti M40 (host and target); NOKIA MPS-10 (host and target); Honeywell DPS6 (host and target); and Christian Rovsing CR80/DAMOS (host and target). It is planned to develop a compiler version having VAX/UNIX as host and target computer, as well as compiler versions hosted on a VAX having the Intel 8086 family land other microprocessor families as targets.

IMPLEMENTATION REPORT
THE KARLSRUHE ADA SYSTEM
GUIDO PERSCH
GMD FORSCHUNGSSTELLE KARLSRUHE
C/O FZI UNIVERSITÄT KARLSRUHE
POSTFACH 6380, D-7500 KARLSRUHE 1,
FEDERAL REPUBLIC OF GERMANY

The Karlsruhe Ada System is a co-operative effort of GMD (Gesellschaft für Mathematik und Datenverarbeitung) Research Laboratory Karlsruhe and SYSTEAM KG Dr Winterstein, Karlsruhe. Work was started in 1979 at the University of Karlsruhe producing successive versions of Ada on a Siemens 7000 computer running under BS2000. In 1984 the compiler was adapted by GMD and SYSTEAM to ANSI-Ada. It will be validated with ACVC 1.4 in summer 1984. The host/target for GMD is Siemens 7000/BS2000, for SYSTEAM it is VAX/VMS. There are further host/targets under development by GMD and SYSTEAM, e.g. a Motorola 68000/UNIX system. The Karlsruhe Ada system is also used by other companies, e.g. SDL (System Designers Limited, UK) for retargeting to MIL-STD-1750A.

The compiler is decomposed in three parts: front end, middle end, and back end. The front end uses an LALR(1) parser for syntax analysis and an attribute grammar for semantic analysis to produce the intermediate language DIANA. It is supported by a library management system called SEPAREE.

The middle end transforms DIANA with expanded generic instantiations into AIM by an attribute grammar with attribute-driven tree construction. The DIANA tree reflecting the Ada source program structure is shaped into a form which is suitable for code generation with the help of DIANA attributes and attributes computed by the middle end.

The intermediate language AIM represents Ada programs by a sequence of basic blocks where each block consists of a sequence of AIM statements. Aim statements are essentially expression trees. The back end allocates the objects of the program and generates machine code. The machine code selection is automatically generated by CGSS, the Code Generator Synthesis System. Input to this system is a description of the target machine by AIM operators. With the aid of this system, the compiler can be retargeted in 1 to 3 man years.

Several tools have been constructed around the compiler; most of them are based on DIANA. They use the semantic information stored in DIANA attributes and the source recreatibility of DIANA to write language-oriented tools. For static program analysis there are tools for finding non-initialized variables, cross-reference listing generators over module boundaries, name expanders for documentation, and a control flow analyzer over module boundaries.

The dynamic program analysis tool (debugger) starts from a run-time image and can answer questions about the procedure/task hierarchy and the program text. The inspection of data will be added in 1985.

The Library User System (LUSY) enables inspection and manipulation of program libraries and provides an Ada binder with sophisticated help to find a valid elaboration order.

The Karlsruhe Ada System is partially financed by the Bundesamt für Wehrtechnik unde Beschaffung (the West German Ministry of Defence) and is the reference compiler with the SPERBER environment,

Evaluation of commercially available retargetable and rehostable Ada systems

A. Ardö
Department of Computer Engineering, University of Lund
P.O. Box 725, S-220 07 Lund, Sweden

L. Philipson
Department of Computer Engineering, University of Lund
P.O. Box 725, S-220 07 Lund, Sweden

Abstract. A request for proposals for portable and retargetable Ada systems hosted on VAX/VMS was sent out. The request contained an Ada system specification and a questionnaire. Answers from 9 possible vendors were received. Three answers were complete enough to permit further evaluation. These systems are described in detail. Evaluation of compilers must be done using several criteria apart from compiler validation.

1 Background

As part of a research project on design principles for tightly coupled multiprocessor computers, an experimental multiprocessor system has been designed (Philipson 1984). One of the ideas behind this system is to permit experiments on different levels, ranging from VLSI implementation to program behaviour. For this reason a high level parallel language has to be implemented with the experimental architecture as target. Based on earlier studies Ada has been chosen as the first candidate for this language (Ardö 1983; Ardö 1984; Jones & Ardö 1982).

In order to minimize our work it was decided to buy a retargetable and portable Ada system hosted on VAX/VMS. The compiler has to be retargetable i.e. it must be possible to substitute the code generator for another code generator with our multiprocessor computer as target. It is desirable that the compiler also is portable to make it possible, in a later stage, to port the whole Ada system to the multiprocessor.

2 Request for proposal

A request for proposals for a portable and retargetable Ada system hosted on VAX/VMS was sent out to 16 possible vendors.

A detailed specification of the desired Ada system and a questionnaire covering features of special interest was included in the request. The following sections contain a summary of the specification.

Evaluation of Ada systems 10

2.1 Compiler

The compiler must accept the ANSI standard Ada as defined in ANSI/MIL-STD-1815A.

There must exist a version of the compiler with VAX/VMS as host and target.

Since the intention is to retarget the compiler, it is essential that the interface between the front-end and the back-end is clean and well defined. The intermediate language used shall not be so low level that all decisions about the run-time data structures etc are already made.

Decisions about run-time data structures, memory management and scheduling shall be deferred to the back-end. It is desirable that there is some kind of representation for pragmas in the intermediate language.

In order to make evaluation possible the intermediate language used as interface between the front-end and back-end shall be described in detail. Also the data generated by the front-end for use by the back-end shall be described in detail as to structure and format.

2.2 Interfaces

The dependences and interfaces between the different parts of the system is of special importance in this project. Therefore the interface between the key components (in the context of retargeting the compiler) in the system shall be described. If any of these components are dependent on some other part of the system this dependency must be described as well. The interfaces compiler - linker, compiler - operating system and executable code - run-time system are considered being the most important interfaces.

2.3 Portability

For the Ada system to be portable it must be delivered in a format that makes porting possible (source or intermediate language). Furthermore the interface to the host operating system must be clean and well defined. Also the dependence on operating system functions by the executable program and the run-time system must be clearly defined. An elaboration on possible ways to port the Ada system, problems likely to occur etc are invited.

2.4 Environment

A clear description of how the Ada environment is structured and used in the Ada system shall be supplied. This shall include such things as which tools are available, the structure of the database, how the library functions interfaces with the rest of the system, the dependence among each other for the various tools and databases needed by the system.

2.5 Performance

The compilation shall be fast enough to be used in a production environment (compilation speed of at least 200 lpm etc).

The generated intermediate code shall be of good quality and efficient with good code optimization carried out. The optimization must be controllable so that exact identification between source code and intermediate code can be made possible.

3 Received answers

We received answers (in one way or another) from 9 of the 16 vendors we asked. The answers varied from complete proposals to phone calls. We were surprised to find that many of the vendors were not interested in selling portable Ada compilers. They considered the internals of their compilers (even the specification of the intermediate languages) as confidential.

Dansk Datamatik Center, Lyngby, Denmark sent a complete proposal for their Ada system. The proposal was very detailed and included system components like debugger etc.

Digital Equipment Corporation, Maynard, Massachusetts, USA indicated, in a phone conversation, that they are committed to make Ada available on VAX but presently pointed prospective customers to TeleSoft.

Gensoft, Pittsburgh, Pennsylvania, USA indicated in a phone conversation that they were not interested to sell a rehostable/retargetable compiler on the terms stated in our request.

Irvine Computer Sciences Corporation, Irvine, California, USA answered that their product did not meet our specification yet.

SPL, Stockholm, Sweden and Abingdon, England offered their VAX/VMS port of the Ada compiler originally developed by the University of York. Unfortunately they could not supply the necessary information on the intermediate code they use as well as other crucial details of how tasking is handled. This made further evaluation impossible.

Systeam, Karlsruhe, Germany sent a partial proposal for their VAX/VMS version of the Karlsruhe Ada compiler.

TeleLOGIC, Nynäshamn, Sweden markets the TeleSoft front end with their own VAX/VMS back end. They had no time to make a complete proposal but they indicated that they were willing to cooperate with us on developing a back-end and they made information available to make evaluation of their TeleSoft Ada system possible.

TeleSoft, San Diego, California, USA indicated in a phone call that they had no time to answer our request for a proposal due to more urgent work on their new compiler.

US Army CECOM, Washington, USA sent the following answer: "The Ada Language System (ALS) is being released only to U.S. Industry and to foreign governments within NATO and SEATO for the sole purpose of rehosting and/or retargeting, which will result in a quality production product. We therefore cannot release the interim Ada Language System to you at this time."

4 Evaluation

After screening the answers, three serious candidates remained, namely Dansk Datamatik Center, Systeam and TeleLOGIC. These three companies had all declared themselves willing to supply us with enough information to make evaluation possible.

All of these three compilers can be used for retargeting and rehosting. All compilers were said to be designed for portability. They all have appropriate intermediate languages to start retargeting from.

At the time of the evaluation none of the vendors, however, had a reasonably complete compiler to sell, but all aimed for validation during the first half of 1984.

We visisted all three companies during November and December 1983 in order to get more detailed information for the final evaluation. They were all very cooperative but none of them had a reasonably well working compiler with tasking to show us. All information about the three compilers, summarized below, is based on information available at that time.

4.1 Dansk Datamatik Center (DDC)

The Ada compiler developed by DDC is part of the effort by the Commission of the European Community known as the Portable Ada Programming System. This project is carried out by three partners, Dansk Datamatik Center, Christian Rovsing (both in Denmark) and Olivetti (Italy).

The compiler consists of a front-end and a back-end (Meiling & Pedersen 1983). The front-end has six passes and generates an intermediate language called IML7 (Clemmensen & Pedersen 1983a). The front-end is target-independent except for some target-dependent constants. The back-end transforms IML7 into Abstract A-code (AA-code) which is a sequential intermediate language (Clemmensen & Pedersen 1983b). This transformation includes the main code generation task as well as memory allocation.

In the first phase, the following four computers will be used as targets: the A-machine (firmware emulation on CR80 by Christian Rovsing), VAX/VMS (DDC), the Finnish NOKIA MPS 10 and the Olivetti M40 (a Z8000 based computer).

Intermediate languages. **IML7** is a high level tree structured intermediate language which contains most of the structural information of the original Ada program. There are predicates attached to the nodes of IML7. These predicates are truth values yielding information about certain properties of the node (such as no bound checks necessary, static bounds, etc). The predicates are used to guide the the code generation.

In IML7 no memory allocation is done. Also all Ada tasking constructs are available.

Abstract A-code is a sequential intermediate language suited for code generation for a stack machine. Most instructions use implicit operands taken from the stack. AA-code is an abstraction of A-code (which is the instruction set of the A-machine (Ibsen et al 1982)). The abstraction is aimed at making the instruction set more orthogonal and maintaining flow and structural information from the Ada source. This makes code generation easier.

Tasking is still present in AA-code in constructs closely corresponding to the Ada constructs. For example there are tasking instructions like Create_task, Abort_task, Call_entry_timed etc. Addresses are represented as base-offset pairs in the usual sense.

Retargeting can be done on several levels. It is possible to use both IML7 and AA-code as well as A-code. Using IML7 as start for code generation allows the implementor total control over the code to generate. This implies construction of a new code generator which is a substantial task because of the high level of IML7. On the other hand the code generator can be targeted specifically towards the target machine and an optimal production quality code generator can be made.

AA-code can be used as basis to generate native code for a wide range of computers. The main code generation task is already performed by the IML7 to AA-code transformation.

Evaluation of Ada systems

Emulation of the A-machine can be done (in software or firmware) with a limited amount of work.

Documentation. DDC has extensive and good documentation of their product. This documentation includes specification of the various intermediate languages used as well as descriptions of the run-time system and the virtual machine they are using.

4.2 Systeam

This compiler (Winterstein 1983) is developed from the Ada 80 compiler developed at University of Karlsruhe (a complete Ada 80 compiler running on a Siemens computer). The compiler generation is automated to a large extent. The main tools used for generating the compiler are a parser generator (PGS), a generator for attribute grammars (GAG) and a code-generator generator system (CGSS).

The compiler consists of three passes a front-end, a middle-end and a back-end. The front-end generates DIANA. The middle-end transforms DIANA into AIM which is a low level intermediate language. The back-end (Jansohn & Landwehr 1983) generates object code from AIM. Most of this compiler is automatically generated from attribute grammars describing the Ada to DIANA to AIM transformations.

Tasking is resolved completely in the middle-end. This is done by translating Ada tasking constructs into sequential Ada with some calls to the run-time system. All support for parallelism is contained in the run-time system. Tasks are implemented as coroutines.

Intermediate languages. DIANA is a high level tree structured intermediate language for representing Ada programs, developed jointly by groups at University of Karlsruhe and Carnegie-Mellon University (Goos & Wulf 1981). DIANA is not specially tailored for code generation purposes. It was designed as an interface for tools -- formatters, language oriented editors etc. DIANA is neutral with respect to memory allocation and tasking.

AIM (Abstract Intermediate Machine) is a general low level intermediate language. Roughly speaking AIM is a sequence of basic blocks, which contains tree structured statements. The tree structure can be flattened out with the aid of a tree flattener which perform a preorder walk. This flattened version of AIM is used as input to the automatically generated code generator.

Tasking is resolved in the middle end, i.e. before AIM is generated. This has the consequence that AIM does not contain any constructs for parallelism or tasking.

Retargeting can be done either at the DIANA level or the AIM level. Using DIANA as basis for retargeting requires the construction of a totally new code generator which is a substantial task. On the other hand the implementor has complete freedom to generate code for a specific target architecture. Retargeting at the AIM level is easier (Jansohn & Landwehr 1983). This is done using Systeam's automatic code generator generator. The code-generator generator system requires a formal description of the target machine. Doing this formal description is still a nontrivial task (1-6 man months).

Documentation. Systeam has good documentation of their product both in form of technical reports from University of Karlsruhe and documents produced at Systeam.

4.3 TeleLOGIC

TeleLOGIC develops a VAX back-end for the TeleSoft Ada compiler. They proved to be very cooperative, but they are restricted by their contract with TeleSoft with respect to the information they could disclose.

The TeleSoft Ada compiler consists of a front-end, a middle pass and a back-end. The front-end and middle pass are made by TeleSoft and the back-end for VAX by TeleLOGIC. The front-end generates a high level intermediate language called High Form (HF). The middle pass generates a tree structured intermediate language called Low Form (LF) from HF. In the back-end LF is transformed into Sequential Low Form (SLF) from which code generation is done.

Tasking is resolved in the middle pass by transforming the tasking constructs into calls to the run-time system.

Intermediate languages. **High Form** is a DIANA like tree structured high level intermediate language with all tasking constructs present.

Low Form is generated from HF in the middle pass which also resolves all tasking constructs. LF is target independent and memory allocation is not done yet. LF contains no tasking constructs whatsoever. All support for parallelism is contained in the run-time system. SLF is a sequential low level intermediate language, similar to p-code. Thus SLF is aimed towards a stack machine. Memory allocation is done together with the transformation from LF to SLF. Addresses are represented as normal base - offset pairs.

Retargeting can be done at the HF level, the LF level or at the SLF level. Using HF to start code generation from requires an effort comparable to using DIANA or IML7. Neither LF nor SLF contains any constructs for parallelism or tasking since tasking is resolved in the middle pass. Retargeting based on various forms of intermediate languages have been done for several different computers.

Documentation. The documentation that was made available to us consisted of program listings and internal documents.

5 Comments on Ada compiler validation

The official validation procedure for Ada compilers is very ambitious in order to maintain the high level of standardization that was one of the the primary objectives for developing Ada. By compiling and running a large number of sample programs many details of the Ada language reference manual are tested (Goodenough 1981). One must be aware of the fact that validation is no guarantee for correctness or efficiency.

Even theoretically it is not possible to guarantee that a compiler is correct after having correctly compiled and executed only a finite number of programs. To invalidate a compiler, however, takes only one correct program that the compiler can not handle (Ardö & Philipson 1984).

There is always the possibility with an official validation that compilers will be adapted specifically to pass the validation tests. In our opinion there is reason to believe that the first few compilers to be validated will suffer from this effect, at least to some degree. After some experience in the field this will most probably not be so much of a problem.

There are other important aspects of compilers that the validation does not attempt to cover, namely performance and user interface. A compiler can have severe performance limitations and still be validated. Examples of such performance limitations in validated compilers include very slow compilation speed, very long execution times, memory inefficiency and limitations of the size of compilation units.

In summary this means that validation has very little to do with the actual usefulness of a complete Ada system.

6 Conclusions

General. Some general conclusions can be drawn regarding the present situation for Ada compilers.

It is actually too early to buy a complete and portable Ada system. The systems available today are either too immature or not portable or both incomplete and not portable.

Obviously it is very hard to make a production quality Ada system. It is not clear if the people involved in defining Ada were aware of all the aspects. A realistic view is that we will have to wait at least another year or two before any good, complete and portable production quality Ada compilers will be commercially available.

Another obvious remark is that the schedules for most Ada compiler projects are far too optimistic. In this respect not much has changed since the pioneering days of FORTRAN in the mid fifties. John Backus, in charge of the original FORTRAN compiler project at IBM, has made the following historical comment on the nature on their schedule (Leeson 1984): "Occasionally people did ask us how long it would take: 'When are you guys gonna be done?' We would always say, 'Six months. Come back in six months.' We honestly felt all the time that we'd be done in six months from now, but it turned out to be three years." The same situation holds today. Whenever and whoever you ask they are six months from validation! It seems like "six months" is the canonical euphemism for "whenever we will be finished".

In our case it was obvious to the potential vendors that the commercial value was rather small. A few, but not many, of the companies that we approached, may have responded differently if for instance IBM had asked the same questions.

Project specific. Regarding our present decision to chose an Ada system for our project we have drawn the following conclusions.

All three companies made it clear that they would be interested in supporting us with information during the effort.

To be able to experiment with memory management, which is crucial in our case, it is desirable to be able to control the memory allocation and addressing totally. This requires code generation to start at a fairly high level (IML7, DIANA or HF). Unfortunately we have not got the manpower to do a complete new code generator within reasonable time limits so this is out of the question. The next best thing is to get access to the source code of the memory allocation phase of the compiler and be able to change in that to do the experiments. This would allow us to start code generation at a low level intermediate language.

Being able to experiment with parallelism, which is also crucial in our case, requires the tasking constructs to be present in the intermediate language, which is not the case for Systeam and TeleLOGIC.

We are presently discussing with DDC about the details of a possible agreement to acquire their system. This decision was mainly based on the factors described above but it was also influenced by factors outside the scope of this paper.

References

A. Ardö (1983). Considerations for full Ada implementation on an experimental multiprocessor computer. Technical Report, Department of Computer Engineering, University of Lund.

A. Ardö (1984). Experimental implementation of an Ada tasking run-time system on the multiprocessor Cm*. Proceedings of the first Washington Ada Symposium, March 25-27 1984.

A. Ardö, L. Philipson (1984). A Simple Ada Compiler Invalidation Test. To appear in ACM Ada LETTERS.

G. Clemmensen, J. Pedersen (1983a). Portable Ada Programming System, DDC Ada Compiler, Back End Compiler, Specification of the Language IML7. Report, Dansk Datamatik Center.

G. Clemmensen, J. Pedersen (1983b). Portable Ada Programming System, DDC Ada Compiler, Back End Compiler, Specification of Abstract A-code. Report, Dansk Datamatik Center.

J. Goodenough (1981). The Ada Compiler Validation Capability. Computer 14(6), pp 57-64, June 1981.

G. Goos, W.A. Wulf (1981). DIANA Reference Manual. Technical Report, Department of Computer Science, Carnegie-Mellon University.

L. Ibsen, L.O.K. Nielsen, N.M. Jörgensen (1982). A-machine Specification. ADA/RFM/0001, Christian Rovsing.

H. Jansohn, R. Landwehr (1983). A Code Generator for Ada. Technical Report, Institut fur Informatik II, University of Karlsruhe.

A.K. Jones, A. Ardö (1982). Comparative Efficiency of Different Implementations of the Ada Rendezvous. Proceedings of the AdaTEC conference on Ada, pp 26-30, October 1982.

D.N. Leeson (1984). FORTRAN Exhibit & Film. Annals of the History of Computing, Volume 6, No 1.

E. Meiling, J. Pedersen (1983). Portable Ada Programming System, DDC Ada Compiler, Back End Compiler, Global Design. Report, Dansk Datamatik Center.

L. Philipson (1984). VLSI based design principles for MIMD multiprocessor computers with distributed memory management. Proceedings of the 11th Annual Symposium on Computer Architecture, June 4-7 1984.

G. Winterstein (1983). Karlsruhe Ada Compiler Specification. Report, Systeam.

THE INTRODUCTION OF ADA* IN AEROSPACE INDUSTRY

B. Labreuille - M. Heitz
INFORMATIQUE INTERNATIONALE
2 rue Jules Védrines
31400 TOULOUSE

1. INFORMATIQUE INTERNATIONALE has been among the first companies to engage in an industrial software program centered around Ada. An important part of the early activities in this program in an experimentation plan destined to assess the language and its environment (more specifically the ROLM Ada Work Center) from the viewpoint of its introduction in an existing context.

The particular context is that of Aerospace applications at CNES (Centre National d'Etudes Spatiales), in Toulouse, France. The experiment has as its main objective to provide information on the suitability and use of the language, and on the problems to be expected when introducing Ada in an industrial environment. As such, this study is expected to provide significant insights towards a successful Ada technology transfer.

The experiment covers two main areas :

-the introduction of the language (how it is learnt and used in practice),

-the suitability of the language for product development.

A by-product of the experiment is also an assessment of the particular Ada environment used, i.e., the ADE.

The experiment has been in progress since the fall of 1983, and only preliminary findings are reported here. We think those results, although incomplete are of significant interest to the present and prospective Ada community.

We first describe the experimentation plan as a whole, and then report our current experience in the two areas mentioned above.

---

* Ada is a registered trademark of the United States Department of Defense (Ada Joint Program Office).

2. THE EXPERIMENTATION PLAN

Experimentation in the two areas (language introduction and use) follows a uniform approach consisting of four steps :

- definition of the questions to be answered,

- development of related metrics, and definition of data to be collected,

- development of tools for data collection,

- validation and analysis of collected data.

2.1. Introduction of the Language

The objective is to define the requirements for a successful Ada training program, and to constitute a set of guidelines on a "good usage" of the language features.

The main elements on which the recommendations are based are :

- a self evaluation by the trainees, reporting, for each language feature, the difficulty in understanding, in applying, and the quality of the related training material ;

- an analysis of the relative frequencies of the use of the various features, and of the development time spent by individuals in writing some test programs ;

- a hand-made analysis of the structural aspects of the programs.

2.2. Suitability of the Language

The goal of this part of the experiment is to assess the effort, evolution and quality in the development of significant Ada projects in the area of concern. Three such projects have been selected, in the areas of real-time, graphical, and interactive applications. The particular projects corespond to the redesign and implementation of projects already developed for CNES (with the participation of Informatique Internationale).

The evaluation of effort measures time spent by individuals, the skills required, and the volume of the resulting product in terms of number of lines, number of units, etc...

The assessment of evolution is conducted through the number and categorization of errors detected during development and test phases, the resulting modifications and the effort spent.

The quality aspect of the study has as its goal to lay the foundations for adapting classical quality measures to Ada. Those include Halstead and MacCabe complexity measures, measures of data complexity (depth of data type dependencies, number of visible definitions per unit, number of references to other units, number of units referenced, number of units referencing a given unit, depth of dependency tree, etc...).

As with most quality measures, these measures will have to be calibrated, e.g. in the light of the evolution assessment.

The Introduction of Ada* In Aerospace Industry

3. EXPERIENCE IN INTRODUCING THE LANGUAGE

Introducing a language such as Ada inside a team requires a combination of educational methods and material, and of significant exercices. At this stage of the project, the exercices have consisted chiefly in the development and validation of a number of software packages of wide usability. This is not only a training in the features of the language, but also in using it with the utmost effectiveness for the production of software components.

The team participating in the experiment consisted of personnel of differing level and background : among the five persons involved, three were skilled developers with an experience of Fortran and real-time applications, while the remaining two were more junior engineers with a heavier experience of Pascal. The team was thus rather balanced, and not especially predisposed towards the language, although its members had generally been sensitized to the problems of software engineering.

3.1. Learning to use the Language

The training program consisted of a formal three-day seminar, delivered by Alsys, completed solely by personal efforts, using whatever written texts were available (esp. [Barnes 84], [Booch 83], [Gehani 83], [Habermann 83]) in addition to the Language Reference Manual. Indeed, this latter was considered so terse as to be virtually unusable for learning the language (the language barrier that it presents to a non-english speaking team is probably an important factor there).

Problems come mostly in the application of detailed restrictions, with a few sour points : the use of derived types, and of private generic parameters (generics were used extensively in the sample packages). The tasking model was also difficult to grasp at first, and more material seems to be needed in this area. Input-Output facilities were, to say the least, difficult to use as soon as anything non trivial was attempted (e.g. I/O of dynamic types).

The Introduction of Ada* in Aerospace Industry

However, learning the language is not sufficient : it is also necessary to learn how to use it properly, a more delicate task for which little material is available ; it is also necessary to learn how to use the associated tools. From this point of view, the ADE offers a number of sophisticated tools, most noticeably a very good source-level debugger. Learning how to use the tools effectively represents a substantial portion of the overall education process, which is often neglected, if not totally ignored.

All in all, learning the language was achieved within a reasonable budget, which is evidence that the language can be taught effectively.

3.2. Practical use of the Language

The exercice consisted in the development of 10 packages, in various areas, covering :

- general purpose data structures, (stacks, qeues, trees),

- Input-Output, (display handling, indexed sequential I/O),

- real-time, (semaphores, producer/consumers, readers/writers).

[Note to the experts :
Although these applications may seem trivial, one has to bear in mind that the personnel involved in the experiment had no previous exposure to Ada.]

At this stage, measures of productivity or of activity breakdown would be overly biased by the learning time which will be of course lessened over the entire experiment. One can nevertheless observe that productivity -in lines of commented source code per day- tends to be lower for more complex

problems, e.g. real-time, but this should come as no surprise. Perhaps more interesting is that even with the education overhead, productivity tends to be on overage close to accepted standards.

We can already report on the relative use of certain language features. Again, due to the early nature of the experiment, we prefer to withhold exact figures, and describe the trends. These are characterized by the overwhelming domination of variable declarations (over 60 % of the declarations), and of procedure calls (over 50 % of the statements) ; type declarations, assignments, if- and loop-statements were also used, rather more significantly than case-statements. Declarations and statements related to exception handling were also found in a non-negligible ratio.

Since the developments had to do with packages, and not full applications, the number of packages is itself insignificant, although generics and generic instantiations were actually used on a number of occasions.

We draw two preliminary conclusions from these observations :

- the language strongly encourages the development of "well-structured" programs and the introduction of levels of abstraction, as witnessed by the proportion of subprogram calls ;

- an efficient implementation of the language must particularly focus on the highly used features, and especially on subprogram interfaces.

We will delay our general observations on the use of Ada in an engineering context until after a report on the second aspect of the experiment.

The Introduction of Ada* In Aerospace Industry   25

4. TESTING THE LANGUAGE IN AEROSPACE APPLICATIONS

This part of the experiment is obviously lagging behind the introduction of the language, since the language has to be learnt before being applied in its final context.

The plan calls for the (re)development of three applications :

- a real-time scheduler for ground telemetry applications originally developed for the TMSAT program ;

- extensions for interactive application developments ;

- graphics and color display of satellite monitoring data (as developed in the TELECOM-1 system).

At this stage, only the first part of the experiment has been conducted.

The scheduler has to monitor the execution of a number of actions that are performed on telemetry datA (data received from the spacecraft) at the request of a number of monitoring agents.

The system must control :

- the actions themselves,

- the consoles where the requests are entered,

- the various resources (files and communication blocks).

The approach consisted in redesigning the application from scratch, following abstraction-oriented and refinement methods, such as described in [Booch 83]. It is not our purpose to present here the details of the solution that was arrived at, but rather to emphasize some of the salient aspects of the use of the language in this context.

First of all, the package and task structure favors the development of an implementation that follows closely the overall design. It allows a clear separation of the various parts of the program, resulting in a code that is much closer to the design documentation.

Heavy use was made of :

- packages, to group the declarations and operations that deal with a given entity ;

- tasks, to control real-time activities : multiple instances using a task type were found to be especially appropriate in the context ;

- generics, to specify the same type of actions to be performed on different kinds of objects.

In terms of using the language, the result was probably much closer to a "proper" use of Ada than to the original Fortran application. This can be contrasted with some experiments previously reported (e.g. [Duncan 84]. From such a point of view, it seems that Ada can indeed be brought effectively in a team, although the small size of the team requires some caution in such a statement

In terms of the suitability of the language to the application, Ada was found of substantial value allowing one to express a design in terms that were quite natural for the application, and to reach a final implementation that was much closer to the design, and of a much more understandable logic than the equivalent Fortran-T program.
*

* The original system was written in a dialect of Fortran IV, called Fortran-T, providing structured and real-time extensions.

5. GENERAL REMARKS ON THE USE OF ADA

From our early experiences, we can draw a number of preliminary conclusions on the most salient aspects of a practical use of the language and associated tools.

5.1. Using the language

The major aspect of the language is the separation of package specification and body, together with the separate compilation facilites. This has had a drastic influence on the design and development process : the overall architecture of the system is expressed very early in terms of Ada units, and their interconnections ; the global design is completed by completing the visible parts of the various units, thus introducing all the major system interfaces. Such specifications must absolutely be completed by either comments or a design document (or both), but at this stage, on can already use the translator to check the validity of the specification. The design can then gradually evolve towards the implementation, by introducing the missing bodies. This entails fewer iterations on the interfaces.

The rules for separate compilation have been found reasonable in managing recompilations, although more system assistance would have been useful (see below). Thus, the use of Ada has in itself an impact on the development methodology.

A counteraspect is the fact that, due to the gradual introduction of bodies, it would have been nice to be able to link and test a partially implemented system, with references to incomplete parts raising an exception if used. This would further enable the developers to test parts of the system without having to write special test drivers. Unfortunately, the language rules are quite strict there (and rather strictly implemented).

5.2. Using the Environment

The ROLM Ada Development Environment is not exactly an APSE in the STONEMAN sense ([STONEMAN 80]). It is nevertheless a collection of tools that provide some interesting functionalities. Since it is described elsewhere in this conference, we do not give a detailed description here, but rather report on our experiences using it.

Apart from the validated compiler, the most important tool for our development has been the source-level debugger, especially tailored for Ada, and including functions to examine discriminately individual tasks, or to trace exception propagation. The quality of the tool has probably contributed to its enthusiastic adoption within the team.

Considering the use of Ada in early stages, the pretty-printer was found useful. Its various options for gathering statistics are also helpful for the analysis of the resulting programs.

Having a text formatter in the environment has also been useful, leading to a complete handling of all documentation on the machine.

On the other hand, the lack of maintenance tools specifically oriented towards Ada was sourly felt. In this respect, substantially more help could come from the library manager. The library manager is a necessary part of any Ada implementation, and is the part that manages all the relationships between the units. As such certain complementary functions could easily be provided, which were felt as badly missing. These are :

- an indication of recompilations induced by a change, and possibly an automatic triggering of recompilations ;

- a graphical (or semi-graphical) representation of the architecture of the system, in terms of units and their relationships.

Another important shortcoming is due to limitations of separate compilation features in using multiple libraries, i.e. a body unit has always to be compiled in the same library as its corresponding specification unit. This rather complicate the development process in the context of a multi programmer team.

These comments are not made to criticize the ROLM tools, which, after all, still provide better facilities than anything we know on the market, but rather to indicate to other Ada implementors that such limitations have been felt by a small team engaged in a limited-scale experiment, and are likely

to be even more of a problem for real-life projects. The functionalities offered by the tools is therefore an important aspect of an implementation.

6. CONCLUSION

Although our experimentation is far from being complete (final results are expected by the end of 1985), it is interesting to report some of our preliminary findings.

The most important ones are :

- Reaching an acceptable level of proficiency in Ada could be done reasonably well ; reaching a level of expertise in particular areas (e.g. generics, tasking, I/O) would require special training, for which little has been available (to us).

- The use of the language has an interesting (positive) impact on the development method, allowing one to use Ada for expressing certain aspects of the design.

- Ada induces a certain programming style that implies going through several layers of interfaces.

- The use of a number of tools is of significant help. One should not forget that learning how to use the tools effectively is almost as important as learning the language, and takes some time and effort as well.

We are looking forward to being able to report more about our experiences, and also to generalize our use of the language for a variety of applications.

AKNOWLEDGEMENTS

This work has been done in the context of a contract with CNES (Centre National d'Etudes Spatiales) an we are grateful to the following people who give us the authorization of publishing this preliminary results :

DIVISION GENIE INFORMATIQUE

CNES - CST - TOULOUSE

REFERENCES

[Barnes 84] J.G.P. Barnes : "Programming in Ada", 2nd edition, International Computer Science Series, 1984

[Booch 83] G. Booch : "Software Engineering with Ada" The Benjamin/Cumming Publishing Company, 1983

[Duncan 84] A.G. Duncan et al. : "Communication System Design using Ada", proc. 7th International Conference on Software Engineering, Orlando, Florida, March 1984.

[Gehani 83] N. Gehani : "Ada - An advanced Introduction", Prentice-Hall, 1983

[Habermann 83] A.N. Habermann : "Ada for Experienced Programmers"

[STONEMAN 80] U.S. Departement of Defense : "Requirements for Ada Programming Support Environments", 1980

Ada[r] as a Programming Design Language for a Telematic Services Project

O. MAUREL
TECSI-Software, 29 rue des Pyramides 75001 Paris, France

C. BONNET
TECSI-Software, 29 rue des Pyramides 75001 Paris, France

Abstract : This paper discusses the experiences of using Ada as Programming Design Language for a large industrial videotex project. The specificities of a large telematic services project that deals with both telephonic and telematic problems make the methodologies used in standard telephonic project not completely adapted : the lack of semantic descriptions of the actions as well as the lack of data representation in these methodologies led us to choose a PDL approach.
The first part of this paper presents the approach and the definition of an Ada PDL for specifying telematic protocols. The main characteristics of this Ada PDL which is a "pure" Ada subset are given.
This Ada PDL was used to design the presentation layer of the Architel protocol implementation. This layer defines a general set of services used by the application level to manage a virtual videotex device and had not been previously implemented.

The second part discusses the effects of this approach on the design : for each feature of the PDL some results are mentioned, concerning data structure analysis, software modularity and error handling. The significant benefits conferred on the final product are listed and the problem of designing in Ada without "Ada support" is mentioned. In conclusion, the possible extensions of this work to the validation and the simulation of telecommunication protocols are presented.

1 INTRODUCTION

Telematic services software differs from standard telephonic software in two major aspects :
- the protocols used are both telephony and data transmission protocols,
- the implementation mixes standard telephony problems (real time, events...) and "large software" difficulties like virtual device management.

The telematic protocol specifications defined for this videotex project are a new proposal of the French PTT and have not yet been implemented ; this protocol is named Architel, (ARCHITEL, 83) and follows the Open System Interconnection (OSI) recommandations (CCITT, Z70).

It consists of six layers :

layer 1,2,3 : X 25 protocol (CCITT)
layer 4   : transport layer (CCITT for class ∅)
layer 5   : session layer (S62, ECMA75)
layer 6   : presentation layer

The five first layers are either standard CCITT protocols or proposed standards layers (4,5). The most original part of the Architel protocol is the presentation layer which defines a general set of services used by the application level to manage a virtual videotex device.

This virtual device includes extended memory capabilities and predefined or end-user defined data acquisition programs to facilitate the videotex Data Base application design.

In the context of the production of telephonic software, several methodologies are defined, and used. $SADT^r$, SDL (CCITT, Z104) are well known tools for module interaction and automata description. These tools have powerful techniques to describe the interface with the environment, but fail to describe complex algorithms and data management. These were the main reasons which led us to look for a new design approach for this telematic services project.

2   WHY A PDL ?

At the beginning of the project, we started from a <u>natural language</u> specification of the protocol which describes the external interfaces and the services of the layers : the French language allows a great flexibility in the description, but does not avoid ambiguity or incomplete specifications. Applied to this specification a manual transformation to produce a graphic SDL (or flowchart) description was a "Roman work" without real methodologic result.

SDL gives a good representation for the data flow analysis and message interfaces. But we faced some drawbacks :
- lack of flexibility : since the specifications written in French language evolved during the project, the corresponding evolutions of the specifications written under flowchart form were difficult to apply without powerful graphic tools ;
- the lack of semantic descriptions of the actions generates ambiguities and incomplete specifications ;
- lack of data representation techniques essential for a virtual device description ;
- discontinuity between the specification phase and the later phases of the project due to the lack of semantic information.

After this first analysis, we felt that the complexity of the SDL specifications and of the associated functions, coupled with the necessity to maintain the software during long life cycles, make necessary the definition of a coherent approach to the different steps of the software specifications and realisation.

We wanted to have maximum consistency during these phases to avoid loss of information and to identify at the beginning of the project the implementation difficulties of this new protocol.

This led us to choose a programming design language approach for the specifications.

A Programming Design Language or <u>PDL</u> offers many advantages : syntactic clarity and uniformity of a programming language and the flexibility necessary for software specification or design. (see Boehm 1980, Sammet 1980). When this PDL is a <u>subset of a high level language</u>, the same general syntax can be used during the different phases of the project, which is a great advantage for a large project. The other reasons for defining a design language as a subset of an existing programming language has been discussed elsewhere (see Sammet, 1981). We wanted essentially to take advantage of a well documented language which has a sufficient level of abstraction for defining software as data + algorithm.

3   Ada AS PDL / DEFINITION OF A PDL FOR TELEMATIC SERVICES PROJECT

Ada was chosen, not for the availability of a good compiler, but for the following reasons : it is well defined (US Mil Std and ANSI) and supported by a large organisation. It will probably become a common reference for the designers and programmers of large systems in the coming years. It allows abstraction facilities and supports the modular programming required by relevant software engineering principles.

Our PDL is a proper subset of Ada. "Proper" because the complete language is not necessary for a designer, and a " subset" in order to avoid any syntatic confusion between specification and coding and to make our PDL acceptable to any tool or program which supports Ada. We deliberately omitted the implementation oriented features which are too specific for a design language.

An efficient Ada PDL must be easy to use, easy to learn and must keep the essential features of Ada, allowing, for instance, the definition of abstract data types.

We wanted to define, not a general purpose Ada PDL, but a design language tailored to our project. What are the characteristics of the implementation of the Architel Protocol ?

First, the software size and the software development costs - 300 000 source lines of high level language and 120 man x year - are too large to ignore the problem of software production. The consistency of the software must be maintained throughout its life cycle : design, development, documentation and maintenance.

The OSI architecture imposes the use of standardized protocol procedures (defined on the protocol as services of a given layer) and a predefined modularity : a layer is an abstract machine.

In particular, for the Architel presentation level, the protocol describes the data structure and the functionalities of the virtual device known to the application. The error handling and, in this case, the interaction with the other layers, are part of the protocol specification.

In addition to these points, our Ada PDL keeps the "basic" features of Ada, for example :

- library, separate compilation

We want to benefit from this fundamental property of Ada. The software decomposition is easily deduced from the library organisation. Our development system SDL2020^r offers a library management which increases the software consistency.

- Package specification, package body

This feature allows the separation of <u>data</u> and <u>algorithms</u> and increases the flexibility for the intended state machine definition which implements the protocol services for each layer.

- Application oriented package

To support some videotex features not described in the protocol. (Example : list of videotex pages, array of videotex characters...).

- Abstract data type

A major advantage of Ada is to authorize user defined types and subtypes. The data specification (virtual device organisation) is a complex part of the protocol (layer 6).

- Control structures

The complexity of the algorithm and the necessity to describe the functionalities require using of the complete set of the control structure of the language.

- Statements

Assignments and subprogram calls.

- Error handling

The basic idea is to keep the exception definition of Ada and to have "application defined" exceptions. Each module must contain an exception handler section - but the text of this section is kept as comment for design purposes.

The result of this approach is a readable subset of the language, understandable by a non Ada specialist, but naturally containing more than "a classical PDL". This subset includes type and object declarations, assignment, subprogramm call(s), classical control structure(s) and offers all the components, design facilities and some exception handling facilities. The task constructs of Ada are not kept in the PDL definition, because they impose a particular run time model (rendez-vous).

4 SPECIFICATION OF THE PRESENTATION LAYER USING THE Ada PDL

After the PDL design phase and the methodology analysis, we decided to use this "Ada PDL" to design the presentation layer of the Architel protocol implementation (ARCHITEL 83).

The first step of our development methodology consisted in the protocol layer specification. The second step was to define the software architecture of the product, and the third one, before coding, to produce a specification for implementation.

Starting from a natural language specification, we defined a protocol specification which exactly describes the functional contents of the implementation. As two additional results we got a better idea of the software size and an evaluation of its complexity. These points were critical because the protocol had not yet been implemented.

The software development environment used for this work is not an Ada environment, like an APSE, but offers similar facilities and is based on UNIX[r] system :

SDL2020[r] is a configuration management system which guarantees the consistency among the various software parts or components used in a module. SDL2020 is processor and environment independent. It offers solid bases on which to build an advanced methodology - like our protocol analysis - and it maintains a complete history of the evolution of a software product.

Ada for a Telematic Service Project

5 CONSEQUENCES FOR OUR DESIGN

There is no doubt that the choice of an Ada PDL has some consequences on the specification of a high level protocol implementation.

For each feature of the PDL, some results are listed.

5.1 Data Structure Analysis

The presentation level of the Architel protocol defines a data structure : the <u>virtual device</u>. This structure is known to the external videotex data base. The protocol clearly gives the data structure, the functions and the external interface of this device. A major advantage of the Ada PDL during the preliminary specification phases was the possibility to introduce the notion of the virtual device as an <u>abstract data type</u> and to start a <u>consistent</u> study of the data representation.

The main benefits derived from this analysis were the following :

- the establishment of the consistent abstract data type definition for the virtual device requires thinking about the basic protocol notions, such as model, profile, document structure, page structure, and to avoid possible ambiguities in the definitions. A natural language description of a data organisation describes the objects and their relationships and does not define a unified view of their representation.

- It was advantageous to list exhaustively the existing entities and to define the associated basic operations. This was useful to evaluate the complexity of the implementation and to deduce the development effort.

- It is also an advantage to introduce a unique and complete definition of the objects manipulated by the semantics of the protocol and to avoid data discrepancy.

5.2 Software Modularity

Another issue is the deduction of the coherent set of software components from a protocol interface definition. In our case, the software modularity is a characteristic of the PDL and is increased by the SDL2020 environment. The consequence of using these tools together is a very high level of control of the software architecture consistency.

Each semantic component of an Architel presentation layer defines either an action of the virtual device or a "communication event". In the former of case, the virtual device abstract data type defines the basic set of operations and, the PDL describes :

- the general mechanism used by the semantics. These functions are for example the services used for the basic data manipulation and are gathered in specialised packages.

- The actions on the data are described, not in terms of "abstraction", but with the <u>explicit references</u> to the data structure. To avoid a <u>too low level description</u> of the semantics, the access to the data is encapsulated within "access functions" like get-model (document-reference) (these functions are part of the general service package).

- The internal treatments performed by the semantics are given in the body of the associated subprograms. This relationship between the subprograms and the semantics is due to the characteristics of an OSI protocol which defines the <u>services</u> as functionalities of the layer. For each semantic, the references to the protocol specifications are given.

- The treatment of a communication event is done by the protocol automata which are described as "case statements" ; these automata are generally described in the protocol with a good level of abstraction and the benefit of the PDL description is a better readability.

5.3 Error Handling

The exception mechanism is used to define both :

- the exceptions which are described by the protocols and sent to videotex subscribers ;

- the exceptions defined to catch software anomalies.

A complete error dictionnary has been available since the analysis phase, and the problem of the error propagation has been systematically studied. This increases confidence in the quality of the final product.

6 CONSEQUENCES FOR THE FINAL PRODUCT

The consequence of using our Ada PDL is a top down oriented approach :

- with a great modularity of the specification and a good definition of the interfaces ;
- exploiting the general mechanism of package definition ;
- and with the possibility to introduce an initial Ada library architecture before the beginning of the implementation phase.

The Ada library architecture is directly deduced from the analysis of the different modules and, after a complete overview of the first package decomposition, it is relatively easy to organize the development library.

This point is important in the actual transition phase with unexperienced Ada programmers, because a good definition of the Ada program library has a direct consequence on the quality of the data program (no semantic problems for example).

The term of "abstract software architecture" can be used to define this general analysis of the protocol specification.

Finally, the approach stimulates the effort to complete the knowledge of the presentation level protocol specification and suppress possible gaps. The systematic analysis of the data-semantic threads leads to a protocol implementation of a good quality : specialized tools (like cross referencer) give an automatic validation of these links.

This synthetic view of the protocol has had some bottom-up effects on our design : the creation of "general utility" packages, and a functional organisation of semantics, which are described in the specifications as "specific" services.

The PDL description of the presentation layer is the "result" of our analysis of the protocol and of the semantic problems which need to be resolved by the implementer : more than hundred questions were raised by our analysis of the original document.

7 PERSPECTIVES AND CONCLUSION

In the future, this approach can lead to an automatic simulation of the protocol as described in /PDIL-83/ with a "superset" of Pascal. All the basic features, necessary for this work are included in Ada : multimachine description for describing protocol functions in a hierarchical way, data structures with extended data type (protocol oriented events, queues...), non deterministic control of interactions (done for example, by decision functions), "user" error handling.

It is relatively easy to deduce from the Ada PDL specifications an executable program describing the studied protocol level. This last point means that the complete description in Ada PDL of the layer of the Architel protocol can be used to build a tool for checking the behaviour of a <u>completely specified service</u>, and a machine for the evaluation (<u>i.e. validation</u>) of different implementation hypothesis (<u>i.e. simulation</u>).

In our opinion, there is no doubt that the choice of an Ada PDL has significant positive effects on the design of a large system. In our case, the use for the development phases of an <u>"Ada compiler"</u> is not necessary in order to benefit from the design work. The transition to an other programming language (C, Pascal) is relatively easy if the data structures, the interfaces and the components are well defined. The SDL2020 environment offers a sophisticated support for this translation with the notion of product management, which makes possible the consistent association between code and source program, the corresponding documentation and the generation procedures. The definition of an "abstract software architecture" seems to be a good basis for the implementation phase providing also a representation for estimating the human effort necessary for the effective implementation of the product. The main advantage of this approach is that the implementer may concentrate entirely on the architecture and on a good understanding of the specifications. Adding simulation tools based on "pure Ada" will be certainly the future step before the proposition of a complete development methodology for the communication protocols.

Acknowledgments :

This work was done in the spring of 1983, as an experiment of using a high level programming language as a specification language.
This study was done in the context of a Telematic project inside CIT Alcatel (PAVI Point d'Accès Vidéotex Intermédiaire, one of the Telematic applications of E10S).

The authors are grateful to the following people who had used this PDL and for their constructive contribution in its definition :

    JF. CAILLET (CIT Alcatel)
    P. GELLI (CIT Alcatel)

Trademarks :

Ada is a registered trademark of the US Department of Defense.
Unix is a registered trademark of Bell & ATT Laboratories, (USA).
SDL2020 is a registered trademark of TECSI-Software, (France).
SADT is a registered trademark of SOFTECH, (USA).

References

ANSART J.P. et al. (1983). Description, Simulation and Implementation of Communication Protocols using PDIL In ACM SIGCOMM 83 SYMPOSIUM on Communications Architectures and Protocols, University of TEXAS, AUSTIN (8-9 MARCH 1983)

BOEHM, B.W. (1980). Software Engineering - as it is in Software Engineering (H. Freman and P. Lewis, Eds), Academic Press, PP. 37-73.

FRENCH PTT (1983). ARCHITEL, STUR Service de presentation Architel de type terminal virtuel videotex, NT/PAA/DIR/943 & NT/CNR/DIR/12.

SAMMET, J.E. et al.(1982). PDL/Ada, - A Design Language Based on Ada In Ada Letters, volume II, number 3 PP. II-3.19, II.3.31.

THE ADA[+] "PROGRAM LIBRARY":
ITS MEANING AND ITS IMPLEMENTATION
IN AN EXISTING GENERIC ENVIRONMENT IN INDUSTRY

K. Ripken
Laboratoires de Marcoussis, CR-CGE, F-91460 Marcoussis, France

Abstract. The concept of the Ada "program library" is clarified by characterizing it in two ways: as an auxilliary term of the language definition mechanism as far as the enforcing of language rules in the presence of separate compilation is concerned, and as an important concept of the Ada environment which assures that a valid program of a program library is always in a consistent state from the point of view of version control and configuration management. A practical implementation of program libraries is sketched using the mechanisms of the generic object-oriented production and configuration management system MOSAIX on top of UNIX[+].

[+] Ada is a registered trademark of the US Government (AJPO), and UNIX is a registered trademark of Bell Laboratories.

INTRODUCTION

In the Ada language, a "program" is a collection of one or more compilation units where each unit corresponds to the specification or implementation part of one of the program structuring constructs (subprogram, package and task) (DoD 1983a, section 10(1) - further references to the Ada Reference Manual will only be made by section -). In addition to this concept, the definition of Ada introduces the concept of a "program library" as the container for all the compilation units of a program (Section 10.1(3)). This paper attempts to clarify the latter concept by characterizing it in two ways: as an auxiliary term of the language definition mechanism as far as the enforcing of language rules in the presence of separate compilation is concerned, and as an important concept of the Ada environment which assures that a valid program of a program library is always in a consistent state from the point of view of version control and configuration management.

With respect to this latter role of the program library as an environment concept, the paper goes beyond the Ada language by investigating how the evolution of a program library itself can be controlled. As an example, the paper will discuss how the program library can be implemented with the mechanisms offered by the generic production and configuration management system MOSAIX. This system, marketed and in industrial use, can be viewed as the framework for an Ada Programming Support Environment (APSE) on top of UNIX (Ripken 1983 ; Ripken 1984). Its functionality could probably, at least to a large extent, be implemented on top of the Olivetti KAPSE or the CAIS (DoD 1983b).

Tichy (1982) has presented the design of a database for Ada programs, providing a detailed view of the relations between the Ada units, however not treating the concept of the Ada program library.

Most of the material of this paper results from a study on "Life cycle support in the Ada environment" , conducted for the Commission of the European Communities (Systems Designers & TECSI 1983), but has not been included in the publication of the study in (McDermid & Ripken 1984).

THE MEANING OF THE "PROGRAM LIBRARY"

An auxilliary concept of the language definition

Besides the introduction of the program library concept in section 10.1(3), the language definition devotes the entire section 10.4 to it. In this section, a possible mechanism of the compiling environment is indicated which can guarantee the enforcement of the language rules "in the same manner for a program consisting of several compilation units (and subunits) as for a program submitted as a single compilation." This mechanism is the "library file" which "enables the translator to perform type checking across separately compiled units exactly as within a given compilation unit" and allows for the checking "that a given compilation does not use information from other units that have in the meantime become obsolete" (Ichbiah et al. 1979, section 10).

In fact, strictly speaking, the program library is an environment concept and plays only the role of an auxilliary concept in the language definition in the same way as, for instance, the concept of a "declarative region" in section 8.1. For, the abstract definition of a valid program, composed of several compilation units, could very well be given without a program library concept. Some existing rules would suffice in conjunction with the language rules from other sections than section 10 (e.g. "For each subprogram declaration, there must be a corresponding body." (6.3(3))) :

- The "main program" is a subprogram which is not a subunit (10.1(8)).
- The simple names that appear in context clauses must uniquely identify units which are not subunits (10.1.1(3)). These names must not be identical to names of non-overloadable entities in the package "STANDARD" due to the rule that a library unit is visible as if declared immediately within this package (8.6).
- The simple names of all subunits that have the same top ancestor unit must be distinct identifiers (10.2(5)).

The Ada "Program Library"

Thus defining a valid program as a set of units with certain properties means excluding all environmental aspects. The definition of the CHILL language, for instance, takes this approach (CCITT 1980, section 7.6). In the existing formal definition of Ada (CEC 1982), the program library is of the type "static environment" which indicates its auxilliary role as a part of the overall static environment of a complete program.

Guaranteeing development consistency

If the program library concept is of minor importance as a definitional vehicle, its role as an environment concept is essential. This role demands that the compiler maintain all the information on the compilation units of a library which is necessary for guaranteeing the consistency of an Ada program development at any point in time. Consistency means that the library contains only each (potential) unit of one or several programs which has been successfully compiled given all the other units of this library in its actual state.

Information maintained in a program library. As an example consider the following simple Ada program

> **with** A;
> **procedure** P **is**
> -- declarations
> **procedure** Q (...) **is separate** ;
> -- more declarations
> **begin**
> -- statements
> **end** P;

where A is a package having a body.

This example exhibits the main relations between Ada compilation units :
- the relation "library unit / library unit body" , e.g. between package A and its body
- the subunit relation, e.g. Q is a subunit of P
- the with-dependency relation, e.g. procedure P is compiled with the information represented by package A.

These relations affect the compilation process.

Another relation, the elaboration-dependency relation, states in which order library units and their corresponding bodies have to be elaborated. With-dependency and elaboration-dependency define a partial ordering which must be respected when the compilation units are elaborated before the execution of a program.

The program library has to maintain these relations. Besides, it should also keep an intermediate representation (e.g. in DIANA form) or/and a symbol table for each compilation unit so that the compiler can do identification, type checking, and code generation across compilation unit boundaries in an efficient way. Moreover, some information resulting from the compilation process may be more closely related to the program library, as a collection of units, than to a single unit.

Compilation process. In fact, the compilation process may be arbitrarily complex depending on the number of steps and intermediate results reflecting the various options of compiling. In order to simplify the following argumentation, compiling is considered a two-step process. In a first syntactic and semantic analysis step an intermediate representation ("IR") is created. This is the input to the code generator which, in a second step, creates an object for a specific target machine.

Therefore, it is from now on assumed that a program library contains the above relations as well as the IR's of the compilation units which have been successfully compiled into it.

Separate vs. independent compilation. The compilation of a unit, therefore, generally requires the inspection of a set of IR's of previously compiled units on which the current unit depends. The crucial point is the control of these IR's. This control is provided by the concept of the program library.

The program library is supposed to contain at most one IR for each unit and only a valid one, i.e. one which is the result of a compilation using only valid IR's. If a unit is recompiled on which other units depend in the sense of the above-mentioned relations then the IR's of the dependent units become obsolete, are deleted from the library, and only added again after a recompilation of their corresponding units.

At any time during the development of a program, i.e. during the sequence of edit-compile cycles of its units, the development results as documented by the program library are consistent. This continuous consistency in the case of Ada's separate compilation contrasts sharply with the continuous danger of inconsistency in the case of independent compilation of programs in other languages, e.g. PL/1 and PL/1-like languages, C, FORTRAN etc. In these languages, common definitions which are shared between compilation units are generally included at the textual level. For external interfaces there exist sometimes specific include files which have to be maintained in parallel with the source files containing the actual defining occurrences. In general, the definitions of these languages do not prescribe any actions to control the consistency of the "includes" at translation time. If the language environments do not provide adequate means then inconsistent programs are frequent. In such a case it can be very difficult to detect the inconsistency as an inconsistent program can very well be a running one.

The result of this discussion can be summarized as follows. In the case of independent compilation without an environment controlling configurations, a program which is correctly compiled can be inconsistent. In the case of Ada's separate compilation, a program which violates consistency cannot be compiled correctly.

AN IMPLEMENTATION OF PROGRAM LIBRARIES

The Ada language definition represents the program library as a means for controlling the evolution of its compilation units. In software engineering practice, however, the scope must be broadened : since a pogram library corresponds to a project, the evolution of the program library itself has to be controlled. For, it is clear that in practice obsolete units in the sense of the language definition are not necessarily obsolete ; they may well be different versions which have to coexist in different program configurations. These different program configurations correspond to different states of the program library.

In the following sections, the paper will, so to speak, walk along the boundary between the language and environment issues by showing how the program library can be implemented so that the requirements for version control and configuration management (cf. McDermid & Ripken 1984) are met. As an example, an implementation with the mechanisms contained in the MOSAIX environment on top of UNIX will be discussed.

The implementation environment

MOSAIX is a modular open support approach to software development on top of UNIX, proposed by TECSI-Software. Its basic component MOSA-COM is a generic production and configuration management system, formerly called SDL 2020 (Keller & Levy 1983) and derived from SGDL, a product of CIT-Alcatel (Maisonneuve et al. 1981).

MOSAIX views software development as a production process : a final product (complete system with all its deliverables) is produced in a sequence of steps which each produce "products". Products resulting from an earlier step generally are intermediate products in the sense that they are input components to the subsequent step. Each step is characterized by a production procedure which invokes a tool. (MOSAIX is open in the sense that any tool can easily be inserted into it.) A principal property of MOSAIX is that it keeps track of the evolution of all the products which, in practice, results from the continuous iteration of the overall production process. Moreover, MOSAIX allows to organize a project by assigning the responsability of products to so-called "managers" thus implementing controlled sharing of products in the presence of evolution.

Product evolution. MOSAIX is based on the principle that all the data objects which have to be put under configuration control can be dealt with in the same way, independent of their type. All these objects are, in fact, considered products of a production activity and their way of evolution is described in the same fixed database schema as far as the entities are concerned. (Attributes can be freely defined.) This schema is unusually elaborate as it distinguishes three levels of evolution : version, edition, and iteration level, corresponding to functional variants, decomposition variants and simple revisions, resp.

All coexisting incarnations of one product are represented by uniquely identified paths from the root to the leaves of its product tree. Each invocation of the product's generation procedure which is an attribute on the edition level generates a new product iteration as a leaf of the tree. Further below, the program library will be viewed as a product for which a new iteration is generated with each compiler invocation.

According to its functionality as a configuration management system, MOSAIX offers the operations of determining all the input component products of a product, and all the products which possess a given component product ; furthermore, MOSAIX can verify whether a product has exclusively been produced using the last iterations or/and editions or/and versions of component products ; and, most importantly, MOSAIX can automatically regenerate products.

Product space structuring. Products are grouped into libraries called "managers". These correspond to persons or teams with a specific role on a project (development, integration, qualification,...). Managers can be arranged hierarchically and searched for products in hierarchical order. The transfer of products between managers expresses product state changes, e.g. from "under unit test" to "in integration". Managers belong to "databases" ; this latter concept need, however, not be explained for the purpose of the further discussion.

The program library product and its evolution

The sources of the Ada compilation units, their intermediate representations, and their object codes are, of course, considered products in MOSAIX. The information about these products which has to be maintained in the program library is kept in a product of type "Ada program library" (APL). When an Ada unit is compiled the last source iteration and APL iteration are taken as input components to the compilation process. This process exploits the information in the APL iteration in order to determine the compilation context, i.e. to retrieve the IR's of the units of this context. The process then produces an IR iteration for the current compilation unit, and, finally, generates a new iteration of the APL product which reflects the new library state as required by the language definition.

The Ada "Program Library" 49

For this mechanism to function, the information of the APL iteration consists of two parts :
(a) The relations between the Ada compilation units mentioned above
(b) A mapping of the compilation units, which have been successfully compiled into the library, to their uniquely identified IR iterations which have resulted from the compilation. The units are characterized by their name and their properties of being a library unit or a subunit and a specification or a body.

Part (a) is exploited by the compiler to determine the compilation context, part (b) is used to retrieve the intermediate representations of this context. The total information is established and retrieved by a program library handler which is a simple environment tool. The important points are shown in an illustrative way with the small example program shown above.

Edit/compile cycle. Let "L.APL" be an Ada program library product with the last iteration "L.APL/V/E/n" (The version and edition level node names are only incompletely mentioned in the iteration name ; they are not necessary for this discussion. n is a positive integer.). This iteration may correspond to the state where the package A, its body, and the procedure P have been compiled successfully. The information in **L.APL/V/E/n** then is

```
P with A
A_BODY is body of A

(A, library unit, spec) -> A.IR/V/E/i
(A, library unit, body) -> A_BODY.IR/V/E/j
(P, library unit, body) -> P.IR/V/E/k
```

where i, j, and k stand for the iteration numbers of the IR iterations.

If the package A is now edited then the IR iterations A.IR/V/E/i and A_BODY.IR/V/E/j become obsolete in the sense that they do no more correspond to the last iteration of the source A. However, L.APL/V/E/n is still coherent and valid under the assumption that the previous source iteration of A has not been deleted. In MOSAIX, an iteration cannot be deleted as long as it is a component of another product. Here, the source is a component of the IR which in turn is a component of the APL.

This step, therefore, shows that a source revision need not affect the program library. Indeed, sources should be separated from program libraries since they can very well be compiled into different libraries.

If the package A is now recompiled, say with the command "compile A L.APL" , - MOSAIX takes the last iteration of A and L.APL by default -, then a new iteration **L.APL/V/E/n+1** is generated which will contain :

Body required for A
(A, library unit, spec) -> A.IR/V/E/i+1

Note that A.IR/V/E/i+1 is now mentioned. It is this new IR iteration of A which will be used for the subsequent compilation of the body of A and of P unless A is again recompiled.

The important point is that the previous iteration n of L.APL is still around if it is not deleted explicitly. All its components, the three IR's, and their respective components, the sources, are also still around so that the development can get back to this consistent state if necessary. Furthermore, the general function of MOSAIX which verifies whether a given APL iteration is only built on the basis of the most recent IR iterations can be exploited to find out which recompilations have become necessary.

Sharing of program units. Let us now assume a simple organization on a project : the project members Meyer and Smith develop and Dupont integrates.. Each of them will be responsible for the products in his MOSAIX manager. Dupont may just have "stolen" a stable version of the package A, its body, and their IR's from Meyer and given visibility of his manager to both Meyer and Smith. These latter two may independently continue developing programs which use the package A. For this purpose they may both create and use their own program library products.

The interesting point we want to make is now the following. A compilation of A by Smith into his program library need not be a real compilation. It may simply consist of a modification of Smith's library making its new iteration dependent on the IR-iteration of A found in Dupont's manager. (Note that the corresponding source iteration can be traced back as a (MOSAIX-) component of the IR-product.) In this way, duplications of compilations of shared Ada program units can be avoided.

CONCLUSION

The paper has distinguished the two roles of the Ada program library, to serve as an auxilliary concept for the language definition, and to serve as an environment concept which guarantees development consistency.

An implementation of the latter role has been sketched using the existing object-oriented configuration management system MOSAIX. This implementation shows that the library concept is a practical one which, properly implemented, leads to a minimization of duplications of objects and compilations while maintaining the necessary derivation history. The Ada program library can, in the given implementation, also be exploited to deliver a coherent program collection with all its constituents and to regenerate such a collection automatically.

The Ada program library, essentially an environment concept and as such underlining Ada's need for a suitable environment with configuration control, is yet another example of Ada's concern for quality assurance in large systems development.

REFERENCES

CCITT (1980). Definition of the CHILL language.

CEC (1982). Formal Definition of the Ada Programming Language. Commission of the European Communities : Reference Nr. III/1645/82-EN.

DoD (1983a). Reference Manual for the Ada Programming Language. US Department of Defense. ANSI/MIL-STD-1815 A.

DoD (1983b). Draft Specification of the Common APSE Interface Set (CAIS), Version 1.0. KIT/KITIA CAIS Working Group for the AJPO, US Department of Defense.

Ichbiah, J.D., et al. (1979). Rationale for the Design of the Ada Programming Language. SIGPLAN Notices, 14, no.6.

Keller, J.P. & Levy, J.P. (1983). SDL2020 - Un outil pour assurer la coherence d'un logiciel pendant tout le cycle de vie. In Printemps Convention '83, SICOB, Paris.

Maisonneuve, M. et al. (1981). SGDL, a Microprocessor Software Development and Management System based on PWB/UNIX. In Proc. of the 4th Intern. Conf. on Software Engineering for Telecommunications Switching Systems, Coventry, pp. 83-88.

McDermid, J.A. & Ripken, K. (1984). Life cycle support in the Ada environment. The Ada Companion Series. Cambridge: Cambridge University Press.

Ripken, K. (1983). Coherent management support in the Ada environment. In Proc. ESA/ESTEC Software Enginering Seminar (ESA SP-199), Nordwijk, pp. 161-166.

Ripken, K. (1984). The role of configuration management. In Proc. NATO Advanced Research Workshop in Munich on "Program Transformation and Programming Environments" , ed. P. Pepper, to appear in Springer Lecture Notes on Computer Science.

Systems Designers Ltd. & TECSI Software (1983). Life cycle support in the Ada environment. Final report of a study for the CEC. Fleet (Great-Britain), Paris (France).

Tichy, W.F. (1982). Adabase : A Database for Ada Programs. In AdaTEC '82 Conference on Ada.

DISCRETE EVENT MODELLING IN ADA - IMPLEMENTATION AND APPLICATION

Valerie A Downes and R Tellaeche Bosch
Department of Computing, Imperial College, LONDON.

ABSTRACT

This paper describes work that has been done at Imperial College, London, in developing an Ada library to support the application of Ada to discrete event modelling.

Discrete event simulation (DES) is a powerful technique that has been widely used in industry and commerce to investigate the behaviours of real-world systems. A full DES project consists of a several phase life-cycle which may be outlined as follows:

> Analyse the real system;
> Design a model of the system;
> Implement the model;
> Analyse the model's behaviour;
> Postulate change;
> Iterate through steps 2 to 5;
> Apply change to real system.

The modelling tools described in this paper cover the second and third steps in this life-cycle, and provide for output to assist step four.

An Ada simulation library (ASL) has been implemented with the underlying philosophy that the simulation primitives should appear to the user as a homogeneous extension to the language. The ASL supports the process interaction method of modelling and all the details of the housekeeping are hidden in library packages. The ASL has also been based on the objective that no restrictions should be imposed in the use of them.

This paper describes the problems that were encountered in meeting these objectives and the methods that had to be used to implement the simulation primitives. A multi-tasking model was chosen to represent the independent entities that exist in a model since this approach seems to match the natural conceptual model of systems. The choice of this approach caused several difficulties concerned with providing indivisible primitives, entity representation, mutual-exclusion, queueing, virtual time synchronization and deadlock avoidance. The techniques used to overcome these problems are discussed. In addition, facilities provided for sampling and data-collection are summarised.

A simple Ada/ASL program for a single server queue is presented as an example and a critique of the ASL is then included, based on experience with model building of several systems.

1. INTRODUCTION

Discrete event simulation is a long established and widely used modelling technique which has a considerable range of applications. The main components of discrete event models are entities, representing real world objects, and conditions that trigger state changes in the entities corresponding to events that happen at discrete time intervals. The driving mechanisms for the state changes are usually stochastic in nature. For example, the sampling of a service time from a normal distribution of service times, with a given mean and standard deviation, can be used to schedule an end-of-service event. These models are used to investigate the behaviour of real world environments and to produce statistical measures of expected behaviours. They provide a number of advantages over experimenting with change in the real environment, advantages of cost, time and accessibility.

Many of the applications of discrete event simulation have been in the area of computer systems. Models of operating systems are used to investigate the efficiency of various scheduling algorithms for the allocation of resources. Models of computer systems are used to predict performance. More recently, models of functional requirements have been used to illustrate the expected behaviours of a specified system [BAR84].

Because of the wide applicability of this modelling technique it seemed a suitable case for support by tools in an Ada programming support environment. Ideally, such tools should cover all the steps in the creation and evaluation of a simulation model, from initial analysis of the real system through model building and testing to the statistical analysis of the results. However, the work reported here has been concerned only with building libraries to support the generation of models as Ada programs. The objective of the project was to provide the language primitives for discrete event models so that they would appear to the programmer as a natural extention of Ada, whilst at the same time imposing no restrictions on the use of Ada facilities in the simulation programs. The internal workings of the Ada Simulation Library (ASL) were to be completely hidden from the user. The following sections describe the route taken to meet this objective and the extent to which it has been satisfied by the current version of the ASL.

Discrete Event Modelling

2. DESIGN DECISIONS

2.1 Model Structure

Several special purpose simulation languages have been developed in the past, some as extensions to FORTRAN or Algol and some as fairly primitive statistical packages. From the work done in designing these languages three distinct methods of model building have emerged [FIS73]. The first two of these, activity scanning and event scheduling, have developed from the historically sequential view of programs. The third method, process interaction, attempts a more natural representation of the real world by defining separate processes to represent entities and then allowing them to interact in ways that model their real interactions [FRA77]. In Simula this method is supported by co-routines where there can be only one active process in any activity involving more than one entity; the other processes must remain passive. The first design decision for the ASL was to use the process interaction approach and to use Ada tasks to model separate processes so that, if necessary, more than one process could be active at the same time.

2.2 Entity Representation

Entities which form part of a system to be modelled can take several forms. There are entities that form a single, permanent part of the system and these are represented by single tasks of an anonymous type, for example:

```
task DOCTOR is
    -- any user defined entries
end DOCTOR;

task body DOCTOR is
    -- code to model the Doctor's life cycle
end DOCTOR;
```

There are entities which are also a permanent part of the model but conform to the same basic type and these are represented by named instances of a given task type, for example:

```
task type NURSE is
    -- any entries
end NURSE;

task body NURSE is
    -- code to model a nurse's life cycle
end NURSE;

MARY, ADA, JOHN : NURSE;
```

Discrete Event Modelling

Some entities are transient to a model and here the task type and access type is used. For example, a mechanism for creating patients can be set up:

```
task type PATIENT is
    entry COMPLAINT(THIS_ILLNESS : in ILLNESS);
end PATIENT;

task body PATIENT is
    MY_ILLNESS : ILLNESS;
    ....
begin
    -- code for current illness accepted
    accept COMPLAINT(THIS_ILLNESS : in ILLNESS) do
        MY_ILLNESS := THIS_ILLNESS;
    end COMPLAINT;
    -- code to model a patient's life cycle until
    -- discharge from treatment or death
end PATIENT;

type PATIENT_ID is access PATIENT;
NEXT_PATIENT : PATIENT_ID;
```

and patients can then be generated by another process:

```
NEXT_PATIENT := new PATIENT;
```

and given any personal attributes through entry calls:

```
NEXT_PATIENT.COMPLAINT(INGROWING_TOE_NAILS);
```

Finally, there are some entities which are totally passive but whose existence is essential to the life cycle of active entities, such as the beds in a hospital. These entities are modelled by a simple count.

2.3 Time

Fundamental to any discrete model is a means of representing and manipulating the elapse of simulated time. It was decided to use the type DURATION for the virtual elapse times in the model since it provides the necessary degree of accuracy and has the operations of the package CALANDAR.

It was also decided to provide mechanisms for finding the current simulation elapse time, resetting this to zero, and suspending the execution of an entity until a given time.

2.4 Process Interactions

Simulation models are used to investigate the effects of the interactions between various entities, for example the expected queuing

Discrete Event Modelling

times for customers being served in a bank by cashiers. Model primitives must, therefore, allow for interaction between the tasks representing the entities. The Ada rendezvous mechanism was not suitable for these interactions for several reasons. There has to be provision for queuing for one of several servers, for the elapse of simulated time, and for several entities to come together for a single activity.

Interactions in the ASL are through actions on queues of processes. A process may join a queue where it halts execution and waits for reactivation by another process. Processes can enqueue and dequeue other processes and activate dequeued processes at a given time.

2.5 Entity Data-sets

Looking at the requirements of most modelling applications it was decided that these could be met by the provision of three data-set disciplines. The standard first-in-first-out (FIFO) queue, a last-in-first-out (LIFO) stack and a priority queue with the best-in-first-out (BIFO). Following standard practice in simulation literature all these data-sets are referred to as 'queues'.

In addition, it was decided that simple resource pools were needed to control the supply and demand of passive entities.

2.6 Sampling

The stochastic nature of simulation models means that it was essential that procedures be supplied to cover random number generation, sampling from standard distributions with given parameters and from user defined distributions.

2.7 Data Collection

A simulation model is of no value if it can not be used to predict expected behaviours and this is done by monitoring certain paramenters during the execution of the model. Some of these results can be expressed as a single value, such as the maximum length reached by a given queue, others are expressed as a range of values with mean and varience, such as customer queuing times. To aid such data collection it was decided to supply ASL queues with functions giving length, maximum length and number of additions, and to provided histograms for data collection during model execution with summary results available for reporting at the end of execution.

3. IMPLEMENTATION

The features required in the ASL fall into three main categories - those needed to organize the simulation model, those for providing the statistical distributions and those that handle the histograms. To reflect this division the library provides three packages as the user interface, SIMULATION, DISTRIBUTION and HISTOGRAMS. The ASL has also been supplied with a TRACE package which allows the user to select optimal trace output to monitor the behaviour of the simulation, the queues, the sampling or the histograms.

It would not be appropriate to cover in this paper all the details of the implementation of the ASL. Instead, a few issues that caused particular problems are described. A user's guide to the full facilities of the ASL is available [TEL83a] and a lengthy description of the implementation of the full library is given in an MSc thesis [TEL83b].

The first major problem was to choose a representation of the event list, an ordered linked list of any tasks suspended by the simulation mechanism from which they would be reactivated at the correct point in simulated time. An implementation had to be chosen that would allow tasks of any type to be put on the list and this was done by introducing an intermediary task of the following type:

```
task type COMMUNICATION_TASK is
    entry SIGNAL;
    entry WAIT;
end COMMUNICATION_TASK;
```

Every time a user task, representing an entity, makes a call to the HOLD procedure in the package SIMULATION by:

```
HOLD(Reactivation_Time => Later);
```

then, unknown to the user, a new communication task is created and named by an agent:

```
type AGENT is access COMMUNICATION_TASK;
```

the agent is then added to the event list which is set up using the types:

Discrete Event Modelling

```
type EVENT_NOTICE;
type EVENT is access EVENT_NOTICE;
type EVENT_NOTICE is record
    TIME    : DURATION;
    PROCESS : AGENT;
    NEXT    : EVENT;
end record;
```

the Hold procedure then calls the WAIT entry of the communication task, which has the following body:

```
task body COMMUNICATION_TASK is
    accept SIGNAL;
    accept WAIT;
end COMMUNICATION_TASK;
```

The effect of this call is to suspend execution of the entity task until there is a SIGNAL call on the communication task. This signal is given by the underlying simulation controller when the clock is advanced to the time given as the value Later.

The second, and not unrelated, problem was how to know when to advance the simulation clock. Because true parallelism is used in the modelling of processes the clock advance mechanism must only be activated when no entity tasks are running. This will happen when entities have either left the model, are waiting in the event list, are waiting in queues or are waiting for resources. To keep track of the number of entities the user must include calls to three procedures in his program. The first, Set_Entity_Count(N), to initialize the number of entities present at model start-up, the second, Include_Entity, every time a new entity is generated and the last, Exclude_Entity, every time an entity terminates. The clock will then automatically advance when there are no free entities in the system. Note that this does not prevent the programmer including Ada tasks that are not representing entities but are there for say data protection.

The procedure call When_Simulation_Ends_Do is used to halt execution of the main program until there are no active entities and the event list is empty. At this point the programmer will want to print out the results of the simulation before terminating the program.

Implementing queues gave similar problems to those of the event list, and a similar solution was found. However, a model has only one event list but may have numerous queues. The ASL provides the user with queue types for BIFO, FIFO, and LIFO and these are implemented by hidden manager tasks which enqueue tasks using the same technique as that of the event list manager. There was also a problem in providing a general way of dequeuing and this was done by introducing a Mailbox task. When a task issues a Dequeue call on a given queue then a mailbox is created by the queue manager with Granted and Collect entries, each having an agent as a parameter. The requesting task then calls Collect and waits for the queue manager to provide the first entity in the queue through a call on Granted. If the queue is empty then the requesting task will be blocked.

Various instances of resource pools, distribution generators and histograms are also supported by task managers generated when these objects are declared.

Implementation was initially carried out using the University of York's version 0 compiler, and later transfered to version 1. Some of the implementation decisions were due to the limitations of the compiler, in particular a generic implementation of queues would have been more satisfactory.

4. A SIMPLE MODEL

To illustrate the use of the ASL a simple model of a single server queue is considered and the program shown in figure 1. Customers are created by a customer generator at one minute intervals, they record their arrival time, wait in Line for service and then add their waiting time to a histogram before terminating. The server task is a permanent part of the model, it selects customers from Line and holds them for a sampled service time from an exponential distribution of mean 1.0.

At the end of the simulation, which covers the service of 50 customers, the server task is aborted and a histogram of waiting times printed out.

5. CONCLUSIONS

The version of the ASL that has been implemented using the University of York compiler has shown that the objective of implementing process interaction primitives within the framework of Ada is feasible. Other work has been reported on using Ada for simulation but none of this has used the ASL approach of exploiting the full parallelism of Ada, rather it attempts to provide features which emulate Simula [BRY84].

Experience with using the library for a variety of applications has shown it to be a good tool for rapid model development by programmers

Discrete Event Modelling

```
with Simulation, Distribution, Histograms, Text_IO;
use  Simulation, Distribution, Histograms, Text_IO;
procedure Single_Server_Queue is

    Line          : Fifo_Queue;
    Waiting_Time  : Histogram_Manager;
    Service_Time  : Exponential_Distribution;
    WTH : Histogram(1..10);

    task type Customer;
    type ID is access Customer;
    task body Customer is
        Arrival_Time : Duration;
    begin
        Arrival_Time := Sim_Time;
        WAIT(Line);
        Update_Histogram(Manager => Waiting_Time,
                    Observation=> Sim_Time - Arrival_Time);
        EXCLUDE_ENTITY;
    end Customer;

    task Customer_Generator;
    task body Customer_Generator is
        New_Customer : ID;
    begin
        for I in 1..50 loop
            INCLUDE_ENTITY;
            New_Customer := new Customer;
            HOLD(Sim_Time + 1.0);
        end loop;
        EXCLUDE_ENTITY;
    end Customer_Generator;

    task Server;
    task body Server is
        Being_Server : Process;
    begin
        loop
            DEQUEUE(Queue => Line, Entity => Being_Served);
            HOLD(Reactivation_Time => Sim_Time + Sample(Service_Time));
            ACTIVATE(Being_Served, Sim_Time);
        end loop
    end Server;

begin
    -- initialize model
    Set_Entity_Count(2);
    Set_Parameters(Distribution => Service_Time, Mean => 1.0);
    Initialize_Histogram(Manager => Waiting_Time
                    Cells => 10, Width => 0.5, Lower => 0.0);
    WHEN_SIMULATION_ENDS_DO;
    abort Server;
    Read_Histogram(Manager => Waiting_Time, Hist => WTH);
    New_Line;
    Put_Line("Waiting_Time");
    Print_Histogram(Hist => WTH, Lower => 0.0, Width => 0.5);
end Single_Server_Queue;
```

Figure 1

familiar with Ada. The programs produced are concise and easy to understand, following the Ada rules of readability.

However, there is still a considerable amount of work to be done on the ASL. Firstly, there are restrictions on the facilities of Ada imposed by the language restrictions of the York compiler, particularly in the area of generics. Secondly, the present implementation leads to very inefficient object code due to the heavy use of tasking and the rendezvous to implement the simulation primitives. Finally, the sampling and data collection facilities, which were not the main area of this study, need to be considerably enhanced.

In addition, the use of truly parallel tasks to model processes, rather than co-routines, means that runs of a model may behave non-deterministically depending on the Ada run-time scheduler. This problem has not been investigated because the York compiler does not have such a scheduler.

The ASL development project is continuing with the transfer of the library to a fully validated Ada implementation on a Data General machine. However, enough work has already been done to justify the prediction that simulation tools will form a useful component of any APSE.

REFERENCES

[BAR84] Bartlett, A J; Cherrie, B H; Lehman, M M; MacLean, R I; and Potts, C; "The Role of Executable Metric Models in the Programming Process - Final Report"; Department of Computing, Imperial College, June 1984.

[BRY84] Bryant, Ray and Unger, Brian, editors of the conference proceedings : "Simulation in Strongly Typed Languages: Ada, Pascal, Simula ..."; Simulation series Vol. 13, No. 2, The Society for Computer Simulation, February 1984.

[FIS73] Fishman, G S; "Concepts and Methods in Discrete Event Simulation"; John Wiley and sons, 1973.

[FRA77] Franta W R; "The Process View of Simulation"; The Computer Science Library, 1977.

[TEL83a] Tellaeche Bosch, R and Downes, V A: "ASL : User's Guide"; Technical Report DOC 83/24, Department of Computing, Imperial College of Science and Technology, 1983.

[TEL83b] Tellaeche Bosch, R : "Discrete Event Modelling in Ada"; MSc Thesis, Department of Computing, Imperial College of Science and Technology, 1983.

PART II ADA - PROGRAMMING SUPPORT ENVIRONMENTS

A MINIMAL ADA PROGRAMMING SUPPORT ENVIRONMENT

J.K. Romanski
Systems Designers, 1 Pembroke Broadway, Camberley, Surrey,
GU15   3XH, England

Abstract. Perspective is a software product used for the development and management of computer systems written in Pascal. Ada is a modern programming language covering a wide application domain which includes the sorts of systems envisaged for Perspective. It is natural for an Ada compiler and the Perspective support environment to be integrated to provide an Ada Programming Support Environment.
        The amalgamation of the two systems is described. There are certain fundamental principles in both systems that may not be changed: the Ada language cannot be extended; the Perspective development method has to remain valid for Pascal and other languages in addition to Ada.

General Description of Perspective

Perspective is a software development system produced by Systems Designers (SDL). The Perspective system is hosted on a powerful minicomputer which performs configuration management, editing, compilation and system building functions. Applications software can be loaded into the target hardware (such as a single board microcomputer) through a simple communication line and tested by using the Perspective host system to inspect and control the target system. This approach combines the advantages of the friendly and familiar environment of the host computer, with the ability to test application software on the actual target hardware.

The Perspective system is intended to be used by a project team during the development and maintenance of a software system. The sources of all software components are held on the host machine in a multi-user, multi-access database specially created and maintained by Perspective. Sources can be shared between projects and/or applications, with all uses of each item being recorded in the database. Multiple versions of a given source item can be held and the build configuration of any applications system or component can be obtained by a simple database query.

The Perspective Ada Compiler

Karlsruhe University developed an Ada '80 compiler funded by the German MoD which formed part of the SPERBER project. Members of that project team have continued work on the compiler in the two companies Systeam KG and GMD and have evolved the work into a full ANSI Ada compiler for the VAX machine.

SDL have a development and marketing arrangement with Systeam. It was a natural evolutionary step to integrate the Ada compiler with Perspective and extend it by providing code generators for microprocessor targets, source language debug facilities etc.

User Domains

Perspective is used to organise, manage, develop and maintain software systems. It provides an environment in which the structure of a system can be expressed and maintained.

Perspective is organised into a hierarchical set of user Domains each of which is given a unique name within the database. The topmost Domain within a Perspective database is called "Root" and this Domain always exists in a database.

Domains contain permission attributes which may prevent a user from using certain facilities within a Domain. A password may be associated with a Domain to prevent unauthorised access. An attribute is associated with a Domain which defines a default language context. Context is used to distinguish between tools which have the same name and perform similar functions but on objects associated with different languages; e.g. invocation of a Coral or Ada compiler would not need a language to be nominated explicitly because it is identified by the context. A user Domain is created by the command

CREATE USER domain_name [WITH permission_list]
[CONTEXT context_name]

Once a Domain has been created a user may start a

Perspective session by using the command

>SET USER domain_name

If the Domain requires a password, it must be given for the session to commence.

The context may be changed during a session by use of the command

>SET CONTEXT context_name

This permits the careful user to mix code developed in different languages.

Creating Items

A Domain is a receptacle for items, each of which is typed and has a unique name within the Domain. The types allowed depend on the context at the point at which the item is introduced to the Domain. Each context provides a list of all typenames which may be used.

Items are introduced by a create command which provides the type and name and has two optional parameters for supplying references to text. The text falls into two categories, one of which is known to Perspective commands and is used for configuration management (config_source) and the other supplies source text for the compiling and building tools (source_text). The command is of the form

>CREATE item_type item_name [FROM config_source]
>   [TEXT source_text]

the effect of this command depends on the context in which it is used.

The Pascal Compiler in Perspective has been extended to accept configuration information in headers as part of the program source. Create in the Pascal context requires only a config_source option. If it is present then the type information from within this source is checked against the item type to ensure that they correspond.

In the Ada context, Ada source is provided via the

source_text parameter which identifies a host file containing text in pure Ada form consisting of one or more compilation units. If no configuration source is provided then the source text will be treated in isolation and will not form part of a set of source items which depend on each other. The configuration source expresses relationships between items, the order in which they must be submitted to the compiler and the Program Library into which they are compiled. Automatic compilation and re-compilation sequences are derived from the configuration source and without this information all compilations must be invoked manually.

Configuration sources are expressed in a simple design language which records dependencies between items. It is envisaged that users would be able to produce these source forms by use of specialised requirements specification and analysis systems e.g. CORE [SDL 78] or PSL/PSA [Teichrow and Hershey (1977)].

An item in a Domain may be a Program Library, as defined in the LRM[DoD (83)], and it would be introduced to a Domain by a command of the form

CREATE prog_lib lib_name FROM target_lib_name

where prog_lib is the type of the item, lib_name its name and target_lib_name identifies a Program Library which may be a standard library for the target or one that is partially completed and requires further development. An error message is generated if an attempt is made to create a Program Library item in a non-Ada context.

Removal of Items

Items in a user Domain which are no longer required may be removed by the DELETE command. An item which is depended on by other items will not be removed unless the user insists on this explicitly. Deletion will be prevented if the item is in use and the use dependency cannot be removed.

Several versions of an item may exist concurrently which are distinguished by a version qualifier (see Versions). The PURGE command is given a full item specification which includes an item name and a version qualifier. The effect is equivalent to a number of uses of the

A Minimal Ada Programming Support Environment

Delete command for all versions of the named item except for the one given in the purge command.

Installation

A created item may be installed in a Domain by the INSTALL command. This analyses the configuration source to find other items on which the item being installed depends. If they are not so already, these other items are installed recursively so that all transitive items have obtained the installed status.

The act of installation records interdependencies between items in the database and their manipulation or removal is carefully monitored and indeed prohibited unless suitable permission is granted.

Error messages are generated if an item is not available to form a link in the database or if mistakes are detected during the analysis of any configuration sources.

Compilation

The Ada compiler is invoked in Ada context by a command of the form

COMPILE item_name [lib_name][FULLY][FAMILY]

The source text of the installed item identified by item_name is compiled into the Program Library called lib_name. If the item_name had a library identification in its configuration source and lib_name was not given then the item_name library identification would be used.

If the option FULLY is given, then the dependency structure derived from the installed items is used to invoke the compiler to compile or re-compile all units upon which this unit depends, prior to the compilation of the given item. This is done transitively on all units.

The option FAMILY is used to specify that the item nominated via the parameter to the command is submitted to the compiler and if successful, then all items which depend on this item are also compiled or re-compiled transitively.

The two options may be used in combination, in which case a

compilation sequence is determined by first applying the rules for the
FAMILY option and then preceding every item in sequence by a list
derived from the FULLY option. Multiple occurrences of each item are
then removed to provide an optimal compilation sequence.

After an item is compiled successfully this is recorded in
the database and a list of the compilation units present in the source
text is associated as an attribute of the compiled item.

The status of the item is changed from installed or compiled
(in the case of re-compilation) to compiled and the Program Library into
which the item was compiled is recorded as a dependency to ensure that
changes or disposal of items are properly policed.

Program Library

The Program Library supports the forest structure of
compilation units which have been compiled successfully in the knowledge
of each other. There is at most one version of any compilation unit in
the Program Library at any one time. The compiler guarantees that the
rules of the language have not been violated and that the necessary
dependencies introduced by subunits, elaborate pragmas, inline pragmas
and generic bodies are checked and recorded in the Program Library.

The Program Library provides a mapping between compilation
units and the bulk storage containers used to hold intermediate forms of
the Ada source, object code, symbol tables, debug tables and so on.

Given the recorded relationships between items and the
Program Library, the compilation unit names and their bulk containers,
the various construction and debug tools are able to find the
information they require.

The user is provided with a tool with which a Program
Library item may be interrogated. This tool would be used to
investigate which unit bodies were missing in a Program Library, to find
if there is a legal elaboration order and so on.

Increasing Visibility of Items Across Domains

A user Domain contains lists of items which have been
created in the Domain itself. An item in a Domain may be made available
for use in other nominated recipient Domains by the PUBLISH command.

A Minimal Ada Programming Support Environment

This command makes an item name visible in the Domains nominated but does not affect usability of the item itself. It has one or two parameter lists. The first provides a list of items to be published and the second, if present, provides a list of recipient Domains. If the list of recipient Domains is not given then a standard distribution list associated with the donor Domain is used. Facilities exist for a user to amend his own distribution list.

Items that are used by items being published are also published, automatically. Items which have been published are under strict control and changes are prohibited by Perspective.

Acquisition

An item which is visible may be made available by use of the Acquire command. The form of the command is

ACQUIRE item_name_list [TO lib_name][FULLY]

The items named in the list must have been published by some other donor Domains to the Domain issuing the ACQUIRE. A Domain name may be used to identify an item uniquely and the names may be written in the form "domain_name.item_name".

Acquisition does not imply physical copying of an item between Domains, but as far as the recipient is concerned, the effect would be the same.

An item may be dependant on some other items which have not been acquired. The acquisition will always ensure that the dependant items are already acquired or that they are acquired implicitly.

Option FULLY specifies that not only are the nominated items acquired, but so are all the items which are dependant on it transitively throughout the donor Domain.

The optional parameter lib_name is used to nominate a recipient Ada Program Library. The donor Program Library is supplied by the attribute associated with the compiled item being acquired.

When a Program Library is nominated, then the item and the compilation units associated with the item are transferred. There are strict rules which govern the legality of such acquisitions e.g. the

Program Libraries must be compatible. Appropriate checks are made to ensure that the Ada rules of separate compilation are not violated.

It is possible for the user to have several Program Libraries in one Domain. Acquisition within a single Domain will generate a new version of the item and acquire compilation units between Program Libraries. When acquired items or compilation units are no longer required, the user may relinquish all uses of an item by the DISPOSE command. The command causes all dependent items to be disposed as well as the nominated items.

A command exists to WITHDRAW an item from the visibility list of nominated Domains. This does not invalidate existing uses of an item across Domains but it does prevent new ones. The parameters are of the same form as in the PUBLISH command. A warning message is generated to all Domains which use a published item if the item is withdrawn.

Versions

Every item in a user Domain can be uniquely identified. Any operation on an item which changes its source/configuration text or dependency relationships results in a new version of the item being generated, with an update to its version qualifier. Version qualifiers are given as two lists of numbers, the first list governs the configuration control versions and the second list governs the development versions.

The configuration control versions consist of numeric fields which may be given user defined names. Any of these version fields may be used independently such that a user may have a version sequence e.g.

[2.0.4]

meaning

issue = 2, release = 0, frozen = 4

Development versions are lists of numbers separated by periods, whose least significant number is incremented whenever a new version number is produced. e.g.

[2.0.4]1.3.2

Commands exist to demote items from configuration controlled versions to development versions and to promote them back again. During development, items may be demoted several times to an arbitrary level and promoted again. Each change in a version number is checked by Perspective to ensure that the version number sequence is alwaya unique.

Conclusions

In addition to the facilities described, linkers, debuggers and host-target loading are also part of Perspective for Pascal and Ada.

Listing generators, editing and query facilities are integrated to encourage the user to remain within the protective environment offered by Perspective without resorting to programming "on the side". The system is encased in a coherent command language which was specially designed with the needs of a user in mind.

It is envisaged that Perspective will grow with the addition of other compilers and tools. The major new features will include a public tools interface and a means of extending the schema used to define the structure of the database. The extensions will be integrated in a way which does not compromise the principles of a disciplined Programming Support Environment.

References

Department of Defense (1983) Reference Manual for the Ada Programming Language, ANSI/MIL-STD 1815A

Systems Designers (1978), CORE - Controlled Requirements Expression, Seminar Notes.

D. Teichrow and A. Hershey (1977), PSL/PSA: a computer-aided technique for structured documentation and analysis of information processing systems, IEEE Trans. on Software Engineering. SE3, pp 41-48.

A REVISED STONEMAN FOR DISTRIBUTED ADA PROGRAMMING SUPPORT ENVIRONMENTS

J. P. Goodwin

Department of Computer Science
Virginia Tech
Blacksburg, Virginia 24061

ABSTRACT

This paper extends the conceptual model of the "STONEMAN" document to more completely model the interfaces and protocols that exist in the Ada Programming Support Environment (APSE). A previous extension to the STONEMAN model is reviewed and critiqued, the guidelines for the APSE set forth in STONEMAN are reviewed, and an updated model is proposed. The new model is shown to meet the guidelines set forth in STONEMAN, and to include subsequent ideas as well. The new model is then applied to the problem of user communication with an APSE, and it is shown how the new model extends to include distributed APSEs as well as single host APSEs. The issue of security enforcement, as a necessary subset of dynamic validation, is also included in the new model.

INTRODUCTION

A fundamental objective of the Department of Defense (DoD) initiative to develop Ada was to increase the portability and maintainability of embedded software (Carlson et al., 1980). To achieve this objective, the Ada Joint Program Office (AJPO) is working to ensure that Ada remains as independent of specific computing systems and applications as possible. The Ada language has been accepted by the American National Standards Institute (ANSI) as a national standard, and has been proposed to the International Organization for Standardisation (ISO) as an international standard. The Ada Validation Organization (AVO) has been established to enforce and protect the trademark for the language. However, the Ada project has evolved beyond an effort toward a common programming language for embedded software systems; work has been begun to define requirements for a common Ada Programming Support Environment (APSE), a Kernal Ada Programming Support Environment (KAPSE), and the Common APSE Interface Set (CAIS). The CAIS is part of the Ada standardization effort because it will provide a standardized development and runtime environment for Ada programs.

A previous report, "Validation in Ada Programming Support Environments" (Lee et al, 1982), recommended that the Open Systems Interconnection Reference Model be accepted as the underlying model of APSEs, and that there be developed a 'Strawman' to extend Ada systems into a networking environment, based on the OSI Reference Model. The model proposed in that report will be called a LAPSE (Layered Ada Programming Support Environment) in this paper. That report further suggested that the security aspects of the design of APSEs be investigated and that the results of that study be incorporated into the Stoneman requirements (Buxton, 1980). This paper will examine these ideas further, critiquing the LAPSE and proposing an updated and more detailed model, called the DAPSE (Distributed Ada Programming Support Environment). The DAPSE models communication between APSE tools through the use of the OSI Reference Model but takes into account the need to extend Ada systems into distributed environments. This model also incorporates a security layer, as recommended by Lee et al. (1980).

REVIEW OF LAPSE MODEL

This section reviews the LAPSE model (see Figure 1.) as suggested by Lee et al. (1980). In that report, the authors noted that "the original intent of the OSI Reference Model was not to actually represent an implementation strategy but instead to model those elements of a communications environment which need attention" (pg. 8). In other words, the OSI model was not intended to force all implementations to have seven layers, but rather to encourage all implementors to layer their implementations, and to clearly specify the functionality of each layer. Thus an application of the OSI model to a specific implementation could quite conceivably merge several layers into one, and split one of the OSI layers into one or more sublayers. This argument was given as a justification for the LAPSE model. The LAPSE model had three layers, which corresponded conceptually to the upper three layers of the OSI Reference Model. The bottom four layers of the OSI model (typically implemented in hardware) were not indigenous to the LAPSE. The top layer of the OSI model (The Application layer) was mapped onto the top layer of the LAPSE model, called the APSE layer. If the current environment was a Minimal Ada Programming Support Environment, (MAPSE), then the top layer will only include the necessary and

A revised STONEMAN

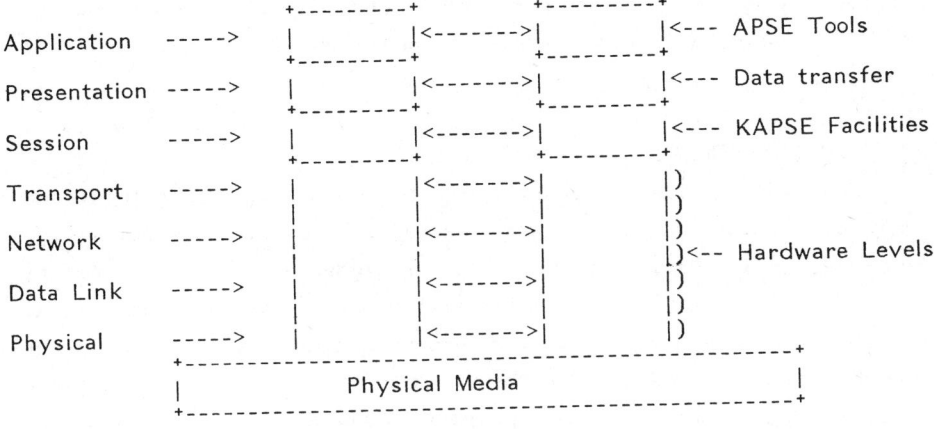

Figure 1. LAPSE Model

sufficient toolset, not the user programs or additional tools. Conceptually, there is no difference between an APSE and a MAPSE. The second layer down (corresponding to the OSI Presentation layer) was named the Data Transfer Layer. This layer was to act as an interface layer between the APSE and the KAPSE, and to implement the validation and security mechanisms suggested in the report. The Data Transfer layer accomplished all matching of formal and actual parameters, and associated typechecking. The bottom layer was the KAPSE Facilities layer, and was mapped onto the Session layer of the OSI model. The report by Lee et al. (1980) suggested that "the KAPSE could be implemented as a collection of Ada packages."

The LAPSE had the advantage that it clearly delineated what interfaces and protocols existed. The report called attention to the existance of certain "hidden protocols" within the STONEMAN model, and noted that these presented a difficult validation problem. In the LAPSE model, these hidden protocols were no longer hidden; they were revealed as KAPSE layer to KAPSE layer communication. Furthermore, the LAPSE model was better than the STONEMAN model because it took into account both validation and security, by modeling the interfaces and protocols that must be validated, and providing a layer where dynamic validation and security checks could be performed. The STONEMAN model was not detailed enough to reveal these problems since it was only two dimensional.

PROBLEMS WITH LAPSE MODEL

The LAPSE model had three basic problems. The first, and most basic, was that it made an unacceptable use of the OSI model. Since the OSI Reference Model is a model of a communications environment, and not a programming environment, it was inappropriate to fit the Ada Programming Support Environment onto only the upper three layers of the OSI model. Nonetheless, the principles of the OSI model are very much appropriate and ought be adopted in the design of the APSE environment. That is, the APSE should be layered, and the internal implementation of one layer should be changeable without necessitating a revision or rewriting of code in the other layers. Furthermore, specific functionality should be assigned to each layer of the implementation, and this functionality should follow the overall design principle of layered abstraction, where the services provided by each layer are implemented only in terms of (and by calls to) the functionalities of the layer immediately below.

A second problem with the LAPSE model was that it failed to take into account (or even mention) the Data Base Conceptual Schema (van Griethuysen, 1982). The APSE model should be integrated with the data base model, so that the design of the total environment is consistent and so that the interfaces between the Data Base and the KAPSE are well defined and easy to validate.

The third problem with the LAPSE model, and the problem with the STONEMAN model before it, was that the model was not well enough developed. It did not show where any the validation mechanisms were to be installed. Lee et al. (1980) stated that all interfaces and protocols must be validated in order to validate the environment, and it was this need that inspired the Data Transfer layer, where validation of the APSE to KAPSE interface was to occur. The problem was that this was not the only place where validation of protocols or interfaces needed to occur. All the horizontal protocols between two instances of layers at the same level must also be validated. For instance, a compiler could be communicating with an editor. Both these programs would reside in the top layer. The compiler and editor would communicate via a virtual protocol which would be implemented by calls through the interface to the Data Transfer layer. The Data Transfer layer services used by the compiler and the editor would also communicate via a virtual protocol which would be implemented by calls through another interface to services in the KAPSE Facilities layer. The KAPSE Facilities services would communicate using an actual protocol. The LAPSE model did not provide a mechanism whereby the virtual protocols could be validated. Another place where the LAPSE model needed further development was in the distinction between dynamic and static validation. The validation mechanisms suggested by Lee et al. (1980) are all static, yet the report suggested the creation of a layer where validation could occur. This validation would be dynamic, and the report did not expand upon the mechanisms by which the validation would be accomplished. It should be noted that there are two types of dynamic validation: dynamic validation during the development cycle, and dynamic validation in the runtime environment. The first type of dynamic validation occurs in the Ada Programming Support Environment on the host machine, and the second type of dynamic validation occurs in the Ada Runtime Environment on the target machine. Both of these sets of validation mechanisms must be considered in any comprehensive APSE model. Dynamic, built-in "validation" might be better termed "verification"; however, some of the connotations of the term verification are outside the domain of this report and thus the term validation is used consistently.

The report also mentioned the need for some security mechanisms, and suggested that they also be implemented in the Data Transfer Layer. However, it did not expand on different types of security mechanisms, nor did it distinguish between friendly and non-friendly or security intensive environments in its discussion of the need for security mechanisms. If a program is allowed to operate in an environment where security is important, and that program is not secure or does not meet the security requirements associated with its environment, then the validity of that environment has been jeopardized. Thus two fundamental principles about security must be recognized: (1) Different instances of Ada Programming Support Environments may have different security requirements, and therefore a program that is valid in one instance of the Ada environment may not be valid in another instance of the Ada environment because it is not secure, and (2), security is a subset of validation, i.e. a program that is not secure (enough) is not correct. These ideas clearly need much more attention before a final model for Ada environments can be approached.

Most of these issues were not addressed in the previous report because it was preliminary and did not go into the level of detail that would be necessary to deal with all these issues. This paper attempts to investigate all these issues and refine the model in the light of its findings. Thus the process of successive refinement of the model is carried one more step, arriving at a new model more complete than the earlier model. No doubt further iterations will need to take place.

REQUIREMENTS

Before updating the previous model, the requirements for the APSE should be reiterated and augmented by the ideas that have been put forward since STONEMAN. The basic STONEMAN philosophy (Buxton, 1980) emphasized fourteen general guidelines. Five among them are (1) long term software support, (2) host to target system software portability, (3) an integrated database and toolset, (4) overall simplicity, and (5) uniformity of protocol. The user interface to the APSE programs or tools should not be direct, but should be a virtual interface to the KAPSE with minimal JCL functions such as LOGIN/LOGOUT, CONNECT/RUN and control character processing. Terminal interface drivers should not be part of the KAPSE, but should interface to it, much as the APSE tools do. This model of user communication with the system is similar to one used in many operating systems; user I/O is handled by a special I/O processor (hardware, software or firmware) and buffered into the kernal of the operating system. A second concept that has received attention since STONEMAN is the configuration or version group, made up of shareable objects, each of which has a name and attributes. Each object in the version group has a date as one of its attributes, with later dated objects superceeding earlier ones in subsequent configurations. A third concept, which is related to the second, is that the APSE environment may in practice be distributed, either between the host and target machine (for down-line loading, trace data collection, or emulation) or between several hosts (for resource or information sharing or communication).

DESCRIPTION OF THE DISTRIBUTED APSE (DAPSE) MODEL

The DAPSE model (see figure 2) is a three layer version of the model presented by Lee et al. (1980). The top layer is called the APSE layer since it includes all APSE tools and application programs. It is analogous to, but not overlayed upon, the Application layer of the OSI Reference model. Conceptually, the user visualizes himself at this level,

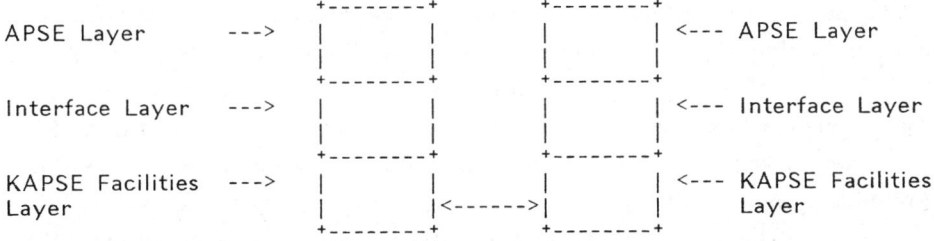

Figure 2. DAPSE Model

since the programs he interacts with are contained in this level: editors, compilers, debuggers, etc. If this layer contains only the minimal necessary tools and not any other tools or applications programs, then it is a Minimal Ada Programming Support Environment (MAPSE). Thus a MAPSE is a minimal instance of an APSE.

The middle layer is called the Interface layer. Interface is meant in the sense that it has been used in STONEMAN, and this layer has grown out of and is an expansion of the interface line between the APSE and KAPSE in the STONEMAN model. The parameter passing mechanisms that match the APSE actual parameters to the KAPSE actual parameters and perform dynamic typechecking between them exist in this layer. These mechanisms, formerly represented as the thick line between APSE and KAPSE, have been made into a level due to their complexity. The security mechanisms called for by Lee et al. (1980) also exist in this layer and work along with the typechecking mechanisms. The principle is to detect and stop security exceptions at as early a point as possible. This layer dynamically prevents protected KAPSE packages from even being called. Static validation mechanisms can show that the Interface layer properly performs its functionalities, and then use that assertion when validating the KAPSE facilities. The Interface layer performs all dynamic interface validation, including but not restricted to typechecking and package access control. In addition, any necessary data transformation operations may be performed within this layer. This layer can, like the KAPSE, be implemented as a set of Ada packages, with a correspondence between the names of the KAPSE level packages and the Interface level ones. The KAPSE level packages will only be visible from the Interface layer, and the APSE programs must call a KAPSE facility by calling the appropriate Interface layer package. The Interface layer will perform its validation and conversion functions, and then invoke the KAPSE package with the validated and possibly modified argument list.

The bottom layer is the KAPSE layer. It is composed of a set of Ada packages that implement the kernal function of the Ada Programming Support Environment. The KAPSE is the only layer that will be implemented differently on different host machines, but regardless of implementation its functionalities will be the same over all instances of the APSE. Part of the KAPSE may be implemented in another language, such as the operating system language of the source machine, but as much as possible should be written in Ada itself, since it is validatable. No other layer should have any non-Ada code. The functionality of the KAPSE should be defined in such a way as to provide a general purpose set of operating system type primitives which are robust enough to use to implement the rest of the DAPSE. The functionality of the KAPSE should not be defined in such a way as to prejudice the implementation of the KAPSE toward any one particular architecture among those on which the Ada environment must run.

Although three layers have been defined, this does not preclude each layer from being broken down into sub-layers in implementation. This is, in fact, anticipated as being the natural outgrowth of the development of a system whose underlying model is a layered one.

RATIONALE FOR A LAYERED MODEL

A layered model follows the guidelines set forth by STONEMAN. It aids long term software support by defining and consistently maintaining the functionality of the KAPSE, so that internal modifications to the KAPSE layer will not affect application software, or any other software above the KAPSE layer. Since any program will only reference those programs (or packages) in the layer immediately below its own, and since the functionality (but not necessarily the implementation) of those programs or packages is fixed across all systems, portability for all software above the KAPSE layer is enforced. Since all protocols and interfaces are clearly defined for the entire system, no hidden protocols exist. By rigidly enforcing one means of inter-tool communication through the KAPSE, an integrated toolset is arrived at and uniformity of protocol is enforced. A layered model is at the same time both simple and complete. For the applications programmer, the APSE is a set of procedures, packages and tasks that are visible to his program. Thus the concepts of the APSE are those of the Ada language itself, and the most straightforward possible. By judiciously grouping the visible packages into a small but well organized set of packages the functionality of the level below can be preorganized for the programmer. Only the necessary portions of the packages need be made visible, and the rest of the underlying layer need not concern the programmer. This model makes the APSE an easy environment to use as a programmer and to maintain as an APSE maintainer, for the same reasons that abstraction makes any system easier to understand and maintain.

RATIONALE FOR THE INTERFACE LAYER

Since the other two layers have been present in both the STONEMAN model and the LAPSE model, there is no need to motivate their presence in the DAPSE model. The Interface layer, however, needs further motivation. The first argument in favor of including this layer in the model is that this layer was really always present. In STONEMAN, the interface between the KAPSE and the APSE was presumed to perform all of the functionality now assigned to the Interface layer. No new functionality has been added, except for the need for security mechanisms as a subset of the validation mechanisms. The case for the inclusion of security mechanisms somewhere in the model has already been made in the previous report (Lee et al., 1980). The Interface layer is where these mechanisms belong, along with the other dynamic validation mechanisms. The second argument in favor of the new layer is that the interface mechanisms are too complex, and their effects are too far reaching for them to be ignored in the design of the APSE. If the interfaces are to be designed then they must be visible as a part of the model. They should not be allowed to fall into the crack between the APSE and KAPSE. Thirdly, since validation is a repeated step in the life of all APSEs, it is better to provide for it ahead of time. This was the basic thrust of the recommendation of the report, that validation requirements be established and included in APSE requirements specifications. Finally, since security must be considered to completely validate an APSE system, it is better that the security mechanisms also be designed into the model from the beginning, rather than added after the design has been completed. This is more true of security mechanisms than of others because of the subtle nature of security failures and the low level at which most security mechanisms are implemented.

DISTRIBUTED ADA ENVIRONMENTS

The concept of an APSE as a distributed system or a configured system is also encompassed by the layered model. As in the OSI model itself, the upper layers do not have any knowledge about the physical location of the peer process with which they are communicating. The KAPSE layer to KAPSE layer protocol is the only place where the actual locations of the source and destination programs must be considered. If the source and destination are on the same physical host, then communication may be as modeled above (see figure 2). If not, then the communication is via the network linking the two hosts. It is intended that the networks used to link distributed hosts also be modeled after the OSI reference model. Thus the model is expanded to the version shown in figure 3 in the case of distributed communication. In fact, only a part of the KAPSE layer, the package specifically concerned with communication, rather than the entire KAPSE layer, need be concerned with whether or not the source and destination are on the same host.

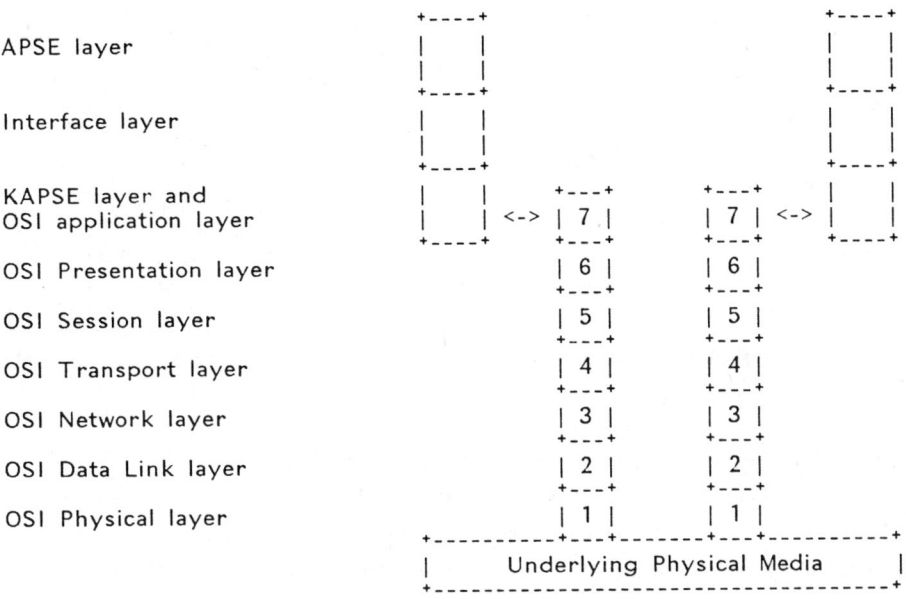

Figure 3. DAPSE model integrated with OSI model

USER COMMUNICATION APPLIED TO DAPSE MODEL

The issue of how a user will interface to the APSE is one that should not be overlooked or put off until late in the design phase if it is to be a natural and consistent interface. The layered approach handles the user much as if the user were in fact an application program: that is, there is no difference between communication with the user and communication with another APSE program. All communication goes through the KAPSE, and the KAPSE routes the 'message' back up through the appropriate layers to its destination (see figure 4).

CONCLUSIONS

The two part model presented in STONEMAN is no longer descriptive enough to model all the considerations that have been added since STONEMAN. A previous report originated the idea that the OSI model be used as the underlying model of APSEs. *It is recommended that a three layered model, patterned after the OSI Reference model, be*

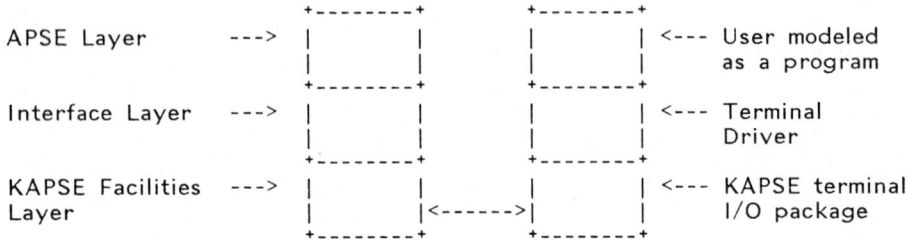

Figure 4. Communication with Users in DAPSE

adopted as the underlying model of APSES.

This report and a previous one have motivated the need for dynamic validation. *It is recommended that an investigation of dynamic typechecking and validation techniques be performed, and that the results be incorporated into the design of the middle layer of the proposed model.*

Security, as a subset of dynamic validation, is a necessary consideration in any validation system. *It is recommended that a security mechanism be designed and incorporated into the middle layer of the proposed model as early as possible* to enforce the assertion that no KAPSE facility can be called unless the appropriate security test has been passed.

It may be found that the security mechanisms proposed by the research recommended above are difficult or impossible to implement in Ada as it is now defined. *It is recommended that subsequent research be undertaken to investigate ways in which Ada could be extended to include security and validation mechanisms as a part of the language, rather than as a part of the APSE or Ada Runtime Support Environment.*

REFERENCES

Buxton, J.N. (1980). Requirements for Ada Programming Support Environments, "STONEMAN". U.S. Dept. of Defense.

Carlson, W.E., Druffel, L.E., Fisher, D.A., & Whitaker, W.A. (1980). Introducing Ada. *In* Proc. 1980 ACM Annual Conference, New York: ACM.

Lee, J.A.N., Lindquist, T.E, Kafura, D.E. & Probert, T. (1982). Validation in Ada Programming Support Environments. Virginia Tech Dept. of Comp. Sci. technical report CSIE-82-12.

van Griethuysen, J.J. (1982). Concepts and Terminology for the Conceptual Schema and the Information Base. ISO TC97/SC5/WG3, ISO TC97 Computers and Information Processing.

CO-OPERATING CHILL AND ADA COMPILER SYSTEMS

E. Meiling,
S. U. Palm
Dansk Datamatik Center, Lundtoftevej 1C, DK-2800 Lyngby, Denmark

Abstract. This paper describes a method which enables the use of Ada program units in CHILL programs and vice versa.

INTRODUCTION

Background and goals

This paper describes a method which enables the use of Ada program units in CHILL programs and vice versa. The method is based on the CHILL and Ada constructs dealing with specification of program properties and the separate compilation facilities.

The presentation in this paper is based on the project "Study of Supporting CHILL on the Commission Funded APSE" which has been carried out jointly by General Electric Company p.l.c. of England and Dansk Datamatik Center (DDC) of Denmark. The project was funded by the Commission of the European Communities.

The programming language CHILL (CCITT(80)) was developed by CCITT (The International Telegraph and Telephone Consultative Committee) for telecommunications applications. It is most likely that both CHILL and Ada will be used in this area. Even though the APSE is developed specifically for Ada programming, many of the tools in an APSE will be equally useful for CHILL programming, and by including a CHILL compiler and CHILL oriented tools in the APSE, a common environment for CHILL and Ada can be developed. However, the *coexistence* of CHILL and Ada might not cover your requirements. What might be needed is language *co-operation*.

The problem of language co-operation is certainly not new, and ways of crossing language barrieres are included in many systems. Different schemes allowing you to include foreign code exist, but most often, you are completely on your own when making use of foreign code, in the sense that checking (e.g. type checking) is no longer provided.

It is the goal of the proposed system that static and dynamic checks should be performed across compilation units, even in the cases where a unit is written in a foreign language. In order to be able to perform such checks, it must be possible to relate the language concepts of the languages involved. The proposed system is not based on source-to-source transformation of executable program parts. Instead, source-to-source transformation is used to transform the program parts specifying the interface (e.g. CHILL spec modules and Ada package specifications).

In should be noted that we are not promoting a programming style in which both CHILL and Ada are used within one program or program system without a good reason. The situation in which it can be useful to import foreign code is when you want to make use of "library facilities" written in the "wrong" language. It is a characteristic of such library facilities that they are declarative in nature. Library facilities will be compilable without any knowledge of the programs by which they might be used. Therefore, we restrict ourself to the exchange of program parts which we in Ada would include by a with-clause.

Basic approach

CHILL and Ada are sufficiently similar to consider the possibility of exchanging program parts. The similarities and differences between CHILL and Ada were investigated using denotational semantics techniques in an earlier phase of the project on which this paper is built (Meiling & Palm 1983 a). The exchange of program parts makes use of the separate compilation facilities. Separate compilation in the Ada sense is not identical to the (proposed) piecewise compilation concept in CHILL; but it turns out that the differences do not hinder the construction of a combined compilation system in which separate/piecewise compilation handlers can co-operate on the exchange of program parts.

Both languages contain constructs by which *properties* of program parts can be specified, and these constructs can also be used even if the program part itself is written in another language. Rules similar to the Ada conformance rules must be introduced to define the interface conformance.

To the compiler system receiving the foreign object code, it must look as if the object code is the result of compiling a program part written in the receiving language. This implies that a number of things must be done in the same way by the CHILL and Ada compiler involved in such an exchange. To emphasize this, we use the term *co-operating* CHILL and Ada compiler systems. The term *compiler system* is in this paper referring to the compiler together with the related tools (e.g. separate compilation handler, linker).

The ideas presented in this paper can also be used in connection with other programming languages containing separate compilation facilities and language elements capable of specifying (static) properties of programs.

Separate and piecewise compilation

The piecewise compilation facilities in CHILL, (CCITT 1983 b), differs in several ways from separate compilation in Ada. The CHILL piecewise compilation sceme is conceptually based on textual replacement, and the CHILL language does not define a library unit concept. Separately compiled units are considered as program *pieces*. The CHILL piecewise compilation unit considered in this paper is the *module,* a construct strongly related to the Ada package.

A missing piece of a CHILL program is indicated by a *spec module* in which the static properties of the missing piece is specified, together with a *remote module* indicating where the piece should be inserted and how it can be located.

The definition of CHILL deals only with the semantics of complete CHILL programs. To obtain a (complete) CHILL program, remote modules are *replaced* by corresponding pieces. The spec module has no semantics in CHILL and should be ignored when the program pieces have been put together. Since the scheme is based on textual replacement, there is no need to introduce special rules to define the elaboration order of separately compiled units.

The CHILL piecewise compilation mechanism is closely related to the Ada subunit concepts. The definition of piecewise compilation in CCITT(83b) gives the compiler system implementor a large degree of freedom in designing a way to handle the piecewise compilation of CHILL programs. Separate and piecewise compilation handlers can be build using the same database mechanism, and some of the separate compilation concepts of Ada are applicable for CHILL as well.

Principles of Co-operation

In order to describe the method of co-operation we introduce some concepts in a language independent way. These concepts describe the CHILL and Ada concept used in the co-operation. The basic concept is the *co-operation unit*, describing the program parts which can be exchanged.

The co-operation unit

The co-operation unit is a syntactical construct (in CHILL or Ada) which, through its specification, offers facilities to programs and other co-operation units. Thus, a co-operation unit may be included in several programs and cannot make any assumptions about its context. A co-operation unit consists of a co-operation unit specification and a co-operation unit body. A *co-operation unit specification* defines the facilities intended for use outside the co-operation unit. The facilities may comprise variables, types, and calling interfaces to subprograms. A co-operation unit specification serves two purposes. To a user, it is a catalog of the available facilities. To a compiler, it indicates how to interpret the code generated for the co-operation unit. For example, the textual placement of a variable declaration within a co-operation unit specification should unambiguously tell the compiler how to access the variable.

A *co-operation unit body* defines the executable part of the co-operation unit, i.e. subprograms and the program part for what in Ada is termed the elaboration.

The facilities of a co-operation unit are made available by means of an *include clause* mentioning its name. A co-operation unit specification or body which mentions the name of another co-operation unit in an include clause, is said to be *co-operation unit dependent* on this co-operation unit. A co-operation unit specification or body must be executed after the co-operation units on which it depends.

A co-operation unit may be gradually constructed from separately compiled *compilation units*, e. g. an Ada package together with its subunits. However, the co-operation is not concerned with incomplete co-operation units, neither is it concerned with the rules for constructing co-operation units from compilation units. You may view a co-operation unit body as a complete collection of the object code implementing the facilities described in the co-operation unit specification.

Co-operating CHILL and Ada compiler systems

In the next sections we will therefore assume that remote modules have been replaced by appropriate source texts (for CHILL programs) and that body stubs have been replaced by the corresponding subunits (for Ada programs).

The co-operation unit in CHILL and Ada

The CHILL language does not contain a concept similar to the co-operation unit. However, it is straightforward to introduce the concept of co-operation units into a CHILL compiler system, and we simply define a CHILL co-operation unit body as a CHILL module marked to act as such. The CHILL compiler system will for a CHILL co-operation unit body enforce the presence of a spec module (CHILL co-operation unit specification), either supplied by the user or automatically constructed on the basis of the module. This is similar to the rules for subprograms as compilation units in Ada.

The CHILL co-operation unit specifications and bodies are defined to be co-operation unit dependent on modules from which they seize (the CHILL term for import) facilities.

Notice that although the CHILL co-operation unit has been introduced in order to enable co-operation with the Ada compiler system, the concept can be useful also in the construction of CHILL programs not making use of facilities imported from the Ada compiler system.

A possible scheme for the use of co-operation units in the development of CHILL software is outlined in the following: When a programmer wants to compile a CHILL program (which may be a sequence of modules), he provides the CHILL compiler with the names of the co-operation units used by his program. The compiler system will generate code corresponding to a (complete) CHILL program in which the user program has been prefixed by a module containing the co-operation units mentioned by the user together with the co-operation units on which these depends (in a transitive manner). The sequence in which the CHILL compiler system includes co-operation units must be consistent with the co-operation unit dependencies.

The introduction of co-operation units in CHILL will not impose restrictions on the use of piecewise compilation in CHILL, since the rules above merely specifies how certain CHILL program pieces can be used as co-operation units.

Considering the Ada case, a co-operation unit specification is defined to be an Ada compilation unit consisting of a context clause and a package specification, whereas an Ada compilation unit consisting of a context clause and a package body is a co-operation unit body. We will use the term package (not defined in the Ada manual) for an Ada co-operation unit. To ease the presentation, we assume that Ada subprograms are always embedded in a package. Context clauses and with-dependencies in Ada correspond to include clauses and co-operation unit dependencies, respectively.

Summing up, we may say that the co-operation unit concept is fairly easy to introduce into the CHILL compiler system and that it is very closely related to Ada language concepts.

The co-operation

A co-operation unit is compiled into *co-operation unit code*. The compilation of the co-operation unit may be accomplished through several compilations, and these compilations may take place at different points in time. However, this aspect does not affect the co-operation, as this only deals with complete co-operation units.

The process of making a co-operation unit available in the receiving compiler system is called *conveyance*, and it consists of two sub-processes:
- Translation of source text.
- Adaptation of code and dependencies.

The *translation* process is the process by which a co-operation unit is made linguistically available in the receiving compiler system. The translation is a source-to-source mapping in which the specification of the co-operation unit in the delivering language is translated into an equivalent co-operation unit specification in the receiving language. The co-operation units on which the co-operation unit specification depends must already have been conveyed, as the receiving compiler system needs their specification in order to be able to interpret the received specification.

The *adaptation* process is the process of exchanging co-operation unit code and co-operation unit dependencies. We use the term adaptation to indicate that very few changes are necessary. As a part of the code exchange, the code for co-operation units on which the body of the co-

-operation unit depends (transitively) are made known to the receiving compiler system. Notice that the specification of these co-operation units are not translated and, therefore, need not be translatable. The code for some of the co-operation units might be known to the receiving compiler system in advance, either because the co-operation units have already been conveyed or because they origine from the receiving compiler system. The term "make known" indicates that transferring of code need not actually take place.

Conceptually, the co-operation unit dependencies are transferred without any changes. However, some changes in the representation may be necessary. The elaboration of an Ada package consists of elaboration of its specification (which has semantics associated as opposed to a CHILL spec module) as well as of its body. However, the specification and the body need not be consecutively elaborated. Rather, a dependency between them exists. This dependency has to be reflected in the CHILL compiler system when a package is conveyed. The splitting of the conveyance process into translation and adaptation has many advantages:

- The user of a received co-operation unit is provided with a specification of the unit and will by no means be aware of the fact that the co-operation unit stems from a foreign compiler system.
- The translation of the co-operation unit specification secures that the facilities of the co-operation unit will be used in a way which follows the rules of the foreign language.
- By not attempting to translate the entire co-operation unit, we have obtained that a co-operation unit is conveyable if ts specification is translatable Hence, the programmer of a co-operation unit which has to be conveyed is allowed to use all the constructs of the language in question when programming the body, as long as he is able to provide a translatable specification.

Translation

Translation is the source-to-source mapping which transforms a specification of a co-operation unit in the delivering language into a specification in the notation of the receiving language, thereby making the co-operation unit linguistically available in the receiving language.

Not all constructs which may appear in an Ada specification are translatable to spec module constructs in CHILL and vice versa. Language elements having no counterpart in the other language (e.g. Ada generics) cannot be translated, and in other situations certain restrictions will be imposed. Translation is defined by a set of *translation rules,* and these rules define the *translatable specification subsets* of CHILL and Ada. The translation rules will, for example, specify the mapping from an Ada *type declaration* to a CHILL *newmode definition statement,* and from a CHILL *quasi procedure definition statement* to an equivalent Ada *subprogram declaration.*

The translation rules must ensure semantic consistency of the translation, and they must therefore be based on a comparative description of CHILL and Ada. Such a study has been undertaken by Dansk Datamatik Center as part of the project on which this paper is based (Meiling & Palm 1982 and 1983 a). The investigation showed that a common description of central concepts like the concept of values can be found. A possible set of translation rules is reported in Meiling and Palm (1983 b).

Co-operation unit specifications are to be considered as purely *descriptive.* There is a drastic difference between a CHILL spec module and an Ada package specification in this sense, since the elaboration of an Ada package specification is an execution-like process while, in CHILL, no semantics are associated with a spec module. The dynamic aspects of an Ada package specification, such as object initialization, is not considered as a part of the specification of a co-operation unit and it is not translated into CHILL (or translated into a CHILL comment), but the object initialization is still performed as a part of the execution of the co-operation unit. The initialization is, in effect, moved to the package body.

It is not difficult to construct Ada programs in which the action above will be incorrect. To express the nature of an Ada package in CHILL, two CHILL modules must be created, one for the package specification and one for the package body. We have chosen not to do so, since we believe that elaboration of a co-operation unit specification should serve only to introduce the facilities of the co-operation unit. The facilities supplied by a co-operation unit should be kept independent of the sequence in which other facilities are introduced. Consequently, the translation rules should forbid translation of Ada package specifications in which it is not possible to elaborate the package specification and package body as one unit.

Translation Examples

In the following, some examples illustrating translation rules are given. Apart from Ada initializations, almost every rule is symmetric. In the examples, the CHILL construct shown in the left column are translatable to the Ada construct given in the right column and vice versa. The entities which may appear in a translatable co-operation unit specification comprise CHILL locations/Ada objects, CHILL modes/Ada types and CHILL quasi procedure definition statements/Ada subprogram declarations. From this point on, these entities will be termed variables, types, and calling interfaces, respectively.

Co-operation Unit Specification Translation

M: SPEC MODULE	with P; use P;
SEIZE P ALL PREFIXED;	package M is
...	...
GRANT ALL PREFIXED;	end M;
END M;	

The *SEIZE P ALL PREFIXED* imports all entities exported by the co-operation unit *P* and (because of the suffix *PREFIXED*) removes the prefix *P* from their names. Thus we require that the names of exported CHILL entities are prefixed with the name of the co-operation unit exporting them. Under this assumption, *SEIZE P ALL [PREFIXED];* is equivalent to *with P; [use P;]*, and, in both specifications, M is co-operation unit dependent on P. In CHILL the names of the entities exported have to be explicitly mentioned in a grant statement. *GRANT ALL PREFIXED* will export all the entities defined in the spec module and prefix them with *M*.

Variable Translation

DCL X T;	X : T;
DCL F BOOL;	F : BOOLEAN;
DCL I INT (3 : 8);	I : INTEGER range 3..8;

The types involved should conform to the Ada subtype indication or the equivalent form in CHILL. The only restrictions on a translatable variable are those on its type.

Type Translation

```
NEWMODE S1 =                      type S1 is
    STRUCT (B BOOL;                   record B : BOOLEAN;
            I INT);                          I : INTEGER;
                                      end record;
    SYNMODE S2 = S1;              subtype S2 is S1;
```

Nearly all types have a counterpart in the other language. Arrays cause some problems as their bounds are known at compile-time in CHILL, whereas this is not always the case in Ada. However, it turns out that row variables in CHILL plays the same role as dynamic array variables in Ada and, hence, Ada array types are sometimes translated into row modes and sometimes into CHILL array modes.

Calling Interface Translation

```
F : PROC (X,Y INT IN)             function F (X,Y : in  INTEGER)
        RETURNS (CHAR);               return CHARACTER;
END F;
P : PROC (B BOOL OUT)             procedure P (B : out BOOLEAN);
END P;
```

The translation as such causes no problems. Nevertheless, we are here faced with an unsolved problem. In CHILL, the names of the exceptions which may be raised at the point of call have to be explicitly mentioned by the subprogram (and the calling interface), whereas an Ada subprogram may raise any exception at the calling point. These two conventions are not compatible. On the one hand, we miss a notation in CHILL for specifying that any exception may be raised at the point of call, and on the other hand, we have no possibility of preventing an Ada subprogram from raising an exception. The calling interface for any CHILL subprogram will be translatable, but the calling interface for an Ada subprogram is only translatable if the subprogram does not raise any exceptions. Unfortunately, this can not be checked. As a consequence, the translation outlined above is in fact not preserving the semantics.

Notice that the translation of calling interfaces allows the use of constructs in the foreign language which have no counterpart in the native language. For instance, a CHILL user may via a calling interface to an Ada subprogram start a task.

Input/output

Input/output requires special attention, since it involves the non-translatable Ada concept of generics. The proposed suggestion for input/output in CHILL (CCITT 1983 a) is unlike Ada input/output in several ways, but the differences does not preclude co-operation in this area.

Translation will not directly relate CHILL and Ada input/output concepts, since translation, as a semantics preserving process, cannot relate semantically different concepts. Instead, the translation can be viewed as a way to obtain access to the input/output concepts of the other language. The translatability of input/output concepts depends on the way generics is implemented in Ada. The translation must define a mapping of Ada generic package specifications like SEQENTIAL_IO into CHILL spec modules. The object code corresponding to SEQUENTIAL_IO must be made available to the CHILL compiler system, and this requires that the Ada compiler system implements generic instantiation of input/output packages by code sharing. Similarly, the code for CHILL input/output facilities must play the part of shared generic code in the Ada compiler system. We estimate the cost of implementing such facilities to be higher than the benefits can justify.

In many situations you want to use your native input/output concepts to manipulate files produced by a program written in the other language. In such cases it might be sufficient to translate the type of the data on the file, whereafter you can treat the file as a native file.

Compiler Requirements

The co-operation as outlined in this paper will impose several constraints on the compilers involved. These constraints are summarized below.

- In order to allow for exchange of code, the compilers must employ the same linkage format.
- If simultaneously active CHILL processes and Ada tasks are allowed, these must be implemented by means of the same kernel operations for scheduling of processes and for storing/retrieving of process contexts.
- The two compilers must use a common representation of values for all translatable types.
- The addressing scheme of the compilers involved must be compatible in order to make it possible to access variables and call subprograms in the foreign language.

- The subprogram call mechanism used by the compilers must be indentical.

- Exception handling must be common for the two run-time systems in order to allow exceptions to propagate between the two systems.

In the paper by Meiling & Palm (1983 a) the authors suggest to combine some of the compiler components in the CHILL and Ada compilers. The sharing of compiler components will make it easier to fulfil the requirements above.

Acknowledgement

The authors wish to acknowledge the help received from colleages at DDC and GEC. We would like to thank Prof. Bernd Krieg-Brückner for many valuable suggestions, and we would like to thank the Commission for funding the project "Study of Supporting CHILL on the Commission Funded APSE".

References

CCITT (1980). CHILL Language Definition, CCITT Recommendation Z. 200.
CCITT (1983 a). Draft Proposal for Basic Input/Output Facilities in CHILL. CCITT.
CCITT (1983 b) Proposed Draft Recommendation for Visibility and Piecewise Compilation in CHILL. CCITT.
Meiling and Palm (1982). A Storage and Environment Model for CHILL and Ada.
Meiling and Palm (1983 a). A Comparative Study of CHILL and Ada on the Basis of Denotational Descriptions. Lisle, Illinois.: CHILL Conference Proceedings.
Meiling and Palm (1983 b). Co-operating CHILL and Ada Compiler Systems", Copenhagen, Denmark: Dansk Datamatik Center.

APSE TOOLS - ROLM'S EXPERIENCE

J.K. Elliott, D.M. Klein, and J.S. Williams
ROLM Corporation, San Jose, CA, 95134, USA

Abstract. ROLM Corporation was the first company to bring a production quality validated Ada* compiler and Ada programming support environment (APSE) to market. Customers have been using this system — the Ada Development Environment (ADE™) — to gain experience with Ada and to develop software for one and one half years. Feedback from this actual user experience has been the driving force in maturing the ADE concept and defining directions for the future. This paper highlights ROLM's experience with the development and maturation of the ADE and presents plans for future enhancements.

INTRODUCTION

Since our presentation at the March 1983 AdaTec meeting here in Brussels, Ada has been on the move. At that time, ROLM had released its first version of the ADE but the Ada compiler had not yet been validated. Today, three versions of the Ada Development Environment have been released with increasing functionality, performance and user friendliness in each release and the Ada compiler has been successfully retested against the ACVC validation suite. ROLM remains committed to Ada's future; we have joined forces with Data General Corporation to continue enhancing the ADE and the existing 32-bit code generator and we are now developing new 16-bit code generators for ROLM's MSE/14 and 1666B computers.

ROLM CORPORATION'S COMMITMENT TO ADA

In 1969, ROLM Corporation was formed with the objective of becoming the leading manufacturer off-the-shelf computer subsystems for embedded applications. In 1969, using a standardized off-the-shelf technology within embedded systems was a radical concept. In 1984, the technology is accepted and ROLM has been highly successful as the leading manufacturer of such systems.

Ada, and the notion of a standard language to be used within embedded systems, has undergone a similar progression. The first Ada

---

* Ada is a registered trademark of the Ada Joint Program Office
  ADE is a trade mark of ROLM Corporation.

Language Reference Manual was issued in 1979 amid scepticism in some quarters. At ROLM though, Ada was serious business; it's emergence and clear impact on our marketplace mandated that we capture the initiative as a pioneer and leader in Ada technology. Our strategy was to offer our customers a full implementation of the Ada language mated to an integrated support environment; our solution was the Ada Development Environment.

In October, 1982, we announced the Ada Development Environment and three months later we installed our first system. As already noted, we validated in June of 1983. We were the second implementation to validate and the first implementer not associated with the AJPO to go to validation. It was a difficult and painful process, but we succeeded. Our success in turn provided credibility to the entire Ada effort. Ada was a reality; it could be implemented and validated.

Validation, though, was merely a birth certificate — a beginning. Since last year we have steadily worked to enhance the ADE and add to our Ada product offerings.

THE INITIAL RELEASE OF THE ADE

The system demonstrated and used here in Brussels at the March 1983 AdaTec meeting was essentially the same as the first delivered system. It was hosted on and targeted for ROLM's MSE/800 — the mil-spec version of Data General's powerful 32-bit MV/8000 computer system. It provided a full tool set and a complete Ada compiler, but the compiler had not yet been validated, and the APSE had not yet received the benefit of extensive exposure in actual user applications. Release of a complete compiler and associated toolset was essential in order to get meaningful input from users on the effectiveness of Ada and the ADE in a production environment. Our view was that a partial implementation, or an implementation lacking an integrated environment would only serve to give users an unbalanced and inappropriate view of the Ada concept and would not solve the development life cycle problem.

A complete system

One of the main objectives of the initial ADE release was to provide a complete, integrated toolset, including a full Ada compiler, that could be used to effectively develop and maintain Ada application programs. We satisfied this objective.

All required features of Ada were available to users in the first release including fixed point, generics, overloading, separate compilation, I/O packages, machine code package, tasking, etc. The validated version of this compiler was first installed at customer sites in June 1983.

In addition to the compiler, the ADE included configuration control, full screen editor, document formatter, pretty printer, file maintainer, math package, runtime support routines, Ada linker, and a command line interpreter that processed a set of ADE unique commands.

The ADE supported the concept of Ada libraries, known as ALIBs, which contained all information about one or more Ada program units. Several "categories" of an object existed in an ALIB and any particular object was referenced by specifying its name, category, and possibly version. Multiple versions of an object of category x could exist. For example, TEST/CATEGORY=ADA referred to the Ada source code in file TEST. TEST/CAT=BINARY referred to the object code corresponding to the source code in file TEST. And TEST/CAT=ADA/VER=2 referred to version 2 of the source code in file TEST. To make use of these rather long names, the ADE commands had to first map them into real operating system file names. Because the ADE commands were implemented as AOS/VS (the underlying operating system) command language interpreter (CLI) macros, the name translation and consequently the execution time of ADE commands tended to be slow.

The Ada environment

One of the other objectives of the initial release was to provide the Ada user an insular environment that shielded him from the underlying operating system. We wanted the Ada user to be immersed in the ADE; he would not need to be concerned about the AOS/VS command language, file system, and other support features. A set of ADE commands all beginning with the letter "A" was created to help distinguish ADE commands from AOS/VS commands. Commands ACOPY, ATYPE, and ADELETE for example performed the same functions as the standard COPY, TYPE, and DELETE commands.

This shielding turned out to be an impossible, and indeed, an unpopular objective to meet. The underlying operating system kept showing through. For instance, actual AOS/VS file names rather than ADE object names would be displayed in diagnostics and output listing headers. In addition, users wanted capabilities available in AOS/VS which were denied them in ADE.

EARLY USER EXPERIENCE

Lockheed Missiles and Space Company in Sunnyvale California was our initial Beta test site. They received early versions of the ADE and we worked closely with them to test and evaluate the compiler and environment. Lockheed's objective was to gain Ada expertise by using it in a real application -- developing a GKS graphics interface for Ada. (Some results from this project were reported at the October 1983 AdaTec meeting in Dallas. Over 50,000 lines have been written.)

CR2A and Informatique Internationale, both located in France, were also early customers. Both these companies had their first exposure to our ADE at the March 1983 Brussels AdaTec meeting. In fact, we received significant and useful feedback at AdaTec meetings held here in Brussels, and in Cherry Hill and Dallas.

Comments and suggestions expressed by both casual and long term users has proven invaluable; both have had an impact on subsequent improvements made to the ADE. Besides instigating new tools and tool improvements, this ongoing dialog and the friendly proddings of our users led us to abandon the concept of isolating the ADE user from the AOS/VS operating system.

THE ROLM/DATA GENERAL PARTNERSHIP

In April, 1983, ROLM and Data General entered into a new agreement for joint marketing, joint development, and technology exchange in Ada systems. Data General -- a major minicomputer manufacturer -- like ROLM, saw enormous potential and impact in the emerging Ada technology.

Supplying industry with powerful systems for software development has been a major thrust in Data General's business strategy. The MV Series -- a compatible family of 32-bit systems -- has enabled Data General to emerge as the price/performance leader within this market segment.

APSE Tools

ROLM's business emphasis has been embedded processors deployed in Mil-Spec applications. The agreement forged between ROLM and Data General is synergistic. ROLM Corporation concentrates upon developing code generators and supporting the embedded target processors. Data General focuses on the host development facility and enhancing the ADE and the 32-bit Ada compiler. By joining forces, ROLM and Data General provide users today with a complete, fully supported Ada solution, unmatched in the industry.

THE CURRENT ADE

The ADE has matured significantly since its first release, due in part to input from actual user experiences. New tools have been added, old tools have been improved, the compiler has been upgraded, and the user interface simplified. Some of these enhancements are summarized below.

<u>Ada environment</u>. The concept of an Ada environment providing special tools and capabilities to support Ada programmers has been retained. Special ADE commands and on-line help are still available, but so are non-Ada capabilities. A user can now compile a FORTRAN program while in the ADE for example. The user is no longer shielded from the operating system; the full power of AOS/VS is now accessible. For example, full utilization of the hierarchical file system with its protective access control scheme and commands for creating, listing, and manipulating files of classes of files is now possible.

<u>User interface</u>. All commands conform to the standard CLI syntax. Specially named commands that duplicate standard CLI commands are no longer needed. Name mapping, converting object names such as TEST/CATEGORY=ADA/VER=2 into their actual file names, is no longer necessary. Users deal directly with AOS/VS files. Source files, object files, associated documentation files, etc. are distinguished by file name extensions just as they are everywhere else in AOS/VS. For example, TEST.ADA and TEST.OB refer to the Ada source and object code files for TEST.

<u>Configurability</u>. The ADE system manager can exercise a variety of

controls over all projects operating in the ADE. He can specify that all compiles and links be done in background batch streams for example. Individual project managers can also excercise certain controls over their project members. As an example, they can specify that users always be asked to record the reason for changes when an edit session is complete.

Directory structure. The ADE now directly supports and encourages the use of a hierarchical file directory structure for project organization. Individual project members can have their own working directory or directory structure while code and Ada program libraries of compiled library units common to all project members are maintained at a higher level. In fact, a project can now organize its libraries and files into any structure it deems appropriate. The compiler and linker can now compile into and link from Ada libraries in any directory for which the user has write access. If desired, multiple Ada program libraries can exist within a single directory. ADE commands to move up and down the directory structure have also been provided.

Ada compiler. Many improvements have been made to the compiler. Error messages are more intelligible and semantic error messages are now inserted in the listing after the offending statement unless an errors only list is requested. The standard compiler listing is greatly improved. Pragmas LIST and PAGE are now functional. Conditional compilation of specially marked source lines is now supported. (These lines must begin with "--/name" so that they are treated as comments unless the compiler is specifically requested to compile such lines.) Pragma INLINE is now supported. Representation clauses for record layout are now supported (with some restrictions). The compiler can now compile into any named Ada library rather than just the default library. And, of course, many bugs have been fixed. All of the approximately 1900 tests in the version 1.3 ACVC test suite are now processed correctly.

Pretty printer. The pretty print tool has been enhanced to produce program statistics and a cross reference list if desired. It can also format a program into a publishable form with reserved words underlined.

APSE Tools   109

Tasking support. Tasking support has been improved so that some Ada tasks can continue to execute while others are pended waiting for input data.

Library manager. An Ada library manager tool is now available. This tool gives the user the ability to interrogate and modify his program library. He can see what units have been compiled into a particular library, what other units a unit WITHs, who WITHs a particular unit, when units were compiled, and what the source and object file names are for a given unit. He can determine if a program is complete in the Ada sense, i.e. if all dependent units have been compiled and compiled in the correct order. He can also remove bodies of units or complete units from a library.

Import non-Ada code. It is now possible to import foreign code into an Ada program library so that procedures written in other languages such as FORTRAN or PASCAL can be used as the body of an Ada procedure. Of course, only objects which have corresponding data types in both languages can be passed. Pragmas INTERFACE, ENTRY_POINT, and LOAD are used to implement the import feature. The ADE IMPORT command simplifies the process.

Math library. The import mechanism has been used to import routines from the AOS/VS common math library into the ADE. These are the same highly optimized math routines used by FORTRAN and other languages. The result is a dramatic 200 - 500 per cent performance increase over the math routines distributed with the initial ADE release.

Screen editor. SLATE, a new more powerful text editor, is now the default editor in the ADE. SLATE provides many new features in comparison to SED, the previous default editor. For example, pattern matching with wild card characters is supported. Note however that it is very easy for the ADE system manager to reinstate SED as the default editor if it is the preferred editor at his site.

Configuration management. A powerful, yet easy to use text control system (TCS) is now available to ADE users to support configuration management. This system provides many features beyond the checkin/checkout capabilities in the initial ADE release. As in release 1, when a file is

checked out, no other project member can check it out for modification and
a new version or cycle is created each time a modified version is checked
in. However, now, only changed lines, not the complete new version, are
recorded when the file is checked in. For large applications this yields
a dramatic savings in the disk storage needed to archive source
modifications. Differences between versions and user comments about why
changes were made can be displayed at any time. A new variation of a file
can be split off from a controlled version at any point. This new
variation can then be modified and tracked separately. In addition, a
unique revision number can be associated with the specific version of each
file contained in a large software product. Thereafter, that version of
each file can be referenced by the one common revision number, e.g.
file/rev=1.0.

<u>Documentation</u>. The ADE documentation has been improved and compacted into
a more portable format. There is now one ADE manual rather than many
separate manuals. The ADE manual contains a good high level overview of
the ADE to familiarize new users to its concepts. In addition Appendix F
of the Ada LRM has been greatly expanded. Examples of how to use
implementation defined pragmas are now included.

FUTURE DIRECTIONS FOR THE ADE

ROLM and Data General are committed to refining and enhancing
the ADE. The three tiers upon which this effort is predicated are
additional code generators, improved 32-bit compiler performance, and new
tools.

16-Bit code generators

ROLM currently has under development Ada Target Development
Tools for our 16-bit processors. The 1666B (AN/UYK-64) processor is used
in many existing programs in the U.S. and Europe. The MSE/14 and MSE/14
Micro are Mil-Spec 16-bit ECLIPSE processors with full software
compatibility with Data General's 16-bit ECLIPSE line. These processors —
with Ada as the implementation language — have already been selected or
are under consideration for use on a number of major programs.

Developing code generators targeted to the MSE/14 and 1666B has yielded new challenges: Incorporating an Ada program file, including runtime support, into the 16-bit address space; generating efficient code suitable for the real-time, embedded environments in which these processors are typically deployed.

For both code generators, we decided to augment the operating system calls on the target to support the Ada tasking model directly. This enables elimination of tasking support from the user's runtime support library. A side benefit of this approach is true multitasking: Ada tasks are equivalent to tasks created at the operating system level. Supported by other design refinements such as the conditional loading of runtime support routines, the result has been a dramatic reduction in system memory requirements and more space for user code. In addition, an automatic overlaying mechanism has been implemented.

In a similar fashion, efficient code generation was a clear performance goal for the design teams. We met this goal. Local code optimizations, plus optimizations specific to the Ada language (such as eliminating redundant constraint checking) have yielded runtime speed and memory performance that begins to compare favorably with PASCAL, FORTRAN and other high level languages.

Finally, pragmas; representation clauses and specifications; LOW_LEVEL_IO; LONG_FLOAT and LONG_INTEGER; and other implementation specific features of the language are supported, far more completely, in the MSE/14 and 1666B compilers.

The 32-bit compiler

In the previous section, we discussed the improvements in design and performance that have been introduced into the code generators for our 16-bit processors. The code generator for the 32-bit Ada compiler, in future releases, will incorporate many of these same refinements. To state a few: direct code generation, supporting more of the implementation specific language features, and additional code optimization. Enhancements in other parts of the 32-bit system are also scheduled. Included in this group are conditional loading of the runtime support routines, LOW_LEVEL_IO, interrupt handling, a new parser for better error recovery, and enhancements to TEXT_IO allows access to control characters.

Tools

Finally, new tools will be made available to extend and augment the Ada Development Environment's current capabilities. A Remote Communications Package will aid in host to target development, enabling users on the ADE host to initiate file transfers to the target as well as access the target's virtual console. DIANA Interface Tools will provide all the capabilities required for users to develop their own DIANA-based tools.

Conformance with emerging standards

ROLM and Data General have closely monitored the efforts of the KIT/KITIA and CAISWG to establish a specification for the KAPSE interface and environment compatibility. We have played an active role in the CAIS reviews and the APSE Evaluation and Validation workshops. As a complete and viable standard for APSE compatibility emerges from these efforts, we intend to evolve the ADE towards full compliance with that standard. Finally, our implementation is based on DIANA, and we have closely tracked the evolution of DIANA and remained current with the latest revision published by Tartan Labs.

CONCLUSION

The Ada Development Environment and 32-bit compiler has been available for over a year and a half. The advantage of initially fielding a fully implemented system with a validated compiler is now evident. The ADE has been used in production environments to develop hundreds of thousands of lines of Ada code and the Ada Development Environment has matured as a direct consequence of actual user experience and feedback. We have seen three releases of the ADE — the latest of which supplied a newly certified compiler compliant with revision 1.3 of the ACVC test suite. The Ada Development Environment is now a tested concept and a mature system; the final validation has been at the hands of actual users.

TOWARD AN INTERACTIVE INTEGRATED
DEVELOPMENT ENVIRONMENT FOR ADA*

Arthur G. Duncan

General Electric Company
Corporate Research and Development
Schenectady, NY 12345
USA

1. INTRODUCTION.

This paper describes work in progress on a system called the Advanced Ada Development Environment (or AADE). This work, being carried out at the General Electric Company Center for Corporate Research and Development, is an attempt to bring the power of modern Lisp-based environments, such as the Lisp Machine environment and the Interlisp environment, to bear on the development of systems in Ada.

Using this environment, one would create an initial prototype of a system, in the same way that Lisp programmers now create rapid prototypes of complex AI systems. One would then refine the prototype in a disciplined way, using tools in the environment, to build a a production quality system.

In addition to the development tools, the environment will contain design libraries based on Ada packages and other, higher level, concepts that would allow one to put together initial prototypes (and in some cases even production quality systems) from prepackaged components.

2. THE ENVIRONMENT ITSELF.

The AADE is intended to provide an integrated set of software tools for creating and modifying systems in Ada. These tools will be fitted around a central core, consisting of

- an interpreter,
- a hot editor,
- a graphical input and menu system employing a pointing device, such as a mouse, and
- a window system for display.

The hot editor deserves particular mention here. By a "hot" editor, we mean an editor that

1. can be used interactively with an interpreter, allowing one to halt a program in the middle of the run, make changes to the current program state or to the program itself, and then continue the program from the point at which it was halted, and

2. allows a number of windows (representing program views, test drivers, hardware simulators, etc.) to be bound to one another in such a way that a change in one editable window will cause the other windows to be immediately updated.

About this central core, the environment would have

- an incremental compiler, as well as facilities for calling precompiled Ada libraries;
- very high level preprocessors that allow one, for example, to describe sets, sequences, and higher level control structures;

---

* Ada is a registered trademark of the U.S. Department of Defense.

- very high level application libraries providing idealized descriptions of components encountered often in particular applications (e.g., high level descriptions of multiple beam antennas, inertial measurement sets, etc.);
- simulation tools;
- verification and validation tools, such as consistency checkers and test set generators; and
- project management tools for tracing requirements, recording design decisions, etc.

3. EXTENDING THE ADA ENVIRONMENT TO SUPPORT PROTOTYPING.

In the AADE, the desired output is a system written in Ada that can be compiled with any validated Ada compiler. While the finished product must be legal Ada, the same requirement should not hold for all prototypes of a given system. We hope to facilitate prototyping by creating an interactive environment that (1) relaxes some of Ada's restrictions such as strong typing and (2) provides some higher level extensions to Ada.

Relaxing Ada's Strong Typing.

Ada is strongly typed, whereas most prototyping languages (such as Lisp and APL) are weakly typed. While Ada's strong typing contributes toward efficiency and reliability of a finished system, it tends to force a number of early implementation decisions, particularly with numeric types. For example, in a prototyping environment, it would be useful to have a generic vector space arithmetic package that would work with any numeric scalar type. This is hard to achieve in strict Ada, however, since numeric types passed as generic parameters must be specified as either integer, fixed point, or floating point types (or, alternatively, as private types with all arithmetic operations explicitly passed as parameters).

In the AADE, we plan to allow one to execute programs (or program fragments) without having to declare in advance the types of all variables. However, the system should keep track of all missing declarations so that the user can easily fill them in when refining the prototype to be an Ada library unit.

High Level Extensions to Ada.

Language features that would be useful for prototyping, but are not found in Ada include

- lists, sets, and sequences as types,
- procedures with a variable number of arguments,
- procedures and functions as arguments to other procedures and functions,
- arrays of procedures, and
- higher order functions, such as APPLY and MAPCAR in Lisp.

Suppose, for example, that a particular application can be naturally described in terms of sets of integers. In a prototyping environment one should be able to write

X: Set of Integer;

without having to write a generic set package (which forces a particular implementation) and then instantiate that package with the generic type parameter *Integer*.

An extensive library of higher level design constructs in the form of types and higher order functions would allow the designer to develop prototypes using a vocabulary that is natural to a particular application.

Since the purpose of the AADE is to aid in developing systems in Ada that can be compiled on any validated Ada compiler, it is important that the AADE keep track of all extensions used in a given system and provide automated assistance in converting these extensions to legal Ada. Thus, we would view these extensions as a form of preprocessor to Ada.

A Development Environment for Ada

4. RELATED WORK.

Some related projects at universities and in industry include:

- The Arcturus Project at U.C., Irvine (Standish 1983): Arcturus provides an interactive environment for constructing and interpreting Ada programs. It provides template-driven Ada text editing, an Ada program design language, performance measurement tools, a pretty printer, and tools for automated stepwise refinement from an Ada PDL into executable Ada.
- The PECAN project at Brown University (Reiss 1984): This is a family of programming environments supporting multiple views of a user's program. These views include a syntax-directed editor, expression trees, data type diagrams, flow graphs, and the symbol table. PECAN itself is built on top of lower level modules, including a window system and screen handler.
- Computer * Thought Ada: This system runs on the Symbolics 3600 and provides an Ada editor, interpreter, source-level debugger, and extensive on-line documentation.
- The Basil project at CMU (Furst 1983): This project provides a "hot editor" for the T_EX formatter, whereby one can simultaneously view the T_EX source and the formatted output with changes in the source being instantaneously reflected in the output.
- Some other related systems include the Cornell Program Synthesizer (Teitelbaum and Reps 1981) and ALBE/P (Lewis and Porges 1979).

5. TECHNICAL ISSUES.

In the AADE we plan to follow the lead of Arcturus by relaxing some of Ada's requirements, such as strong typing, in the initial prototyping of systems. We also plan to make effective use of a high resolution graphics display by supporting multiple views of users' programs à la PECAN.

Two constraints on the GE Development Environment are that

1. much of the environment should be usable with languages other than Ada, and
2. the environment should be available on a wide variety of hardware configurations.

The key technical issue is the design of an internal program representation, since this design will affect every other component of the system. This internal representation, or I-Code, should be both generic and extensible, since we cannot know in advance exactly what set of operations we will need to support. Moreover, it must be suitable for

- interpreting,
- compiling,
- generating editor templates, and
- defining extensions to a given source language.

P-Code and Abstract Syntax Trees have both been successfully employed by others to support more than one language; however, neither appears completely suitable for the AADE. P-Code is at too low a level while Abstract Syntax Trees do not appear as suitable for direct interpretation as some other representations.

Efficient interpretation is extremely important, since we expect the interpreter to be used more often than the compiler in developing prototypes. Also, on some systems, the command language itself may be some variant of Ada, in which case a fast interpreter will be needed to give adequate response times.

6. THE DEVELOPMENT CYCLE.

The AADE is now in the initial design phase. In particular, we are still working on the I-Code design. We expect to have the I-Code design in a more or less stable state by the third quarter of 1984 and to have some prototype parts of the Core running by mid 1985.

We plan to do most of the development work for the AADE on a powerful workstation, such as the Symbolics 3600, since many of the facilities we need (for example, the window and menu system) are already in place. As the environment matures, it can be rehosted on a variety of less expensive workstations. Basically, the development cycle will be

1. to develop an initial prototype of the Core on a powerful personal workstation, such as the Symbolics 3600,
2. to iterate on the initial Core design by developing prototypical design and prototyping tools around the Core,
3. to build up libraries of design and prototyping tools around the core, and
4. to rehost the environment on other workstations.

The initial prototype AADE will not provide full Ada but, rather, a suitable subset. It will include packages as the basic structuring facility for systems, but might initially leave out tasking and other features of Ada that are difficult to implement. While the interpreter will be gradually enhanced to support an approximation of full Ada (as well as several extensions), our goal is not to build a validated Ada interpreter but, rather, an environment for creating Ada source programs that can then be compiled with a validated Ada compiler.

Since the area of software development environments is undergoing rapid changes, we want the AADE to be able to "grow" new tools and features easily. Again, the design of the internal program representation will be the main factor affecting the ability of the AADE to evolve. The Interlisp environment, which has evolved gracefully over a period of fifteen years, is a prime example of a successful evolutionary development environment. The AADE would seek to carry on in the same spirit.

7. REFERENCES.

Furst, M. (1983), Private Communication.

Lewis, J. W. and Porges, D. F. (1979), ALBE/P: A Language-Based Editor for Pascal, Proc. of the Eighth Texas Conference on Computing Systems, November 1979, IEEE Press.

Reiss, S. P. (1984), PECAN: Program Development Systems that Support Multiple Views, Seventh International Conference on Software Engineering, Orlando, Florida, IEEE Computer Society Press.

Standish, T. A. (1983), Interactive Ada in the Arcturus Environment, Ada Letters, 1983, pp. III-1.23 to III-1.35.

Teitelbaum, T. and Reps, T. (1981), The Cornell Program Synthesizer: A Syntax-Directed Programming Environment, CACM, *24*, No. 9, pp. 563-78.

ACKNOWLEDGMENTS.

Besides the author, the AADE team consists of Clark Cooper, John Hutchison, and Jonathan Leivent, all of whom are contributing significantly to the project.

PART III ADA - ASPECTS OF IMPLEMENTATION

ADA AND RELIABILITY

J.C.D. NISSEN
GEC Software Limited, 132-135 Long Acre, London

THE IMPORTANCE OF RELIABILITY

The intention that Ada should be suitable for embedded software in military systems which may be "mission critical", meant that it required very high reliability. There have been cases where a software error has ruined or nearly ruined a space mission. Attention has been focused on purely software errors, and little has been said about the combination of software and hardware to obtain high reliability, which is the main subject of this paper.

TERMINOLOGY

There are various aspects of reliability. Availability of a system is the ability to continue performing its normal function in the face of faults and errors. Correctness concerns the ability to produce the appropriate output for a given input. This can be generalized for real-time systems as the ability to respond to stimuli with the right values at the right time; the behaviour must be correct. However, correctness of input is sometimes assumed: integrity concerns maintaining a consistent system (particularly maintaining consistent data within a system) despite input of errors. Security concerns the access to sensitive information within the system, and the authorization of that access. Security can be generalized to include access to function as well as information. Security is rarely of importance in embedded systems, once installed, and is not discussed in this paper.

However, it should be noted that the other aspects of reliability must be covered if security is to be maintained - faults and errors must not lay the system open to abuse.

Availability, correctness and integrity are to be maintained in the face of faults and errors. Before discussing a classification of faults and errors, let us distinguish the terms. By "fault" is meant a hardware malfunction; for example a stuck gate or a failed power supply. By "error" is here meant a wrong value which may have resulted from noise, software malfunction, human mistake, etc. The distinction is somewhat blurred by the possibility of transient faults appearing as noise, pattern sensitivity of hardware appearing as software malfunction, etc. Therefore any classification must be treated with caution.

CLASSIFICATION OF FAULTS AND ERRORS

One classification is according to origin: hardware, software or human. For hardware and software, the whole life-time should be considered. For each there can be errors in specification and design. Such errors are often called "bugs". With hardware there is the possibility of faulty manufacture, i.e. non-exact reproduction. Wrongly manufactured hardware has, effectively, faults built in. The same kind of problem can occur with software, if code or data is corrupted, during loading from host to target, for example. This appears as a hardware-induced error built into the software. Then, in service, there may be faults with hardware, and these may induce errors in the software.

As regards the human factor, errors in instruction correspond to hardware and software specification errors. For example a mistake in the user manual can give rise to human error. If instructions are not followed, the human error corresponds to noise-induced error in software. One could say that it is the software's responsibility to defend against human maloperation, in which case any human error which gets through is due to a software design or specification error.

HARDWARE SOLUTION TO FAULTS

No hardware is perfectly reliable; faults must always be considered. Ideally one would like such faults to be detected, and the software informed, without otherwise affecting the normal processing. A common way of dealing with hardware faults is by replication. For a computer system there would be three or more computers, synchronized, and working in parallel, doing the same calculations. At the output interface, majority decision logic would reject errors induced by faults in one computer. If there are more than three computers, more than one faulty computer can be tolerated. In the case of three, one has "triple modular redundancy", (TMR).

The redundancy techniques above cover faults and fault-induced errors satisfactorily (though there is a problem of ensuring that no single fault in the synchronization mechanism can bring down the whole system). However, they do not cover hardware or software errors (bugs) in the specification or design. Furthermore, the techniques are expensive - not only because of hardware replication, but also because each computer may be slowed for synchronization, there may be much majority decision logic, and input-output highways have to be replicated. Thus the cost/power ratio may be considerably greater than three times a single computer.

AVOIDANCE OF SOFTWARE DESIGN ERRORS

The main thrust of Ada design for reliability has been towards a software solution to purely software problems. By encouraging good programming style and re-use of proven components (packages), software design errors should be reduced. Debugging is simplified, and the chance of introducing further bugs in the process is reduced.

Work on the Style Guide (Nissen & Wallis, 1984) showed that Ada has been excellently designed as regards allowing, if not enforcing, good programming practice as established for other procedural languages. Where style

rules might be required for other languages, they are built
into Ada. The layout recommended in the ARM (Ansi, 1983) has
been carefully thought out, and there are only a few
arguable points. The main disadvantage of Ada is its sheer
size, which means that there is a lot for the programmer to
learn how to use well.

A good start towards re-usable components has been
made, but there is still a long way to go. The package
specification part is little more than a syntactic interface
specification, and does not cover the semantic specification
which is crucial for the user. A systematic means of
specification is required, so that a user can search a
library of specifications to find the one which is closest
to his or her needs.

AVOIDANCE OF COMPILATION ERRORS

By Ada standardization, and rigorous compiler
validation procedures, the chances of errors in the
compilation stage are reduced. (However, the possibility of
hardware-induced errors during compilation should be
considered.) Validation is merely a testing process; the
possibility of verification of a compiler against the formal
definition in a foolproof manner appears remote. As a
general rule, testing should cover the whole of the program
under test, exercising every path. Since supersets of Ada
are not allowed (except via foreign code), every part of the
compiler should be executed during validation. At present
the validation suite is not sufficient to do this.
Unfortunately, extension might be needed for each new
compiler to cover particular limitations and to ensure the
compiler behaves sensibly as limits are reached; furthermore
some such tests might take too long in practice.

We are still some way off being able to persuade
certain military approval bodies that, for software on which
lives depend, they should scrutinize programs at the high
level language level, rather than at the assembly language
or even binary level. However, we now should be able to

persuade them that the high level language level is worth having; being able to check at this level should help to eliminate semantic errors, thus allowing the forest to be seen for the trees.

The potential portability of Ada programs is of benefit since, by following rules (Nissen & Wallis, 1984), porting is simplified and the chances of design errors manifesting themselves only after the porting are reduced. There is a trend towards host-target development, in which programs are developed on a host and only transferred to the target at a late stage. Much of the testing and debugging can be done on the host but, if portability between host and target cannot be guaranteed, the testing will need to be repeated on the target.

SUPPORT FOR SOFTWARE DEVELOPMENT METHODS

What about the early stages in software development, before coding takes place? Ada is not of much obvious benefit here, except as an excellent language (even better than "C"!) in which to write tools to support these stages. However, studies have suggested that Ada may be the best available procedural language as a target for (as output from) state-of-the-art design methods (DoI, 1981). If so, this could ultimately prove one of Ada'a greatest benefits, even if Ada does become something of an intermediate language in a semi-automatic design process. The use of formal (or at least rigorous) design methods is pushing us in this direction. Such methods allow a high degree of quality control and also the possibility of program proving. This surely must be the way to go for highest software reliability. It is envisaged that formal methods will soon be applied in large-scale program development in industrial as well as military applications. Ada is acting as a superb focus for much activity on formal methods, which may actually be essentially language independent!

SUPPORT FOR HARDWARE DEVELOPMENT

Ada can also be of benefit in hardware development. It can be used for writing tools to support all stages of logic, board and chip design. It may even be used as a target language, given a "silicon compiler". Considering the cost of errors in VLSI design, formal methods and good tools are important. Verification and validation, with simulation, are needed before the design is cast in silicon. Ada could prove a good simulation language, having an affinity with Simula which was designed for the purpose.

SOFTWARE SOLUTION TO FAULTS

All the above considerations only concern the impact of Ada in reducing specification and design errors. The possibility of hardware faults has never (to the author's knowledge) been considered and accepted in language design except recently by Barbara Liskov (Liskov & Scheifler, 1983). She has tackled the problem of faulty communication, for example, with a program distributed between nodes connected by a packet-switched network. Not only may a link fail, but packets may not arrive in the order sent. The incorrect ordering could be an embarassment for Ada rendezvous calls, if "first made, first served" is assumed. However, her language has messages rather than rendezvous. There is a strong case for messenger tasks in Ada for such distributed systems. Loss of a packet then leads to loss of a messenger task, and ordering becomes a scheduling/priority issue.

The author believes that, for a multiprocessor or distributed target, the language design must take into account the possibility of faults. Such systems are often intended to continue functioning after a fault: indeed it may be difficult to avoid them doing so. The software which continues running needs to be informed of the failure of part of the system, assuming the faults have not been masked.

With the reduced cost of hardware (processors and memory) the goal of masking all hardware faults by means of hardware detection and correction mechanisms (e.g. Hamming codes for memory) is nearer. However, for at least some parts, TMR will be required, and this may push up the cost too much for certain applications. Other factors such as weight could rule out such hardware solutions, for example in a missile.

A TOTAL SOLUTION

This paper hereafter concentrates on a solution for systems where cost is a criterion, but where reliability is also important. Such systems include communications systems and systems to control expensive or potentially dangerous plant (chemical, steel, atomic etc.). Masking all hardware errors is assumed to be too expensive.

The system of particular interest is a distributed system comprising a network of nodes such that, if one node fails, the processing can be redistributed among the others. This solution is examined in some depth in a chapter of the Cambridge University Press book on Ada and Multiprocessors (Tedd et al, 1984). The author was involved in the preparation of this chapter and acknowledges its influence on what follows below.

Dealing with node faults

A layered approach is possible in each node. Responsibility for detection and recovery from faults and errors is shared between the layers, but a good design should delineate the responsibility clearly. Thus the lowest layer, the hardware itself, should be largely responsible for detecting faults in itself. Hardware detection is much cheaper than hardware correction. For memory, parity checking is cheaper than Hamming correction. For the processor, duplication with comparison is cheaper than triplication with majority decision logic. The cheapest solution is thus to detect the fault and fail the whole node.

The author has already stated his belief that, in a distributed system, the language design must take into account the possibility of faults. On failure of a node, the software on the other nodes must obviously be informed in some way of the failure for two reasons: the load must be redistributed, and that part of the application software running on the failed node has effectively been aborted.

The layer above the hardware is the operating system, or, in Ada terminology, the run-time system. This is assumed to be distributed between the nodes. It will be responsible for redistributing the load after a node failure.

On top is the application software, which must take into account the effective abortion of part of itself. Unfortunately Ada, or more strictly the ARM (Ansi, 1983), does not envisage possible task abortion due to node failure. Indeed the language design appears to neglect altogether the possibility of hardware faults. However, the ARM does not specifically exclude abortion by something outside (or underneath) the Ada program. When the program is distributed, it seems a reasonable interpretation to allow abortion of the tasks on a failed node by the underlying hardware (or run-time system). Indeed compiler validation is unlikely to be able to detect this interpretation and thereby prevent it.

Aborting the tasks on the failed node is not the end of the story. Any current "transactions" involving these tasks will be affected. The transactions will have to be rolled back in order to restore the system to a state where data is consistent. There is also the possibility of a "domino effect" leading to further roll-back.

The transaction issue is one that is crucial to the APSE, and other systems containing a significant database. Transactions are not a part of Ada, so have to be superimposed, or somehow spirited out of the language. One possibility is for a task to be created for each transaction and for the run-time system (or KAPSE) to recognize such tasks. Each rendezvous by the task would be monitored so that data affected can be "saved"; if the transaction is rolled back the data (base) needs to be restored to a consistent state.

Introducing transactions seems to be going too far for many applications; but the need to retain critical data remains. A possibility is to have a worker/standby arrangement of tasks, with the standby having the same code as the worker, but always residing on a different node in the network. The worker communicates any critical data with the standby, so that it can take over in the event of failure of the worker's node.

Dealing with link faults

What about faults in links between nodes, rather than in the nodes themselves? An application program, attempting to rendezvous over a link, could have the TASKING_ERROR exception raised when the link fails. However, a reasonably cheap solution may be of the fault masking type, where an alternative route is provided. The run-time system would steer communication down the alternative route when a link fails, and the application program is merely delayed somewhat. A message, or set of rendezvous parameters, lost at the moment of failure could be retransmitted, a buffer being provided in the sending node to cover this contingency.

Dealing with software design errors

Earlier in this paper the avoidance of design errors was discussed. To recover from any residual design errors, it is necessary to have alternative algorithms. An expensive solution is to have TMR but with each processor running a different algorithm to the same specification of behaviour. The processing is synchronized on output, when the majority decision is made. A less expensive solution is to use recovery blocks (Randell, 1975). After executing the first choice algorithm, its results are tested. This point

in an Ada program would generally be immediately before call
for rendezvous or output statement. An alternative algorithm
is brought in if the acceptance test fails. The alternative
has to start from the same point as the first algorithm did,
so data must be restored. For efficiency a special cache can
be used. In this case the restoration of data is not
specifically programmed. The alternative algorithm could be,
for example, a different body for the same task
specification as the first algorithm. If the first algorithm
fails, the run-time system arranges that the alternative
body is executed with data, including any input parameters,
restored from the cache. The Ada program must be able to
inform the run-time system. If the recovery block is a task,
a self-abort could be used. If the recovery block is a
subprogram, a special exception might be used. Whatever
means is chosen, the Ada program requires special
interpretation which goes beyond the ARM.

Dealing with other errors

Early in this paper an attempt was made to
classify faults and errors. A few kinds remain to be
discussed briefly. Errors induced by transient hardware
faults or pattern sensitivity can be covered by the recovery
block technique. They may often be picked up by hardware
detection mechanisms designed to deal with permanent faults.
Human errors can be guarded against by defensive
programming. However, it may be difficult to program the
system to restore all data to a consistent state. The
concept of the transaction may again be helpful; a
transaction is associated with a set of commands input by
some person and, if required, the transaction can be
aborted, with automatic restoration of data as appropriate.
This can be considered a "user-friendly" feature, allowing a
form of "undo" command.

CONCLUSIONS

Ada is well designed for encouraging a style of programming which will reduce bugs, but it does not cover the requirements of certain kinds of fault-tolerant and error-tolerant systems. Three particular problems have been raised concerning:

  (i) Node failure in a distributed system
  (ii) Recovery Blocks
  (iii) Transactions

For the first, allowance of abort by the underlying run-time system is required. This extends, but does not contradict the ARM interpretation. For the second, a special interpretation of self-abort or of an exception may be required, again going beyond the ARM. For the third, some notion of transactions needs to be incorporated into the language, perhaps for a future version of the language, or its replacement.

ACKNOWLEDGEMENTS

The author would like to thank GEC Software Limited for support for the preparation and presentation of this paper. He acknowledges useful discussions with members of the Ada-UK Multiprocessor Subgroup while he was working with GEC Telecommunications Limited.

REFERENCES

ANSI (1983). Ada Language Reference Manual.

DoI (1981). Report on the study of an Ada-based System Development Methodology. UK Department of Industry.

Liskov, B. & Scheifler, R. (1983). Guardians and Actions: Linguistic Support for Robust, Distributed Programs. TOPLAS, 5, 3.

Nissen, J.C.D. & Wallis P. (1984). Portability and Style in Ada. Cambridge University Press.

Randell, B. (1975). System Structure for Software Fault Tolerance. IEEE Transactions on Software Engineering, $\underline{1}$, 2, 220-32.

Tedd, M., Crespi-Reghizzi, S. and Natali, A. (1984). Ada for Multi-Microprocessors. Cambridge University Press.

Converting to ADA packages

B. A. Wichmann
J. G. J. Meijerink
National Physical Laboratory, Teddington, TW11 0LW, UK.

Abstract. A subroutine library must be designed to cover a wide range of needs with minimum of routines. A proliferation of routines requires a large implementation effort, especially for documentation, and adds to the user's difficulty in choosing the appropriate routine for his application. The design of a specific library, such as the Numerical Algorithms Group Fortran library [5] is influenced by the capabilities of the language. One should not therefore assume that the optimal routine design for Fortran is also optimal for another language. In this paper we consider the conversion of a small routine from Fortran (or Pascal) to Ada. The routine has been chosen both because it is small and because it raises a number of important issues to be faced in the design of Ada packages. No detailed knowledge of Ada should be needed as the issues are largely language independent and an explanation is given of each conversion step.

From Pascal to Ada

Program conversion can often be undertaken successfully without a detailed understanding of the algorithms involved. We routinely accept such conversions, performed mechanically without understanding by high-level language compilers, from the high-level language into machine-code. The example taken here is that of a random number generator. The details of its implementation appear in [1], while [2] gives the results of tests on the randomness of the sequences produced. None of the details are needed to understand the conversion process. We start with the Pascal version which appears in [7] because of the obvious similarity between Pascal and Ada. The Pascal version could be transliterated to Ada by merely changing the syntactic form of the text. However, it is clear that the use of the global variables for the seeds of the generator should be changed to avoid any potential misuse. This can be easily arranged in Ada by placing the variables in a package so that the variables themselves appear only in the implementation of the package and not in its specification. If one does this, then one must provide a means of reading and resetting the seeds to allow the sequence to be repeated (if required). Given this change, the (Ada) specification becomes:

Converting to Ada packages

```
package Random_Numbers is

      function Random return Float;
      -- Returns a random value in the range 0.0 .. 1.0.

      procedure Seeds_Are (X, Y, Z : out Integer );
      -- Gives the values of the seeds.

      procedure Restart ( X, Y, Z : in Integer );
      -- To restart from particular seeds or
      -- from any values in the range 1 .. 30_000.

end Random_Numbers;
```

This specification gives a simple, even elegant, description of the package devoid of implementation details. Ideally, a semantic specification should be given also. However, none of the languages discussed here provide any mechanism for this. Extensions to Ada by means of comments which allow such semantic information are presented in [6]. In fact, one can specify one property of the package; that is including a range constraint (0.0 .. 1.0) on the result of the function Random.

The package body is easy to convert to Ada as follows:

```
package body Random_Numbers is

   IX, IY, IZ : Integer;    -- The three seeds.

function Random return Float is
   W : Float;

   begin
      IX := 171 * (IX mod 177) - 2 * (IX/177);
      IY := 172 * (IY mod 176) - 35 * (IY/176);
      IZ := 170 * (IZ mod 178) - 63 * (IZ/178);
      if IX < 0 then
         IX := IX + 30269;
      end if;
      if IY < 0 then
         IY := IY + 30307;
      end if;
      if IZ < 0 then
         IZ := IZ + 30323;
      end if;
      W := Float(IX)/30269.0 + Float(IY)/30307.0 + Float(IZ)/30323.0;
      return W  - Float (Integer (W - 0.5));
   end Random;
```

Converting to Ada packages

```
   procedure Seeds_Are (X, Y, Z : out Integer) is
      begin
         X := IX;
         Y := IY;
         Z := IZ;
      end Seeds_Are;

   procedure Restart (X, Y, Z : in Integer) is
      begin
         IX := ( X - 1 ) mod 30269 + 1;
         IY := ( Y - 1 ) mod 30307 + 1;
         IZ := ( Z - 1 ) mod 30323 + 1;
      end Restart;

begin

   IX := 1;
   IY := 10001;
   IZ := 4987;

end Random_Numbers;
```

The only divergence from the text of the Pascal version is in the inclusion of the initialization of the three seeds IX, IY and IZ. By placing these in the statement body of the package, the three values are automatically initialized without any action by the user. Note that since IX, IY and IZ are hidden, it is possible to simplify the body of Random as it is no longer necessary to place strict range constraints against each value. The new procedure Restart could raise an exception to signal that the given integers are out of range. Instead, they are converted to a value which is in range.

Portability and Style refinements

The original algorithm was produced as two different variants. They had identical external characteristics but one requires 24-bit arithmetic and the other 16-bit arithmetic. In Fortran or Pascal one could provide both variants leaving it to the user to pick the one appropriate to his machine. In the published Fortran version, one variant is included as a comment. In Ada one aims at producing very high portability because all Ada compilers are supposed to be identical in the language implemented. Therefore one strives to provide the program so that no alteration is needed to the source text. In this case Ada provides a means of determining the size of integers. In fact, the constant Integer'Size gives the size of an integer in bits. The algorithm selection can therefore be made automatic. Under very unlikely circumstances, the choice of algorithm could fail. This is detected by means of inspection of the value Integer'Last so that this can be reported by raising the exception Constraint_Error.

Although the conversion can be regarded as being complete in embodying both of the original variants, a review shows a defect in style. Abstractly, the random number generator has just one seed which determines the subsequent values. The algorithm implements the seed as three integer values. Given that the seed is a concept, this should be mirrored in Ada by a data type. The converted package specification and body can be seen from lines 01-13, 15-84, 95 in the final text at the end of this paper.

Default initialization of the seed

The original algorithm initialized the seed by a simple assignment of constants to the three integers. This is fine if one wants a repeatable random sequence. In practice, a random sequence that starts with the same value is not the default requirement. One trick used to avoid repeatability is to initialize the data with values derived from the machine's internal clock. Ada defines a package Calendar which provides just this ability. This change does not influence the Ada specification and the revised body merely has the lines 14, 85-94 added to it. context clause for the package Calendar):

Successively smaller intervals of time are used to initialize the three integers forming the seed. The Z component is increased by one on every millisecond. The Ada standard specifies that the clock has a resolution of at least 20 milliseconds.

The procedure Restart can be called to give the same repeatable sequence as before, i.e, Restart((1,10001,4987));.

Different sequences and tasking

Although the version produced so far is adequate for many purposes, it actually contains two serious defects. To appreciate these defects, consider the use of the package in an Ada program which simulates a complex process which includes random events.

Corresponding to each random event, a different random sequence may be needed. These sequences may have different distributions from the uniform distribution between 0.0 and 1.0 that is provided. Moreover, during testing in particular, one needs to vary the nature of one sequence while keeping the others fixed. The single sequence with one seed does not permit this. The only solution is to allow the user to construct a new sequence with its own seed.

One might think that a simple solution to this problem is to

Converting to Ada packages 135

pass the seed as a parameter to the function Random. This is not possible in Ada because the parameter would have to be of mode in-out - illegal in Ada. To overcome this, one would have to recast Random as a procedure. Unless one takes a purist view of functions, this is a very unattractive solution which is not pursued here.

Our complex simulation program in Ada could be programmed very elegantly by writing Ada tasks for every independent process being simulated. This provides a more realistic model of the process. However, Ada tasks should not share common variables. Such sharing will take place if two Ada tasks use the same random number generator - the shared variable being the common seed. This prohibition against sharing is most important because the generator could otherwise produce indeterminate results (not random, say nothing but zeros!). The solution here is to allow the user to construct a new generator inside each task so that no sharing of a seed is needed.

In Ada multiple instances of a package can be easily made by making the package generic. The necessity of having multiple instances is noted in [3]. The package specification is changed merely by adding generic, i,e. line 00. The package body is unaltered. However, the generic package cannot be used directly but must be instantiated to give a usable package:

    package My_Random is new Random_Numbers;

The sequence is now obtained by repeated calls of the function My_Random.Random.

A significant problem with the generic version of the package is the requirement for the user to instantiate it. This need will be an inconvenience to those requiring neither multiple sequences nor using tasks (the ordinary simple case). A solution to this follows the guidelines on mathematical software proposed in [4]. This solution provides two packages. A generic one whose name is Gen_Name and a standard instantiation. Hence in this case we would have:

```
generic
package Gen_Random_Numbers is

    -- as before

end Gen_Random_Numbers;
```

The body is as before. The non-generic version can be created by generic instantiation as above.

By providing the same specification, the move needed to enhance a program from a single sequence to a multiple set of generators is minimised. An alternative solution to the tasking problem is to put the generator inside an Ada task. The seed would then be a protected variable within the task. This has two disadvantages: firstly, the call of the generator (an entry) would be a procedure and not a function call, secondly, the efficiency of the generator could be much worse due to scheduling overheads. The approach of using a task would be the natural one for the language Occam designed for the Inmos Transputer [8]. One would still need several tasks to run in separate transputers (which could be programmed as one Occam program).

Conclusions

We have shown that there is a substantial difference between a naive transliteration of a subroutine and an ideal Ada package. The difference arises because of the increased capabilities of Ada which allow one to provide greater functionality. In the example given here, the increased functionality that is not available in the Fortran version is as follows:

a) Automatic selection of two variants according to the machine characteristics.

b) Improved security of the seed to incorrect access.

c) Automatic default initialization of the seed by use of an internal clock (in a machine-independent fashion).

d) Ability to provide multiple sequences giving security in a tasking environment.

Of course, other conversions will result in a different set of additional capabilities. At least in conversion to Ada, one should not expect the ideal conversion to present exactly the same functionality.

Acknowledgements The authors are very grateful for detailed comments on a draft of this paper from I D Hill. Further improvements were prompted by remarks from D A Watt, R S Scowen and D May.

References

[1] Wichmann, B. A. and Hill, I. D., Algorithm AS 183: An efficient and portable pseudo-random generator, Applied Statistics, Vol31 No 2, 1982.

[2] Wichmann, B. A. and Hill, I. D., A Pseudo-Random Number Generator, NPL Report DITC 6/82, June 1982.

[3] Currie, I. F., and Peeling, N. E., Modular Compilation Systems for High Level Programming Languages, Algol Bulletin, No 48, August 1982.

[4] Symm, G. T., Wichmann, B. A., Kok, J. and Winter, D. T., Guidelines for the design of large modular scientific libraries in Ada, Second interim report NPL Report DITC 28/83, July 1983.

[5] NAG FORTRAN library, NAG Ltd, 256 Banbury Road, Oxford.

[6] Hill, A. Towards an Ada-based specification and design language. Ada UK News, Vol4, No4, Oct 1983. ISSN 0264-2085.

[7] British Standards Institution, The Pascal Compiler Validation Suite, Version 4.0, October 1983.

[8] Occam, INMOS Ltd. Bristol 1983.

[9] Wichmann, B. A . and Meijerink, J. G. J., Converting to Ada packages, NPL Report DITC 39/84, March 1984, (an extended version of this paper).

Final converted package

```
00 generic
01     package Gen_Random_Numbers is
02         function Random return Float;
03             -- Returns a random value in the range 0.0 .. 1.0.
04         type Seed is
05             record
06                 X, Y, Z : Integer;
07             end record;
08         function Current_Seed return Seed;
09             -- Gives the value of the seed.
10         procedure Restart ( Restart_Seed : in Seed );
11             -- To restart from particular seeds or
12             --   from any values in the range 1 .. 30_000.
13     end Gen_Random_Numbers;

14 with Calendar;
15 package body Gen_Random_Numbers is

16     Simple_Case : constant Boolean := Integer'Size >= 24;
17         -- Simple_Case determines which algorithm will be used,
18         -- it should be evaluated by the compiler and in consequence
19         -- no additional overhead will be placed on the program.

20     S : Seed;

21 function Random return Float is
22     W : Float;
23     begin
24         if Simple_Case then
25             -- Since 30269, 30307 and 30323 are primes, all sequences
26             -- can be of maximal length (see Seminumerical Algorithms,
27             -- D E Knuth, Addison Wesley 1969, p19).

28             S := ((171 * S.X) mod 30269,
29                   (172 * S.Y) mod 30307,
30                   (170 * S.Z) mod 30323);
31         else             -- not Simple_Case
32             -- The simple steps above cannot be performed without
33             -- overflow on a 16-bit machine. This is avoided by writing:
34             --         Y = k * 176 + r
35             -- where   0 <= k <= 172
36             -- and     0 <= r <= 175
37             -- Then    172 * Y = k * 176 * 172 + r * 172
38             --                 = k * 30272 + r * 172
39             --                 = - k * 35 + r * 172 mod 30307
40             -- Similarly
41             -- with    Z = k * 178 + r
42             --         170 * Z = - k * 63 + r * 170 mod 30323.
43             -- and with X = k * 177 + r
44             --         171 * X = - k * 2 + r * 171 mod 30269
45             -- The values are now bounded for a 16-bit machine.

46             S := (171 * (S.X mod 177) - 2 * (S.X / 177),
47                   172 * (S.Y mod 176) - 35 * (S.Y / 176),
48                   170 * (S.Z mod 178) - 63 * (S.Z / 178));
```

Converting to Ada packages

```
49           if S.X < 0 then
50              S.X := S.X + 30269;
51           end if;
52           if S.Y < 0 then
53              S.Y := S.Y + 30307;
54           end if;
55           if S.Z < 0 then
56              S.Z := S.Z + 30323;
57           end if;
58        end if;

59        W := Float(S.X)/30269.0 + Float(S.Y)/30307.0 +
60                Float(S.Z)/30323.0;
61        return W - Float (Integer (W - 0.5));
62     end Random;

63  function Current_Seed return Seed is
64     begin
65        return S;
66     end Current_Seed;


67  procedure Restart (Restart_Seed : in Seed) is
68     begin
69        Seed := ( ( Restart_Seed.X - 1 ) mod 30269 + 1,
70                  ( Restart_Seed.Y - 1 ) mod 30307 + 1,
71                  ( Restart_Seed.Z - 1 ) mod 30323 + 1 );
72     end Restart;

73  begin

74     -- Check that Integer has sufficient range
75     -- for the generator to work at all.
76     if Integer'Last < 30323 then
77        raise Constraint_Error;
78     end if;


79     -- Check that Simple_Case gives correct selection. Raise
80     -- Constraint_Error in unlikely case that Simple_Case does
81     -- not give correct distinction.
82     if Simple_Case and then (Integer'Last < 5212632) then
83        raise Constraint_Error;
84     end if;

85     declare   -- Initialize the seed.
86        use Calendar;
87        T : Time := Clock;
88        Count: Integer := Integer(Seconds(T)/3);
89                 -- in range 1 .. 28801, increases every 3 secs.
90     begin
91        S := (Month(T),
92              Day(T) + Count,
93              Integer(1000*Seconds(T) - 3000*Duration(Count)) );
94     end;
95  end Gen_Random_Numbers;
```

TOWARDS A SYSTEMATIC AND SAFE PROGRAMMING OF EXCEPTION HANDLING IN ADA

Michel BIDOIT, Marie-Claude GAUDEL, Gérard GUIHO

Laboratoire de Recherche en Informatique
Université de Paris-Sud
Bâtiment 490
91405 Orsay - Cedex, FRANCE

Laboratoires de Marcoussis
Centre de Recherches de la C.G.E.
Route de Nozay
91460 Marcoussis, FRANCE

INTRODUCTION

Modular development of robust, large sized programs in ADA leads to an intensive use of exception handling features of the language. This is especially true in the telephone switching area.

This kind of programmation results in new development constraints:

* As a strong requirement, one needs to know at any moment the origin of an exception and its subsequent propagation.

* As far as programs are developed in a modular way, an exception which is propagated out of a program unit must be handled as soon as possible. Indeed, when an exception is propagated from modules to outer modules, its meaning decreases. Moreover, in ADA it may become anonymous.

In ADA, an exception becomes anonymous when it is not handled within the scope of its identifier. More precisely, an exception declared as local to a procedure body must be handled inside this body. The same thing holds for task units and packages.

Handling anonymous exceptions can only be rather general, thus dangerous. Moreover, dealing with anonymous exceptions may be confusing: what happens when an exception E, propagated as anonymous, is caught by a handler where the exception identifier E is used? Or what happens when an anonymous exception is propagated back into its scope again?

In this paper, we describe a method for programming exception cases in ADA. This method ensures that no anonymous exception will be propagated out from a public unit. By public unit, we mean procedures or functions which appear in the visible part of a package specification, task units and packages.

With any public unit declaration is associated a list of "exportable" exception identifiers. This list includes a special identifier for any unit U: error_in_U. This exception name is used to rename exceptions which are not locally handled and which are not "exportable".

To this feature is added a systematic way of writing "complete" handlers for any public unit, and a completion algorithm of user-designed handlers is provided.

Neither modifications nor extensions are introduced in ADA. The methodology may be supported by a preprocessor which guides and check the program development process. This preprocessor is described in section II.1.

I - EXCEPTIONS IN ADA

The authors of the ADA language explain their choices relative to exception handling in the **Rationale for the design of the GREEN programming language** [1]. This document, as well as the **Reference Manual for the ADA Programming Language** [3] will be used in the sequel.

In ADA, an exception is defined as an exceptional situation that arise during program execution. When an exception is raised, normal program execution is abandoned and the control is transferred to an exception handler. Therefore, the exception handling mechanism chosen in ADA follows the "termination paradigm", i.e. any unit is abandoned as soon as an exception is raised during its execution. This choice is especially well-suited for dealing with errors, that is with situations that should not arise, but is less convenient for dealing with exceptions, that is with situations that are considered as being normal but unusual. Once an exception has been handled, there is no possibility of transferring back the control to the point where the exception has been raised; the situation is quite different in MESA, where the execution of the sequence of statements may be resumed.

Other peculiarities distinguish the exception handling mechanism of ADA from that of other programming languages. In ADA, exceptions can not be parameterized unlike what is allowed in CLU or MESA. There is no way to associate an exception name to a procedure or a function, as can be done in CLU or CHILL. Lastly, exception handlers should occur at the end of a block statement or at the end of the body of a subprogram, package, or task unit exclusively. They can not be attached to elementary statements.

As was pointed out in the introduction, our claim is that one needs to know at any moment the origin of an exception and its subsequent propagation in order to be able to handle it in a safe and precise way. Unfortunately, this is not always possible in ADA and we detail below some deficiencies of the language with respect to exception handling. In the sequel a block statement or the body of a subprogram, package, task unit or generic unit will be called a **frame**.

Since exception handlers can not be attached to a statement nor an expression, it may be impossible to determine within which statement or which expression a given exception has been raised. This may occur for instance when distinct subprograms that may raise the same exception are called in the same frame, or when a subprogram is called many time in the same frame.

It is also useful to know which exceptions may be propagated out of subprograms. This possibility was chosen in CHILL, CLU or GYPSY, but unfortunately not in ADA. This would allow the programmer to know that a given exception may be raised by some call to a subprogram, even if he does not know the body of the called subprogram. Hence a better encapsulation would result from such a possibility. Moreover, this would also help when looking for the raising point of an exception, and could also be used to statically check that handlers have been provided for the exceptions, avoiding unhandled exceptions.

A last criticism that can be levelled at the ADA exception handling mechanism is related to anonymous exceptions. When an exception is propagated out of its visibility scope, it becomes anonymous. By definition, it is impossible to determine the raising point of an anonymous exception and handling anonymous exception can only be performed through the use of the **WHEN OTHERS** exception choice. Therefore, handling anonymous exceptions can only be done in a rather general and imprecise way.

II - A METHOD FOR PROGRAMMING WITH EXCEPTIONS IN ADA.

II.1 - MOTIVATIONS.

We propose a method where all exceptions are propagated but , as far as possible, their propagations are controlled.

In ADA, we shall focus on avoiding anonymous exceptions; more precisely, we shall avoid the propagation of anonymous exceptions out of public frames, that is frames that can be used by other people than the programmer of the frame. Local anonymous exceptions will be left to the programmer's responsibility.

In order to avoid the propagation of anonymous exceptions out of public units, we shall associate to each public unit a list of "exportable" exceptions. This will be done by means of RAISE comments added to procedure headers. Furthermore, we shall provide a systematic way of writing the exception handlers of public units in order to ensure that only exportable exceptions may be propagated out of these units. However, our method should be easy to use and should be supported by computer tools. No method can be fully automatized, but we describe below a **preprocessor** that will help the programmer in writing "good" ADA programs with respect to exception handling. The programmer will write his program following the rules given in the next sections and then submit the program to a preprocessor. This preprocessor will assume the following tasks:

* It verifies that the program is consistent w.r.t. the provided rules of exception handling, especially the fact that each exception propagated out of public units is an exportable one.

* It adds (if necessary) and verifies exception declarations.

* It completes the exception handlers provided by the programmer, in order to ensure that exceptions that could be propagated as anonymous are renamed.

Thus, the preprocessor produces as output an ADA program where the exception handlers may have a large size. We therefore shall define a short version of these handlers. These short versions will be displayed through a special-purpose

displayer that comes with the preprocessor. The overall organization of the preprocessor and the displayer may be described by the following picture.

THE PREPROCESSOR AND THE DISPLAYER

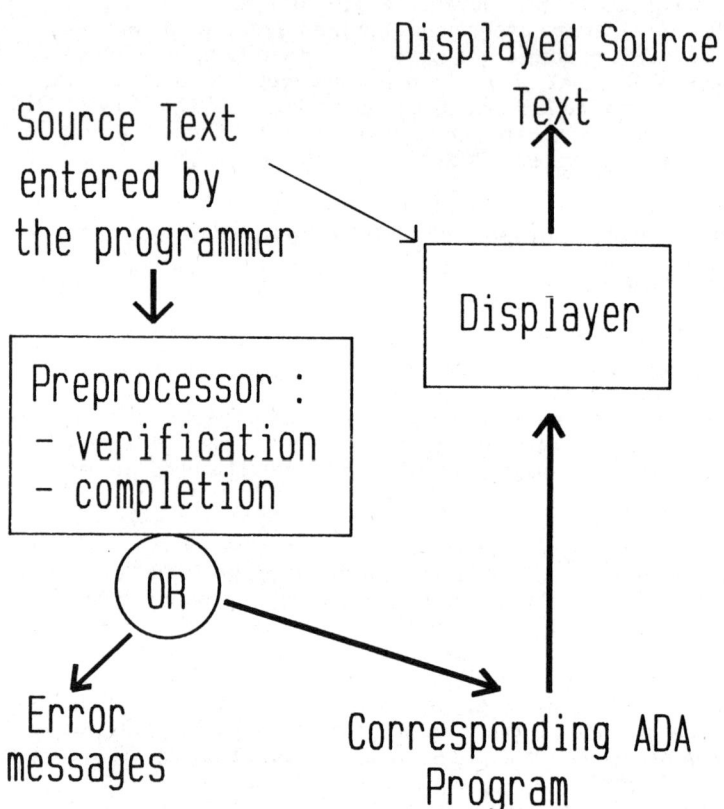

II.2 - BASIC HYPOTHESES.

In order to be able to check the scope of an exception which is exported by a procedure, it is convenient to assume that any procedure (but the main program) is embedded in a package. Then it is possible to define the scope of a procedure with respect to the scope of this package: either the procedure is a visible one and its scope is the scope of the package, or it is a private procedure and its scope is the body (or a part of it) of the package.
But in both cases, the scope of exceptions which are possibly raised by this procedure must contain the scope of the procedure.

Thus we shall consider that a program is a set of packages which are declared in a main procedure. This is a restriction of course, but the expressive power of

Systematic & safe exception handling in ADA

the considered programs is the same as full ADA programs: it is always possible to surround a procedure by a package. Moreover, structuring a set of procedures into a set of packages is quite in the spirit of ADA.

We make the same assumptiom for tasks: they are embedded in a package and their scope, and the scope of the exceptions they export, can be defined with respect to the scope of this package.

Consequently, we are going to consider that the scope unit for exceptions is the package: it implies a true restriction of the language since an exception which can possibly be exported by a public procedure (or a task) has the same scope as this procedure (or this task): the scope of the embedding package. Thus it is impossible to declare the same exception name as local to two different procedures of the same package. It is not a serious restriction: if these exceptions may be exported, it is better to distinguish them.

These assumptions are the only ones which are needed to apply our method. In this paper, in order to avoid too much technical considerations on exception names prefixing, we shall assume that there is no redefinition of the same exception name in nested packages. But the method works as well in this case.

We follow the general rule for declarations of ADA: it is illegal to use an exception name in a RAISE comment and to declare it later.

II.3 - ASSOCIATION OF EXCEPTION NAMES WITH PROCEDURES: THE RAISE COMMENT.

The reason of this systematic way of annotating procedure declarations has been given before: it is necessary to know precisely what procedure exports what exceptions. Thus the names of these exceptions must appear in the header of the procedure. Here it is done by comments.

Thus procedure headers look like:

```
PROCEDURE pop( s:IN OUT stack ) ;  -- RAISE underflow
FUNCTION  top( s: stack ) RETURN element;  -- RAISE empty_stack
```

This RAISE comment is fundamental for those procedures and functions which are public i.e which appear in the visible part of the package specification. Only these procedures indeed can be used as "black boxes" from outside the package.
However in order to keep homogeneous procedure declarations, it is natural to put this comment as well for private procedures and functions i.e. for procedures and functions which are local to the package. In this case, the presence of this comment is left to programmer's responsibility: the preprocessor will take the comment into account if it is present. In the case of a public procedure or function this comment is supposed to be there, and if it is not, an error message will be generated by the preprocessor.

The rules for using RAISE comments and exception declarations are the following: if an exception name occurs in the RAISE comment of a public procedure or function, it must be declared at the beginning of the specification part of the package. If the procedure or function is a private one, then the exception name must be declared at the beginning of the body of the package, if it is not declared in the specification part.

If the same exception name appears in the RAISE comment of two different procedures, then it denotes the same exception and its scope is the largest one.

The preprocessor will ensure these rules and add the exception declarations which are needed in the right place. The programmer does not need to declare exceptions which occur in a RAISE comment. However he may declare exception names, provided these rules are satisfied.

Following the rules above, the example below is considered as erroneous by the preprocessor:

```
PACKAGE p IS
    PROCEDURE pr ; -- RAISE e
END p;

PACKAGE BODY p IS
    e : EXCEPTION;
END p;
```

But the following construction is correct:

```
PACKAGE p IS
    PROCEDURE pr ; -- RAISE e
END p;

PACKAGE BODY p IS
    PROCEDURE h IS -- RAISE ee
    END h;

    PROCEDURE pr IS -- RAISE e
        BEGIN
    END pr;
END p;
```

The preprocessor will add a declaration for e at the beginning of the specification part of p, and a declaration for ee at the beginning of the body of p.

These simple rules become a bit more complicated to put into use as soon as there are nested packages. Let us consider the following package specification:

```
PACKAGE p IS
    PROCEDURE f ; -- RAISE e
    PACKAGE pp IS
        PROCEDURE g ; -- RAISE ee
    END pp ;
    PROCEDURE h ; -- RAISE ee
END p ;
```

Is the ee raised by g the same one as the one raised by h? For clarity reasons, the program reader would like a positive answer! But, to say the truth, it depends on the programmer. There are two possibilities in this case: ask for explicit declarations to the programmer or decide that the scope of an exception name is the scope of the more external package where it appears in a RAISE clause.

This last solution was choosen although it is not quite satisfactory since it could mask errors or at least unclarity in the program.

However the preprocessor we present in this paper is limited to non nested packages: nested packages can be simulated by WITH and USE clauses. The program structure is then quite the same as CLU and MESA program structure, since clusters and modules cannot be nested.

The main advantage of the RAISE comment is that it makes possible for the preprocessor to complete user's handlers in such a way that a public procedure or function will only export the following exceptions:

* those exceptions which appear in the RAISE comment of the procedure header;

* the predefined exceptions of ADA;

* the specific exception error_in_name where name is the name of the procedure.

This last exception is automatically declared by the preprocessor with the same scope as the procedure. It does not need to appear in the RAISE comment. Its role is to propagate exceptions which would be anonymous while indicating from where they come.

II.4 - HANDLERS ORGANIZATION.

Our aim is to avoid anonymous exceptions. However, ensuring that anonymous exceptions will never happen would introduce heavy programming constraints. Moreover, anonymous exceptions are not dangerous if they are local. For instance in the following procedure

```
PROCEDURE f IS
   BEGIN
      DECLARE
         e:EXCEPTION;
      BEGIN
         RAISE e;
      END; -- e becomes anonymous
   EXCEPTION
      WHEN OTHERS => ...; -- e is handled
END f ;
```

it is possible to get an anonymous propagation, but this is not observable by a user of f. Such cases are accepted even if this programming style could be discussed.

We are going to consider how to build handlers for four features which are able to produce anonymous exception propagation from a procedure, a package or a task:

* public procedures or functions;

* private procedures or function; declarative part;

* ACCEPT statements.

II.4.1 - Public procedures or functions.

Public procedures follow the rules above, thus a set of exportable exceptions (exceptions which occur in the RAISE comment, ADA predefined exceptions, error_in_N) is associated with each of them. Each procedure handlers are checked and completed by the preprocessor in such a way to ensure that only exportable exceptions are propagated outside the procedure.

Handlers completion must be done carefully in order to preserve programmer's intents. For instance one could just add to the handlers:

WHEN OTHERS => RAISE error_in_N ;

where N is the name of the procedure. This completion satisfies our requirements but it is too much powerful since exportable exceptions which are not raised in the handlers will be catched and renamed into error_in_N.

What we want is to write something equivalent to this variant of WHEN OTHERS:

WHEN NOT_EXPORTABLE => RAISE error_in_N ;

or else

WHEN ANONYMOUS => RAISE error_in_N ;

This last solution is just what we want but it is very costly to implement: it implies that, at run-time, exceptions which are propagated outside their scope are made really anonymous. And it is not simple at all [4].

As we just want to add a low cost preprocessor to ADA environment, we prefer the first solution. It implies to construct for each procedure, a set of handlers which catches all the exportable exceptions and raise them again, and is ended by a WHEN OTHERS which is then equivalent to a WHEN NOT_EXPORTABLE. Thus we have to take care in a specific way of the cases where the programmer provide a handler with a WHEN OTHERS.

II.4.2 - Handler Completion Algorithm.

This algorithm completes as it is described above the list of exceptions the handlers deals with. Besides it checks the body of each WHEN clause: if an exception is possibly raised there, it must be an exportable one.

Algorithm:

Let N be the name of the procedure or function.

Systematic & safe exception handling in ADA

1) If there is a *WHEN OTHERS* clause in the original handlers, skip Step 2.
2) For each exportable exception E, but error_in_N, do:
   * If there is no *WHEN E => body* clause in the handlers, then add
       WHEN E => RAISE E ;
     to the handlers, else do nothing.
   * Add the clause:
       WHEN OTHERS => RAISE error_in_N ;
     at the end of the handlers.
3) Check the bodies associated which all WHEN clauses:
   * If the body is a sequence of statements without block and without call to a private procedure without RAISE comment, verify for each statement that the potential exceptions are exportable ones.
   * If the body includes a block or a call to a private procedure without RAISE comment, then embed this body in a block and add to it the handlers obtained by completing the empty exception part.

End of the algorithm.

The third step needs some comments. In the first case (no block, no private procedure call), the statements of the list may be:

- A public procedure call: check that the exportable exception list of the called procedure is included in the current exportable exception list;

- A private procedure call, where the called procedure has a RAISE comment: do the same check as above;

- A RAISE statement: check that the raised exception is an exportable one;

- Another ADA statement: the potential exceptions are the predefined ADA exceptions, thus they are exportable.

In the case where there is a block, it is possible to have nested handlers and it becomes difficult to perform this check. It is the reason why a new block is added, enclosing the body, and new handlers, whose role is only to signal again exportable exceptions and to catch other ones, are appended.

In the case where there is a private procedure case without RAISE comment in a handler, there is no way to know what exceptions may be raised: it is impossible to check anything and the only solution is to encapsulate the handler statements in a block with safe handlers.

One can notice that this last method could be applied with any procedure body instead of completing handlers. Of course the resulting programs would be much more complicated an a priori less efficient.

Examples of completion.
  original source text:

```
PROCEDURE p IS -- RAISE e, ee
    BEGIN
    EXCEPTION
        WHEN ee => RAISE e ;
END p ;
```

completed handlers:

```
      EXCEPTION
          WHEN e => RAISE e ;
          WHEN ee => RAISE e ;
          WHEN CONSTRAINT_ERROR => RAISE CONSTRAINT_ERROR ;
          WHEN OTHERS => RAISE error_in_p ;
    END p ;
```

The user will not see these handlers and the following text will be displayed:

```
      EXCEPTION
          WHEN ee => RAISE e ;
          WHEN NOT_EXPORTABLE => RAISE error_in_p ;
    END p ;
```

Let us consider the same source text with a block in a handler:

```
          WHEN ee =>
              BEGIN
                  f(a); -- f may raise eee
              EXCEPTION
                  WHEN eee => RAISE ee ;
              END ;
```

It will be displayed as:

```
          WHEN ee =>
              BEGIN
                  BEGIN
                      f(a) ; -- f may raise eee
                  EXCEPTION
                      WHEN eee => RAISE ee ;
                  END ;
              EXCEPTION
                  WHEN NOT_EXPORTABLE => RAISE error_in_p ;
              END ;
```

II.4.3 - Private procedures and packages handlers

A private procedure is declared either in the private part of a package specification or in a package body. A call of this procedure is only possible from a public procedure of the package or from the statement list of the package.
In the first case, the handlers of the public procedure will catch any exception and will rename it, if necessary, in error_in_name of the procedure.
The second case may produce exportation of anonymous exceptions from the package: thus it is necessary to add handlers to each package body. These handlers raise an exception error_in_name_of_package when an exception which is not a predefined one is catched.

It is not necessary to complete the handlers of a private procedure. However, if the programmer provides a RAISE comment in the header of a private procedure, its handlers will be completed.

Package handlers would be also useful to catch exceptions which are raised during the elaboration of the declarative part of the package body, where private procedure calls may occur. However it is not clear in the reference manual that such exceptions are catched by package handlers [3, 7.3]. If it is not the case the only solution is to forbid any private procedure call in the initialization of a declaration.

II.4.4 - Exception propagation between tasks

Exceptions are not propagated outside a task except in the following case: while a *rendez-vous*, an exception is raised in the body of the **accept** statement and it is not handled locally. Then this exception is propagated to both tasks: the task that contains the accept statement and the task which has called the corresponding entry.

The rendez-vous mechanism in ADA is an asymetric one: the task which calls the rendez-vous knows the name of the called task, but the task which accepts a rendez-vous does not know the name of the caller. That means that an exception which is raised in an **accept** statement and that is not locally handled may be propagated without control. It is indeed quite possible that the caller task is outside the scope of this exception: there is no way to check it.

It is thus necessary to limit the exportable exceptions from an accept body in order to avoid such uncontrolable propagations. To ensure that an exception will not be propagated as an anonymous one, we must be sure that it is visible from the caller task. The simplest way to ensure this point is to state that any exception which is exportable by a task has exactly the same scope as this task.

Note that this is exactly the same rule which was used for the procedures or functions.

Thus, tasks are going to be dealt with by the preprocessor in the same way as public procedures: with each task declaration is associated a **raise** comment with an exception list. These exceptions will be declared by the preprocessor at the beginning of the package where the task is declared, with the same rules as in II.4. The handler completion algorithm will be performed on each accept statement. As for the procedures, for each task T there is an exception error_in_T and any potential anonymous exception will be renamed into this exception.

CONCLUSION

We have shown in this paper that it is possible to ensure that no anonymous exceptions will be propagated in a given program. Moreover, this method is simple to implement. There is of course a counterpart to the control of anonymous exceptions: the number of handlers is increased and consequently the size of the programs. It is obvious that some exceptions will never occur. A good program prover would find out such exceptions... however such provers are not yet available and the only current solution is to allow the programmer to remove some (unnecessary) handlers.

Our method is not quite satisfactory: the origin of an unexpected exception is only kept for one propagation step: error_in_N only indicates the last procedure encountered. It would be nice to be able to keep the whole propagation path: this would be possible in CLU or MESA, for instance, by passing as parameter a character string where the successive procedure names are registered. Unfortunately ADA exceptions are not parameterized.

ACKNOWLEDGEMENTS

This work has been partially supported by D.A.I.I. Contract Number 82.35.033. The authors would like to thank the *Software Engineering Group* of the Laboratoires de Marcoussis, and more especially **Brigitte Biebow** and **Rose Dieng**.

REFERENCES

[1] **Rationale for the design of the GREEN Programming Language**, J. Ichbiah and al., SIGPLAN Notice 14,6 - 1979.

[2] **Requirements for ADA Programming Support Environments**, United States Department of Defense, February 1980.

[3] **The Programming Language ADA - Reference Manual**, United States Department of Defense, January 1983.

[4] **Le langage ADA, manuel d'évaluation**, D. Le Verrand (collectif name of the A.F.C.E.T. ADA Working Group), Dunod Ed., Paris 1982.

[5] **ADA: An Introduction**, H. Ledgard, Springer-Verlag, 1981.

[6] **Etude des outils de programmation des cas d'exception et des erreurs dans les langages comportant des mécanismes d'abstraction**, Final Report of D.A.I.I. Contract Number 82.35.033, Laboratoires de Marcoussis, December 1982.

GUIDELINES FOR THE DESIGN OF LARGE MODULAR SCIENTIFIC
LIBRARIES IN ADA

G.T. Symm
Division of Information Technology and Computing
National Physical Laboratory
Teddington, Middlesex, TW11 0LW, UK

J. Kok
Numerical Mathematics Department
Centrum voor Wiskunde en Informatica
PO Box 4079, 1009 AB Amsterdam, The Netherlands

Abstract. While the Ada language has been designed primarily for programming embedded systems, it is generally expected that it will also be widely used for large-scale scientific computations. Accordingly, we and our colleagues have been studying the problems involved in designing and implementing large, portable and modular, scientific algorithms libraries in Ada. In this paper we summarise our main recommendations, under the headings: precision, basic functions, composite data types, information passing, error handling, working-space organisation and real-time environment.

1 Introduction

Preliminary evaluations of the suitability of Ada for large-scale scientific computation (Cox & Hammarling 1980; Hammarling & Wichmann 1982) indicated that several features of the language would require careful consideration if large, portable and modular, scientific algorithms libraries were to be implemented successfully. Consequently, the problems associated with the overall design and implementation of such libraries in Ada have been studied in detail and are discussed in a recent report (Symm et al. 1984). In this paper we present a summary of the recommendations made in that report under the headings of its various chapters.

2 Precision

In order to avoid problems of incompatibility, which can easily arise on account of the strong type-checking rules of the language, we recommend that all library subroutines should use the same real types. In particular, we recommend that a standard set of real types should be assembled into a library package of the form:

```
package REAL_TYPES is
   type REAL is digits D;
```

```
            -- etc. (see section 4 below)
        end REAL_TYPES;
```

to be used by all other scientific library packages. In practice, the number D of digits prescribed for type REAL will be implementation dependent but we would recommend at least 10 digits, if possible, for scientific computation, though 6 digits may have to suffice for many real-time applications.

A library package which uses type REAL may then have a specification of the form:

```
        with REAL_TYPES; use REAL_TYPES;
        package LIBRARY_PACK is
            function FUN(X : REAL) return REAL;
            -- etc.
        end LIBRARY_PACK;
```

in which case we recommend that it should also have a generic form:

```
        generic
            type REAL is digits <>;
        package GENERIC_LIBRARY_PACK is
            function FUN(X : REAL) return REAL;
            -- etc.
        end GENERIC_LIBRARY_PACK;
```

to provide greater programming flexibility, e.g. to make the package available to the sophisticated user who wishes to define his own REAL type. We note that, for efficiency of execution, an instantiation of this generic form, for the particular type REAL used in the non-generic version, may simply result in a call of the latter.

Finally, with reference to precision, we recommend that attributes of real types should be used wherever appropriate to maintain a balance between portability and efficiency of code. For example, if a simple approximation is known to be accurate for 10 digits at most, one might write

```
        if REAL'DIGITS <= 10 then
            SIMPLE_APPROXIMATION;
        else
            MORE_COMPLEX_CODE;
        end if;
```

Guidelines for scientific libraries

where, if the static condition is TRUE, the MORE_COMPLEX_CODE (though it must be valid) need not be compiled.

3 Basic functions

As an example of library design, which would also fulfil an obvious requirement for scientific computation, we propose a package of basic mathematical functions with the following specification:

```
generic
   type REAL is digits <>;
package GENERIC_MATH_FUNCTIONS is
   -- Declare constants.                                                --
   PI    : constant := 3.1415_92653_58979_32384_62643_38327_95029;
   EXP_1 : constant := 2.7182_81828_45904_52353_60287_47135_26625;
   -- Declare the basic mathematical functions.                         --
   function SQRT(X : REAL) return REAL;
   function LOG(X : REAL; BASE : REAL := EXP_1) return REAL;
   function EXP(X : REAL; BASE : REAL := EXP_1) return REAL;
   function SIN(X : REAL; CYCLE : REAL := 2.0*PI) return REAL;
   function COS(X : REAL; CYCLE : REAL := 2.0*PI) return REAL;
   function TAN(X : REAL; CYCLE : REAL := 2.0*PI) return REAL;
   function COT(X : REAL; CYCLE : REAL := 2.0*PI) return REAL;
   function ARCSIN(X : REAL) return REAL;
   function ARCCOS(X : REAL) return REAL;
   function ARCTAN(X : REAL; Y : REAL := 1.0) return REAL;
   function ARCCOT(X : REAL; Y : REAL := 1.0) return REAL;
   function SINH(X : REAL) return REAL;
   function COSH(X : REAL) return REAL;
   function TANH(X : REAL) return REAL;
   function COTH(X : REAL) return REAL;
   function ARCSINH(X : REAL) return REAL;
   function ARCCOSH(X : REAL) return REAL;
   function ARCTANH(X : REAL) return REAL;
   function ARCCOTH(X : REAL) return REAL;
   -- Declare exceptions.                                                --
   ARGUMENT_ERROR : exception;
end GENERIC_MATH_FUNCTIONS;
```

Here EXP_1 represents e, the base of natural logarithms, while the second parameter BASE of the functions LOG and EXP gives the base of the logarithm or the power respectively. Thus, for example, EXP(X,A) gives the value of A raised to the the power X, while LOG(X) gives the value of the natural logarithm ln X. The second parameter CYCLE of the trigonometric functions gives the complete angle at a point in the units of the first argument X; for example, CYCLE := 360.0 when X is measured in degrees while the default value corresponds to X measured in radians. The second argument Y of functions ARCTAN and ARCCOT is such that, for example, ARCTAN(X) delivers the normal arctangent value in the range [- PI/2, PI/2], while ARCTAN(X,Y) delivers the angle between the positive x-axis and the radius vector of the Cartesian point (Y,X) (note the order) in the range (- PI, PI].

If facilities for partial loading are available, we recommend that the program components of the package body should be given as body stubs with separate subunits. The exception ARGUMENT_ERROR should be raised by the function body whenever the argument of a function violates one of the following constraints:

Function	Argument constraints
SQRT	X >= 0.0
LOG	X > 0.0, BASE > 0.0 and /= 1.0
EXP	BASE > 0.0
SIN	CYCLE /= 0.0
COS	CYCLE /= 0.0
TAN	CYCLE /= 0.0
COT	CYCLE /= 0.0
ARCSIN	abs X <= 1.0
ARCCOS	abs X <= 1.0
ARCTAN	not (X = 0.0 and Y = 0.0)
ARCCOT	not (X = 0.0 and Y = 0.0)
ARCCOSH	X >= 1.0
ARCTANH	abs X < 1.0
ARCCOTH	abs X > 1.0

All arguments not listed here take unrestricted REAL values.

4   Composite data types

Since a type COMPLEX might be equally well defined in either Cartesian or polar form, we propose that a scientific library should contain both versions.

For work in Cartesian coordinates, we recommend a package with the specification:

Guidelines for scientific libraries

```
with REAL_TYPES; use REAL_TYPES;
package COMPLEX_OPERATORS is
   type COMPLEX is
      record
         RE,IM : REAL;
      end record;
   function RE(X : COMPLEX) return REAL;
   function IM(X : COMPLEX) return REAL;
   function "abs"(X : COMPLEX) return REAL;
   function ARG(X : COMPLEX) return REAL;
   function C_TO_COMP(R : REAL; I : REAL := 0.0)
      return COMPLEX;
   function P_TO_COMP(M : REAL; A : REAL := 0.0)
      return COMPLEX;
   function "+"(X : COMPLEX) return COMPLEX;
   function "-"(X : COMPLEX) return COMPLEX;
   function "+"(X,Y : COMPLEX) return COMPLEX;
   function "-"(X,Y : COMPLEX) return COMPLEX;
   function "*"(X,Y : COMPLEX) return COMPLEX;
   function "/"(X,Y : COMPLEX) return COMPLEX;
   function "**"(X : COMPLEX; N : INTEGER) return COMPLEX;
   pragma INLINE(RE, IM, "abs", ARG, C_TO_COMP, P_TO_COMP,
      "+", "-", "*", "/", "**");
end COMPLEX_OPERATORS;
```

where the functions C_TO_COMP and P_TO_COMP form a COMPLEX number from its Cartesian and polar coordinates respectively.

For work in polar coordinates, we recommend a similar package with the specification:

```
package COMPLEX_POLAR_OPERATORS is
   type COMPLEX is
      record
         CMOD,CARG : REAL;
      end record;
   function RE(X : COMPLEX) return REAL;
   function IM(X : COMPLEX) return REAL;
   function "abs"(X : COMPLEX) return REAL;
   -- etc.
end COMPLEX_POLAR_OPERATORS;
```

The complete specifications and bodies of both of these packages are included in an appendix to our report (Symm et al. 1984).

Packages which use type COMPLEX, such as COMPLEX_FUNCTIONS, may be made generic with respect to this type, regarded as a private type rather than a record type, provided that they are also made generic with respect to appropriate functions. Thus, such a package may have a specification:

```
with REAL_TYPES; use REAL_TYPES;
generic
   type COMPLEX is private;
   with function RE(X : COMPLEX) return REAL is <>;
   with function IM(X : COMPLEX) return REAL is <>;
   with function "abs"(X : COMPLEX) return REAL is <>;
   with function ARG(X : COMPLEX) return REAL is <>;
   with function C_TO_COMP(R : REAL; I : REAL := 0.0)
      return COMPLEX is <>;
   with function P_TO_COMP(M : REAL; A : REAL := 0.0)
      return COMPLEX is <>;
package GENERIC_COMPLEX_FUNCTIONS is
   function SQRT(X : COMPLEX) return COMPLEX;
   function LOG(X : COMPLEX) return COMPLEX;
   function EXP(X : COMPLEX) return COMPLEX;
   function SIN(X : COMPLEX) return COMPLEX;
   function COS(X : COMPLEX) return COMPLEX;
end GENERIC_COMPLEX_FUNCTIONS;
```

and an instantiation:

```
with GENERIC_COMPLEX_FUNCTIONS;
with COMPLEX_OPERATORS; use COMPLEX_OPERATORS;
package COMPLEX_FUNCTIONS is
   new GENERIC_COMPLEX_FUNCTIONS(COMPLEX);
```

or an instantiation:

```
with GENERIC_COMPLEX_FUNCTIONS;
with COMPLEX_POLAR_OPERATORS; use COMPLEX_POLAR_OPERATORS;
package COMPLEX_FUNCTIONS is
   new GENERIC_COMPLEX_FUNCTIONS(COMPLEX);
```

We recommend this construction, whereby the one generic package provides the required functions for either of the two COMPLEX types by means of an appropriate instantiation.

For vectors and matrices with REAL components, we propose

```
type VECTOR is array (INTEGER range <>) of REAL;
type MATRIX is array
   (INTEGER range <>, INTEGER range <>) of REAL;
```

and we recommend that these types should be included in the package REAL_TYPES, introduced earlier, thus:

```
package REAL_TYPES is
   type REAL is digits D;
```

Guidelines for scientific libraries

```
type VECTOR is array (INTEGER range <>) of REAL;
type MATRIX is array
   (INTEGER range <>, INTEGER range <>) of REAL;
end REAL_TYPES;
```

Then packages for linear algebra should be made generic with respect to types VECTOR and MATRIX, as well as type REAL, thus:

```
generic
   type REAL is digits <>;
   type VECTOR is array (INTEGER range <>) of REAL;
   type MATRIX is array
      (INTEGER range <>, INTEGER range <>) of REAL;
   package GENERIC_LINEAR_ALGEBRA is
   ...
   end GENERIC_LINEAR_ALGEBRA;
```

in which case the instantiation:

```
with GENERIC_LINEAR_ALGEBRA;
with REAL_TYPES; use REAL_TYPES;
package LINEAR_ALGEBRA is
   new GENERIC_LINEAR_ALGEBRA(REAL,VECTOR,MATRIX);
```

will take types REAL, VECTOR and MATRIX from the package REAL_TYPES.

Finally, with respect to composite data types, we recommend that a complex vector should be represented as a vector of complex components, thus:

```
type CO_VECTOR is array (INTEGER range <>) of COMPLEX;
```

and a complex two-dimensional array similarly:

```
type CO_MATRIX is array
   (INTEGER range <>, INTEGER range <>) of COMPLEX;
```

These two types should be grouped in a library package:

```
package COMPLEX_TYPES is
   type CO_VECTOR is array (INTEGER range <>) of COMPLEX;
   type CO_MATRIX is array
      (INTEGER range <>, INTEGER range <>) of COMPLEX;
end COMPLEX_TYPES;
```

preceded by the context clause:

> **with** COMPLEX_OPERATORS; **use** COMPLEX_OPERATORS;

or:

> **with** COMPLEX_POLAR_OPERATORS; **use** COMPLEX_POLAR_OPERATORS;

as appropriate.

5 Information passing

With reference to interface problems which arise when two (or more) items of software are to be used in conjunction with each other, we have considered, in particular, the common situation in which a user has to supply a function to a library procedure.

For a simple function, of a single variable, we recommend that the library procedure should be made generic with respect to the function. Thus, for example, a library procedure to find a zero of a function $f(x)$, for real x in an interval $[a,b]$, to some accuracy e, may have a specification:

> **with** REAL_TYPES; **use** REAL_TYPES;
> **generic**
>   **with function** F(X : REAL) **return** REAL;
> **procedure** GENERIC_ZERO(A,B,E : **in** REAL; Z : **out** REAL);

Then the zero of a particular function $g(x)$, with the specification:

> **function** G(X : REAL) **return** REAL;

may be obtained by instantiating the generic procedure, thus:

> **procedure** ZERO_G **is new** GENERIC_ZERO(G);

and making the call:

> ZERO_G(A, B, E, Z);

with appropriate values for A, B and E.

For more complicated functions, involving certain parameters as well as the real variable x, we recommend the use of generics, as before, together with the block structure of the language. Thus, for example, to find the zero of a function h(x) given by a series of n terms involving prescribed coefficients, we might have:

```
declare
   -- N is imported to this block
   C,D : array (1 .. N) of REAL;
   function H(X : REAL) return REAL is
      SUM : REAL := 0.0;
   begin
      for J in 1 .. N loop
         SUM := SUM + C(J)*EXP(D(J)*X);  -- for example
      end loop;
      return SUM;
   end H;
   procedure ZERO_H is new GENERIC_ZERO(H);
begin
   ...
   -- Initialise coefficients C and D
   ...
   ZERO_H(A, B, E, Z);
   ...
end;
```

Other techniques considered for the treatment of such functions, such as the passing of working-space parameters and the use of reverse communication, are not recommended for general use.

Finally, with reference to information passing, we recommend that parameters with default values should be placed at the <u>end</u> of the formal part of a subprogram specification, contrary to the common practice of putting **in** parameters at the beginning.

6 Error handling

In Ada, run-time errors may be elegantly handled by means of the exception mechanism and we advocate, in particular, the defensive programming approach:

```
if pre-condition not satisfied then
   raise condition violated;
end if;
```

In general, we recommend (when an error occurs) the raising of an exception whose name clearly indicates the pre-condition which has been violated. This will not usually be a predefined exception, but, for example, ARGUMENT_ERROR rather than CONSTRAINT_ERROR for a call of SQRT with a negative argument. Thus the raising of predefined exceptions should usually be "translated" into the raising of exceptions belonging to user-oriented packages.

We recommend that exceptions raised in library packages which are used by other library packages should be handled in these other packages to initiate alternative approaches or to raise further, more meaningful exceptions.

We also recommend that initialisations in declarations should be kept simple, to avoid raising exceptions which cannot be handled locally but have to be propagated.

We realise that the exception mechanism does not provide the most user-friendly system of error handling and that control by the end-user has not yet been fully explored. However, this subject is currently being studied by the Ada-Europe Numerics Working Group and we recommend that further attention be given to it in the future.

7 Working-space organisation

In connection with working-space organisation, we have considered both explicitly- and implicitly-declared storage.

With reference to the former, we make the following recommendations:
- different data types should be used for matrices which require different storage methods,
- documentation of library subprograms should contain sufficient information for the programmer to be able to estimate the amounts of working-space to be claimed for their execution,
- aliasing of subprogram parameters should be avoided and working-space parameters should not be used,
- representation and address clauses should not be used,
- the pragma PACK should be used judiciously to instruct an installation to minimise gaps in storage areas for objects of composite types.

With reference to storage which is used implicitly, we recommend that:
- range constraints on array objects should always be separated from their type declarations,

- dynamic storage should be freed when values of the relevant access type are no longer accessible (because the unit containing the declaration of this access type is left),
- if dynamic storage must be given to a user program, the access type should be a limited private type, to prevent the user from copying accesses,
- in real-time situations the user should do his own storage management,
- library packages should not be too large and body stubs and subunits should be used to permit separate compilation.

8 Real-time environment

Considering the particular problems associated with the design of scientific libraries for use in real-time processing, we note, in particular, that such libraries are likely to have different subprogram bodies from those used for batch processing. Correspondingly, our first recommendation is that services requested by tasks should always be granted by tasks.

With reference to shared variables, we recommend that tasks should not access such variables for simultaneous reading and updating. The best solution to this problem is to perform all accesses through a central task. We do not object to direct access to shared variables for reading purposes only (i.e. shared data).

With regard to error handling in a real-time environment, we recommend that all exceptions must be handled when using tasks.

Considering examples of tasks, we particularly recommend the use of a "mailbox" construct, whereby results of a server task are sent to an agent task which may be inspected by the calling task whenever necessary.

Finally, we recommend further investigation of the tasking facilities of Ada as a tool for the development of new algorithms for computations on distributed processors.

9 Conclusions

We have presented here a brief summary of our guidelines for the design of large modular scientific libraries in Ada (Symm et al. 1984). Though we would not claim to have solved all the problems in this area, we hope that these guidelines will be helpful to those wishing to develop large portable algorithms libraries for scientific computation.

Acknowledgements

We acknowledge here the valuable assistance of our colleagues Brian Wichmann and Dik Winter, the co-authors of our report, who join us in thanking the Commission of the European Communities for supporting this work. We also thank all who have commented on our earlier interim reports on this subject, particularly the reviewers appointed by the Commission.

References

Cox, M.G. & Hammarling, S.J. (1980). Evaluation of the language Ada for use in numerical computations. NPL Report DNACS 30/80.

Hammarling, S.J. & Wichmann, B.A. (1982). Numerical packages in Ada. In The relationship between numerical computation and programming languages, ed. J.K. Reid, pp. 225-244. Amsterdam: North Holland.

Symm, G.T., Wichmann, B.A., Kok, J. & Winter, D.T. (1984). Guidelines for the design of large modular scientific libraries in Ada. NPL Report DITC 37/84 and CWI Note NM-N8401.

NUMERIC TYPES IN ADA

SOME OF THEIR LESS OBVIOUS FEATURES

R. P. Wehrum
Siemens AG, Zentralbereich für Forschung und Technik
Otto-Hahn-Ring 6
D-8000 Munich 83, Germany

Introduction. This note addresses several of the less obvious, but nevertheless interesting - and sometimes strange - language features of numeric types in Ada. Some of these features reflect insufficiencies in the language definition, while others just refer to remarkable or surprising facts. Only a selection of very basic problems mainly centred on the notions of "staticness", conversion, universal types, and exceptions will be covered. Some of these problems were submitted by the author to the Ada Joint Program Office, and discussed in meetings of the Ada-Europe Review and Numerics Working Groups. The subsequent conclusions, statements, remarks, and comments refer to the language definition as given in the Language Reference Manual, ANSI/MIL-STD 1815A 1983 (LRM). Hopefully, some of the language features dealt with in the present paper can be revised in the formulation of the ISO standard.

1 THE NOTION OF "STATICNESS"

1.1 General remarks

Logically speaking, an entity or the property of an entity is *static* if it can be determined solely by inspection of the program text, in other words, if it can be evaluated at compile time. However, in Ada the notion of "staticness" is much more stringent inasmuch as only a subset of the properties which can be fixed at compile time is considered as static. This conflicts with intuition and leads to some surprising results.

To give an example: only scalar types and properties of scalar types may be static (cf. LRM 4.9 (1,13)). The entity A as defined in:
type A is array (1..10) **of** FLOAT;
is a non-static subtype because it is not scalar and the attribute A'FIRST is a non-static expression though it is of the scalar type INTEGER and though its value is known at compile time.

"Staticness" is required in many language constructs, e.g. in numeric type declarations, in declarations of named numbers, in aggregates (for certain discriminant values), in choices of case statements, in certain representation clauses, pragmas, and attributes. The programmer (and the compiler-constructor) must precisely know the places where static expressions are needed. The violation of "staticness" results in an illegal construct.

1.2 Indeterministic expressions

The result of the evaluation of the expression INTEGER (0.5) is non-deterministic; it can be 0 or 1 (cf. LRM 4.6(7)). In principle, the same expression INTEGER (0.5) can assume different values within the same program. The non-determinism of expressions such as INTEGER (0.5) gave rise to the dropping of conversions from the original set of static expressions as given in former versions of the LRM.

This, in turn, has several unexpected implications some of which are dealt with in the sections 2 and 3 below.

2 IMPLICIT CONVERSIONS
2.1 Numeric literals and universal types

From a set-theoretical point of view integer types and enumeration types are quite similar: both specify finite ordered sets of discrete values. Yet, there are several features defined in a non-uniform way. The *values* of enumeration types are directly represented by the corresponding enumeration literals whereas named integer types do not possess literals of their own: integer literals represent the non-negative values of the *predefined anonymous* type universal_integer which reflects the mathematical set of integers. Enumeration literals (which are parameterless functions, actually) can be overloaded; the type of an enumeration literal is resolved by the context. Integer literals cannot be overloaded; depending on the context they must be converted *implicitly* (or explicitly, cf. 2.4) or need not be converted at all. Analogous properties hold for real literals which stand for the non-negative values of the *predefined anonymous* type universal_real reflecting the mathematical set of *rational* numbers. Static expressions of a universal type must be evaluated *exactly* according to LRM 4.10 (4). The important advantage of the language constructs of universal types lies in the fact that they provide an arithmetic which in principle goes beyond the bounds of the most powerful named predefined numeric types, which is *exact* in contrast to the *approximate* model interval arithmetic holding for the named numeric types, and which is thus *independent* of the *target machine*.

Some Features of Numeric Types   167

2.2 On the non-existence of (typed) static constants

Let us consider the following example

C1 : **constant** NATURAL : = 1;   -- (1)
-- NATURAL = STANDARD.NATURAL = predefined subtype
C2 : **constant** NATURAL : = INTEGER (1) ;   -- (2)
-- INTEGER = STANDARD.INTEGER = predefined type

According to LRM 4.6(15) case (1) implies a conversion of the literal appearing on the right hand side of the assignment. Thus, case (1) is *semantically equivalent* to case (2).

LRM 4.9 shows that expressions that involve conversions are never static. This implies that the set of static expressions which can be deduced from rule (d) in LRM 4.9 (6) is *void*: no static typed constants exist, i.e. static constants of non-anonymous types. The only static constants that can be declared in Ada are named numbers; and each named number is a static constant (either of type universal_integer or of type universal_real).

If one wants to avoid this deduction and in order to describe what is (probably) intended by LRM 4.9 (6), a semantic rule must be added such as "An implicit conversion of a static expression is static." or more precisely "An expression resulting from an implicit conversion of a numeric literal, a named number, or an attribute with a static value (of type universal_integer or universal_real) is static."

The above problem is an example in which a *syntactic* definition tries to overrule a *semantic* concept.

2.3 Illegal expressions involving universal_integer values

Consider the following example:

X, Y, Z : FLOAT := ... ;   ...
X := 100 * 100.0 * X ;   -- (3)
Y := 10.0 / 2 ;   -- (4)
Z := 10.0 / T'SIZE;   -- T non-static subtype   -- (5)

Are the expressions on the right hand sides of the assignments in (3), (4) and (5) legal? According to the LRM they are not legal, though there exists a predefined operator "*" (case (3)) which performs the mapping (cf. LRM App. C (11)):
(universal_integer, universal_real) ---> universal_real.
The overloading resolution for the "*" operators in case (3) proceeds as follows: The second "*" needs to have a left operand of type FLOAT (cf. LRM 4.5.5 (2));

so an implicit conversion must be applied; however, an implicit conversion cannot be performed for the expression 100*100.0 but only for its *constituents* because of LRM 4.6 (15); an implicit conversion from universal_integer to a non-integer type is not allowed again according to LRM 4.6 (15).

Case (4) can be analysed in an analogous way: the right hand side of (4) must be of the same type as the left hand side, i.e. FLOAT. The division operator of the kind

"/" :(universal_real, universal_integer) ---⟩ universal_real

provided by the predefined package STANDARD is not the appropriate one in the present context as implicit conversions are only allowed for the "primitives" numeric literal, named number, and attribute of static value (of type universal_integer or universal_real) and neither an implicit conversion of the kind

universal_integer ---⟩ non-integer type

nor an operator of the sort

"/" : (FLOAT, integer-type) ---⟩ FLOAT

exist. Case (5) involves a non-static universal_integer value. Apart from this the same analysis holds as before.

2.4 Ambiguous expressions involving universal_real values

Let

V 1 : SOME_FIXED_POINT_TYPE ;

...

V1 := SOME_FIXED_POINT_TYPE (V1 * 3.14);   -- (6)

The programmer might well expect that the right hand side of the assignment is legal - why not multiply an object of a real type by a real literal? However, according to the LRM it is not. In performing the overloading resolution for the multiplication operator the only promising candidate is of the form

"*": (any fixed-point type, any (possibly different) fixed-point type)
---⟩ universal_fixed.

The type of the literal is universal_real. Thus an implicit conversion of the literal to a suitable fixed-point type determined by the context is needed; but the context does not suffice to define the target type of the conversion; some semantic rule is missing. The expression is *ambiguous* and therefore *illegal*. (Cf. LRM 4.5.5(10), 4.6(15) .)

Of course the above analysis remains the same if dynamic universal_real values are involved (e.g., take T'LARGE for a non-static subtype T instead of the literal 3.14 in the example (6)).

2.5 Illegal discrete ranges

It is surprising that the loop statements

```
for J in -1..10 loop...end loop;                                      -- (7)
for J in 1..2*5 loop...end loop;                                      -- (8)
```

are illegal, whereas the following example is correct

```
MINUS_ONE: constant := -1;                                            -- (9)
for J in MINUS_ONE..10 loop...end loop;                               -- (10)
```

The illegality in (7) and (8) results from the fact that neither -1 nor 2*5 represents a literal, a named number or an attribute as required by LRM 5.5 and 3.6.1 (2). (10) together with (9) show how this problem can be avoided by employing named numbers.

(It might be interesting to note that the ACVC-Test A55B13A, version 1.2 considers the statement

for I in reverse ONE..FIVE+ONE-1 **loop**..**end loop**;
-- ONE and FIVE named numbers

as legal. But it is illegal for the same reason as example (8) above. This error has since been corrected.)

3 ON THE EXISTENCE OF STATIC NUMERIC SUBTYPES

3.1 The non-existence of static fixed-point types

Let us consider the fixed-point type declaration

type F **is delta** 0.1 **range** -1.0 .. 1.0;   -- (11)

Does F denote a static subtype in the sense of LRM 4.9 ? It does not. The declaration of (7) is *equivalent* to the sequence of declarations by virtue of LRM 3.5.9 (8,9):

type ⟨anonymous_fixed_pt_type_X⟩ **is new** ⟨predefined_fixed_pt_type_X⟩;   -- (12a)
subtype F **is** ⟨anonymous_fixed_pt_type_X⟩ **range**
⟨anonymous_fixed_pt_type_X⟩(-1.0) .. ⟨anonymous_fixed_pt_type_X⟩(1.0);   -- (12b)

The range is not static, because of the explicit conversions in the range constraint in (12b). Therefore, F is not a static subtype according to LRM 4.9 (11). Moreover, this requires that no user-defined static subtypes exist at all. The only named (i.e. non-anonymous) predefined fixed-point type is DURATION; it is a non-static subtype because the above logic, i.e. the "equivalence rule", holds once again: we come to the conclusion that non-anonymous static fixed-point types do not exist, though every expression may be required to be static as in type declarations of the form (11).

Are the anonymous predefined fixed-point types static subtypes? Yes, they should be because LRM states in 4.9(11):
"A static subtype is either a scalar base type, other than a generic formal type; or ..."
in 3.5.9(7):
"...an implementation must have at least one anonymous predefined fixed-point type. The base type of each such fixed-point type is the type itself."
Thus it is reasonable to consider each of the anonymous predefined fixed-point types of an implementation as representing a static subtype. One may wonder whether this matters as these types are anonymous anyway. It matters, indeed, since the attributes of these anonymous types can be examined by help of the BASE attribute.

(As a minor point, the formulation cited above, LRM 4.9(11):" A static subtype is either a scalar base type,...; or..." uses an incorrect wording ; in my opinion, the notion of base type needs to have a genitive object: "scalar base type" must be replaced by "predefined numeric type different from DURATION or an enumeration type".)

3.2 The non-existence of static integer types
(defined by integer type definitions)

Let

type J is range L..R;   -- (13)

Is J a static subtype ? According to the "equivalence rule" stated in LRM 3.5.4(4,5,6) it is not, though all relevant entities are known at *compile time*: L and R must be static expressions of some integer types; and at compile time the predefined type to which J must be mapped is known.

The *predefined* integer types (type INTEGER and - depending on the implementation - possibly others) can be considered as static subtypes.

3.3 Can derived integer types be static subtypes?

Consider

type I_DER is new INTEGER range 1..10;   -- (14)
-- INTEGER = STANDARD.INTEGER

The LRM states an "equivalence rule" for derived types in 3.4 (1,2,3). However, this rule is not explicitly given by a sequence of type and subtype declarations but only *verbally*. So no explicit conversions of the values of the bounds of the range appear, such that the property of the "staticness" of the subtype remains unclear. One may argue that because of this fact (and because the bounds are

Some Features of Numeric Types

represented by literals) I_DER is static. However, I would prefer to give a clear semantic explanation by invoking the following formal "equivalence rule" (for the declaration of I_DER):

type ⟨anonym_I_DER⟩ **is new** ⟨INTEGER'BASE⟩;   -- (15a)
-- ⟨INTEGER'BASE⟩ = INTEGER
subtype I_DER **is** ⟨anonym_I_DER⟩
range ⟨anonym_I_DER⟩ (1) .. ⟨anonym_I_DER⟩ (10);   -- (15b)

If this interpretation is adopted, then I_DER is a non-static subtype, of course.

One arrives at the same conclusion given that the bounds in a subtype indication must belong to the base type of the corresponding type mark (LRM 3.5.(4)). So (14) is semantically equivalent to

type I_DER **is new** INTEGER **range** INTEGER(1)..INTEGER(10);   -- (16)

again leading to the property of "non-staticness" for the subtype I_DER.

Let us give two additional examples for the application of the equivalence rule

type I1 **is new** POSITIVE;   -- (17)
-- POSITIVE = STANDARD.POSITIVE is a predefined static subtype.
This declaration may be interpreted as
type ⟨aI1⟩ **is new** ⟨POSITIVE'BASE⟩;   -- (18a)
-- ⟨POSITIVE'BASE⟩ = INTEGER
subtype I1 **is** ⟨aI1⟩ **range** ⟨aI1⟩ (1) .. ⟨aI1⟩ (INTEGER'LAST);   -- (18b)

This interpretation gives the result that I1 is a non-static subtype because of the explicit conversions.

Let us consider another example
type I2 **is new** INTEGER;   -- (19)
-- INTEGER predefined
Is the subtype I2 - at least this time - a static subtype? The declaration is interpreted by us as the sequence of declarations
type ⟨aI2⟩ **is new** INTEGER;   -- (20a)
-- ⟨INTEGER'BASE⟩ = INTEGER
subtype I2 **is** ⟨aI2⟩;   -- (20b)
Now ⟨aI2⟩ is static and consequently so is I2.

3.4 On the "staticness" of floating-point types

LRM 3.5.7(10,11,12) provides an explicit formulation of the "equivalence rule" such that an analysis of the "staticness" can be given similar to the one carried out above for integer types.

3.5 The illegality of length clauses for SIZE

No representation clause for SIZE is allowed for any fixed-point type. In other words, all SIZE representation clauses for fixed-point types are *illegal*. This can be inferred from LRM 13.2(4,5): "The size specification is only allowed if the constraints on T... are static." Because of the explicit conversions (implied by the semantics) constraints are never static (cf. the conclusions mentioned above).

Similar considerations can be presented for integer types and floating-point types:

type INT **is range** 1..10;   -- (21)
for INT'SIZE **use** 16;   -- (22)

The size specification in (22) is illegal. This is a strange situation, to say the least.

Of course, for other reasons no representation clauses can be provided by the user for the predefined numeric types, which would at least satisfy the requirement of "staticness" (apart from DURATION).

4 REMARKS ON EXCEPTIONS

4.1 Illegality versus run-time error

Assume that the predefined package STANDARD provides only one integer type and let

type INT **is range** 1.. SOME_NAMED_NUMBER;   -- (23)

Then it is clear that INT can only be mapped on INTEGER (if it can be mapped at all). Simply invoking the "equivalence rule"

type ⟨a_INT⟩ **is new** INTEGER;   -- (24a)
subtype INT **is** ⟨a_INT⟩ **range**
⟨a_INT⟩ (1) .. ⟨a_INT⟩ (SOME_NAMED_NUMBER);   -- (24b)

would lead to the conclusion that if SOME_NAMED_NUMBER does not fit into the range of INTEGER, the elaboration of the type declaration would produce NUMERIC_ERROR at run-time due to the evaluation of ⟨a_INT⟩ (SOME_NAMED_NUMBER). This conclusion is not correct; instead the illegality of the declaration must be recognized at compile time.

This means that the "equivalence rule" must not be followed blindly; it takes effect only *after* the *successful selection* of the *underlying predefined* type. Nevertheless, one can figure out *legal* fixed-point type declarations, the *elaboration* of which will raise NUMERIC_ERROR: such a limiting case will happen, for example, if the *specified* upper bound exceeds SAFE_LARGE by a positive value not larger than SMALL.

Some Features of Numeric Types   173

4.2 Explicit conversions and errors

Consider the example

X: SHORT_INTEGER: = SHORT_INTEGER(INTEGER'LAST);   -- (25)

-- SHORT_INTEGER and INTEGER predefined

Of course, the elaboration of this object declaration will result in an error, i.e. will raise an exception. Which one? LRM 4.6(12) simply says: "In the case of conversions of numeric types, the exception CONSTRAINT_ERROR is raised by the evaluation of a type conversion if the result of the conversion fails to satisfy a constraint imposed by the type mark." From this one may argue that CONSTRAINT_ERROR will be raised in the above example (25).

A conversion is a two-step process:

1st step: conversion to the target type, this is the base type of the type
            mark denoting the conversion "operator";
2nd step: check the value of the operand against the
            constraints of the target subtype.

The first step can lead to NUMERIC_ERROR (cf. also LRM 3.5.4(10) and 3.5.6(6)); the second step can lead to CONSTRAINT_ERROR.

Thus, NUMERIC _ERROR must be raised. However, the statements in the LRM concerning this problem are not so definitive as the above mentioned analysis. Indeed, logically speaking, NUMERIC_ERROR is nothing more than a kind of CONSTRAINT_ERROR. The LRM does not seem to contradict the interpretation that in (all) cases where NUMERIC_ERROR can be raised CONSTRAINT_ERROR may be raised instead (the converse is definitely not true); so it can not be determined a priori which of the two exceptions will be raised as the result of the evaluation of an overflowing numeric expression. As a consequence the programmer would have to provide two identical handlers for the above mentioned exceptions.

4.3 Implicit conversions and NUMERIC_ERROR

On a two's complement machine one must be aware of the fact that

I: INTEGER: = -2**31;

-- INTEGER'FIRST = -2**31, INTEGER'LAST = 2**31-1

might raise NUMERIC_ERROR though the value -2**31 definitely belongs to the range of INTEGER. This is due to similar reasons as those discussed in section 2.

4.4 Underflow considered harmless

Due to the fact that zero is a model number and that consequently the ranges between -SMALL and zero and between zero and SMALL are considered as perfectly normal model intervals, underflow situations will be ignored; they will not provoke an exception. Thus, Ada plays down underflow though it is clear that it may invalidate all accuracy requirements. NUMERIC ERROR is raised when overflow occurs, but Ada does not strictly require this for real types (cf. LRM 4.5.7 (7)).

4.5 Compatibility of floating-point and fixed-point constraints with type marks

Consider the examples

type FLO is digits 10;	-- (26a)
type NEW_FLO is new FLO digits DIG;	-- (26b)
type FIX is delta 0.1 range -1.0..1.0	-- (27a)
X : FIX delta DEL;	-- (27b)

What happens if DIG ⟩ 10? What happens if DEL ⟨ 0.1 ? Will the illegality be flagged at compile time or will an exception (NUMERIC_ERROR or CONSTRAINT_ERROR) have to be raised at run-time? Note that all values concerned are static: DEL and DIG have to be static expressions, so what one needs to know is known at compile time.

The correct answer is that CONSTRAINT _ERROR must be raised.Cf. LRM 3.3.2(9), 3.5.7(14), and 3.5.9(13). In the final analysis this somewhat surprising result is the consequence of the *uniformity* of the definition for the compatibility of constraints with type marks within subtype indications as given in LRM 3.3.2(9).

5   THE NOTION OF PREDEFINED NUMERIC OPERATIONS, OPTIMIZATIONS AND OTHER SUBJECTS

5.1 Predefined numeric operations

The LRM defines the notions "operations", "basic operations", and "predefined operators" (mainly) in 3.3.3. However, the notion of "predefined operations" and especially "predefined numeric operations" seems to be completely undefined, though it is used (e.g. in LRM 11.1(6)).

For instance, one may ask the question whether the explicit conversion

Some Features of Numeric Types

INT(⟨some numeric expression⟩)

is a predefined numeric operation assuming that INT stands for a user-defined integer type.

5.2 Exponentiation by zero

The undefined form "zero exponentiated by zero" is well defined in Ada; it yields the value one. One might expect that the evaluation of such an indeterminate form would raise an error.

5.3 Integer multiplication with fixed-point values

Fixed-point values can be multiplied (and divided) by values of the predefined type INTEGER. Why not relax this restriction and admit *arbitrary* integer types?

5.4 The attributes MACHINE_OVERFLOWS and MACHINE_ROUNDS

The attributes MACHINE_OVERFLOWS and MACHINE_ROUNDS provide rather crude information because they refer to the predefined real operations as a *whole*. The information obtained by these attributes could be refined by making them one-parameter and two-parameter functions, respectively. A parameter may be introduced to indicate the *operation* considered and - in the case of MACHINE_ROUNDS - another one which reflects the *kind* of rounding.

With respect to MACHINE_OVERFLOWS there are machines in which an overflow condition caused by an adding operation is signalled by the hardware whereas a multiplication will never produce an interrupt. With respect to MACHINE_ROUNDS one may notice that Kulisch's arithmetic (Kulisch 1976; Kulisch & Miranker 1981) and the IEEE proposal (IEEE 1982) consider several different rounding functions.

5.5 The attributes FIRST and LAST for real types

Of course, model interval arithmetic is only approximate; nevertheless one might expect that the values for the lower and upper bounds of a real type represented by the attributes FIRST and LAST are uniquely defined. However, they are not. Furthermore, it seems possible that FIRST and LAST lie outside of the range of model numbers (i.e. F'LAST > F'LARGE, F'FIRST < -F'LARGE for a fixed-point type F).

5.6 Optimizations of floating-point expressions

The intention of the rules given in LRM 11.6 (5) is to provide the basis for certain optimizations of numeric types such as *constant folding*. These rules are appropriate for the folding of *integers* but they seem to be insufficient for floating-point values. Let us consider, for instance, floating-point addition. This operation is not associative (see the example below, cf. also Wichmann 1980) and the condition: "... a real result must belong to the result model interval defined for a canonical left-to-right order ..." cannot generally be met when operators are reordered: the model interval associated with the optimized "non-canonical" evaluation of an expression may be a superset of the model interval resulting from the canonical evaluation order.

If $x+c1+c2$ denotes an expression of the floating-point type F with c1 and c2 representing the compile-time values 1.0 and F'SMALL, respectively, then what is the result model interval of this expression when the variable x assumes the value -1.0 ? The evaluation in canonical order produces the single-valued model interval containing only F'SMALL whereas $x+(c1+c2)$ gives the result model interval 0.0..F'EPSILON. Note that F'EPSILON is significantly larger than F'SMALL because of the relation: F'EPSILON = $2.0**(3*F'MANTISSA+2)*F'SMALL$ and F'MANTISSA ≥ 5. (This situation becomes extreme for values near F'LARGE; e.g. consider the triple $(x, c1, c2) = $ (F'LARGE, -F'LARGE, F'SMALL).)

Acknowledgements
The author would like to thank Brian Ford who encouraged him to write this paper and to Michael Lott, Chris Comer, William Taylor and all the members of the Ada-Europe Numerics Working Group especially Jean-Luc Adda for discussions concerning its contents.

Postscript
Up to now there are no *official* comments on language issues of the ANSI standard. However, there exist recommendations prepared by the Language Maintenance Committee of the Ada Board as to how some of the language problems *should* be resolved.

References

IEEE (1982). A Proposed Standard for Binary Floating-Point Arithmetic. Draft 10.0 of IEEE Task P754. New York.

Kulisch, U. (1976). Grundlagen des Numerischen Rechnens. Mannheim/Wien/Zürich: B.I.-Wissenschaftsverlag.

Kulisch, U. W. & Miranker, W. L. (1981). Computer Arithmetic in Theory and Practice. New York: Academic Press.

Reference Manual for the Ada Programming Language (1983). ANSI/MIL-STD 1815A. United States Department of Defense. Washington D. C.

Wichmann, B. A. (1980). Tutorial Material on the Real Data-Types in Ada. Final Technical Report. National Physical Laboratory, Teddington.

INTERFACING Ada TO FORTRAN

C.G. van der Laan
Rekencentrum Universiteit Groningen
Postbus 800, 9700 AV, Groningen,
The Netherlands

Abstract. The use of FORTRAN numerical program
libraries in Ada via the INTERFACE pragma is
explored. Subroutines with a subprogram as
dummy argument cannot be used via the INTERFACE
pragma, if the corresponding actual parameter is
an Ada procedure. In order to overcome this
difficulty a specification of a FORTRAN pragma is
proposed. Some routines from Forsythe, Moler and
Malcolm(1977) are coupled as representative
examples; the BLAS, the FORTRAN intrinsic functions,
and some routines from NAG, which illustrate
reverse communication and the use of the FORTRAN
pragma for the case of more than one subprogram as
dummy argument, as well as the graphical supplement
of NAG are only mentioned as examples, for
conciseness reasons.

1 INTRODUCTION
Use of FORTRAN routines in an Ada environment is an
example of mixed language programming. The advantages of using
FORTRAN program libraries in other languages are:
- extensive, efficient, fully documented, thoroughly (field)
  tested FORTRAN libraries exist for many computers,
- maintenance of program libraries with transliterations in
  various languages is cumbersome.
The disadvantages are:
- use of FORTRAN routines in other languages is generally
  not elaborated and therefore not standardized and hardly
  provided by manufacturers,
- dealing with more than one language is more complex and
  error prone,
- portability is decreased by mixed language programming,
  unless (trans-)portable, or generally available, operating
  systems or programming environments are introduced as
  environments for compatible compilers,
- error-handling, and I/O in general, is more complicated,
- interfacing overhead, especially for small routines,
- fewer protection mechanisms are available in FORTRAN
  because it is not a strongly-typed language.

Difficulties with mixed language programming are discussed by Einarsson & Gentleman (1984), who distinguish fundamental incompatibilities between languages from incompatible implementations of languages. In this paper we explore the INTERFACE pragma with respect to the creation of virtual numerical program collections in Ada on top of FORTRAN program libraries. Moreover, we specify a FORTRAN pragma, in order to couple routines which have Ada subprograms as dummy arguments. Our proposal is within the syntax of the standard because we believe that modification of the standard will at least take time, if it happens at all. This work is a continuation of our earlier experiences in mixed language programming with ALGOL 68 and FORTRAN (Van der Laan (1981), De Bruin & Van der Laan (1983)); so far we were only able to describe our ideas because we have no access to an Ada compiler. Moreover, the FORTRAN pragma is a proposal which is not yet implemented to our knowledge and not mentioned in Ada Reference Manual(ARM); even the INTERFACE pragma is not generally considered for implementation which will make it practical impossible to use Ada for numerical purposes for the next few years. A more elaborate version of this paper is given in Van der Laan(1984).
Notational conventions.
ARM denotes the Ada reference manual; FRM denotes the FORTRAN reference manual. In the examples the following naming conventions are used. If we start from a FORTRAN program library collection with name X then the FORTRAN bound interface level is called XF, the Ada bound interface level is supplied as a package specification with name X_A, while the virtual Ada collection is supplied as a package with name VIR_X. The latter layer is not specific for the interface but supplied in order to elucidate the X_A level. Packages were chosen as units because we like to couple collections instead of single routines; furthermore the designator of routines as library units are restricted to identifiers. GEF stands for the collection of subprograms published by Forsythe et al.(1977).

2 CORRESPONDENCE OF TYPES

From the logical level point of view the coupling concerns the FORTRAN concepts INTEGER, REAL, DOUBLE PRECISION, COMPLEX, LOGICAL, CHARACTER, (DIMENSION), SUBROUTINE and FUNCTION. From the physical level point of view we assume that the internal representations of the various types in either language are the same. In Ada some types are implementation defined (see annex C ARM), while LONG_FLOAT and COMPLEX can be provided by an implementation and therefore all these types can be implemented with the same internal representations as the corresponding types in FORTRAN.

Interfacing Ada to Fortran

FORTRAN	corresponds with	Ada
INTEGER		INTEGER
REAL		FLOAT
DOUBLE PRECISION		LONG_FLOAT
COMPLEX		COMPLEX
LOGICAL		BOOLEAN
CHARACTER * LEN		STRING (1..len)

LEN is defined in section 8.4.2. of the FRM and len is restricted to those objects. LEN = (*), a dummy array of assumed size, corresponds to an unconstrained formal parameter in Ada. If we denote any of the above types by FTYPE when we mean a FORTRAN type and ATYPE when we mean the corresponding Ada type, then

FTYPE(D[,D])	corresponds with	array index_constraint of ATYPE

where D, the dimension declarator, is prescribed in section 5.1.1.1 of the FRM, and the index constraint is described in section 3.6.1 of the ARM and restricted by the constraints of FORTRAN. We assume that arrays are stored columnwise in Ada, at least by a compiler option.(If not then the matrices have to be transposed on the FORTRAN level.)

For subprograms we have

SUBROUTINE NAMEF	procedure NAMEA
SUBROUTINE NAMEF (...)	procedure NAMEA (...)
FTYPE FUNCTION NAMEF (...)	function NAMEA (...) return ATYPE

with parameter types as mentioned above, and the result of functions restricted to those of FORTRAN. For arrays as formal parameters the unconstrained array definition is allowed in order to abstract from the bound values, which corresponds to the asterisk in the adjusted array declarator in FORTRAN as described in section 5.1 of the FRM. In FORTRAN the bound information for multi-indexed arrays is generally supplied via actual arguments, or filled in by constant values. Furthermore, parameter passing must be such that in-parameters remain unchanged. Procedures and functions as dummy arguments need special attention when the actual procedures and functions are written in Ada, the more so when they take arrays as parameters. So far it did not seem necessary to consider the case when the actual subprograms take themselves subprograms as parameters.

3 CREATION OF Ada VIRTUAL PROGRAM COLLECTIONS

As detailed in Van der Laan (1983a), we consider two language levels: a User Language level (UL) and a Portable Computer Language level (PCL). Within the PCL level we distinguish a program library level and an interface level, because the program library level is generally available via the various numerical program libraries and because we like to have a separate interface level to adapt the program library with respect to shorter parameter lists, and to perform actions with respect to errors signalled by, and in terms of, routines of the program library. (At the moment in our ALGOL 68-FORTRAN interface the PCL bound level is in FORTRAN 77 while the program library is compiled under FORTRAN 66.) In the UL level we have created a virtual program library level above the interface level because it relieves the virtual library from the restrictions imposed by the PCL in the interface level and allows the generality of Ada, e.g. defaults, overloading, and (dynamical) generation of storage. This situation is illustrated by the following figure.

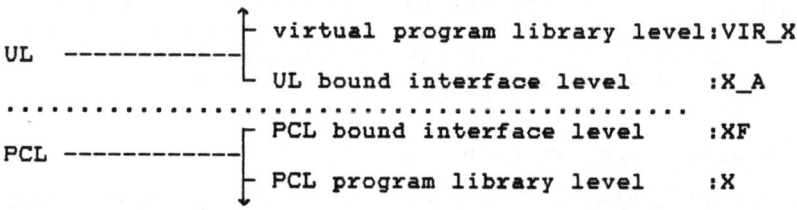

In this paper we have restricted ourselves to Ada as UL and FORTRAN as PCL. So far we have excluded subroutines with labeled common e.g. as used in the PORT library (Fox et al.(1978)). FORTRAN routines, and in general routines written in other languages, can be made available to Ada via subprogram declarations supplied with the INTERFACE pragma, as is given im the ARM in section 13.9 with the following syntax

    pragma INTERFACE (name, name),

where the first name denotes the language and the second name denotes the subprogram. In the sequel of this section the use and the limitations of the INTERFACE pragma are explored.

Interfacing Ada to Fortran

3.1 Coupling the GEF collection

As an example the solution of the linear least squares problem from the GEF collection is considered. More examples are treated in Van der Laan (1984).

```
      SUBROUTINE LINLSQF( A, C, Y, M, N, W)
      INTEGER M, N
      REAL A( M, N), C( N), Y( M), W( 2*(M+1)*N)
C Púrpose:  The linear least squares solution of the
C           overdetermined system  A C = Y  is delivered in C.
C Input:  A REAL array: the coefficients of the linear system.
C         Y REAL array: the dependent values. Not altered.
C         M, N INTEGER constants: the description of the size
C              of the problem,  M rows (dependent values) and
C              N columns (the number of unknowns).
C         W REAL work array.
C Output: C REAL array: the solution of the linear least
C              squares problem.
```

In the sequel frequent use is made of vectors and matrices, which we assume available in the spirit of Symm et al.(1984) in a VECMAT package.

```
package VECMAT is
   type COMPLEX is private;
   type VEC is array (INTEGER range <> ) of FLOAT;
   type MAT is array (INTEGER range <> , INTEGER range <>) of
                                                         FLOAT;
   type CVEC is array (INTEGER range <>) of COMPLEX;
   type DVEC is array (INTEGER range <>) of LONG_FLOAT;
   type INDEX is array (INTEGER range <>) of INTEGER;
-- functions for the above data types should be specified here.
private -- compatible with FORTRAN
   type COMPLEX is record RE, IM: FLOAT; end record;
end VECMAT;
```

Ada bound interface level: part of the package GEF_A.

```
with VECMAT; use VECMAT;
package GEF_A is
   procedure LINLSQF(A: in out MAT; X: out VEC; B: in out VEC;
                     M,N: INTEGER; W: in out VEC);
private
   pragma INTERFACE ( FORTRAN, LINLSQF);
end GEF_A;
```

Part of the virtual Ada GEF collection: the package VIR_GEF.

```
with VECMAT; use VECMAT;
package VIR_GEF is
   procedure LINLSQ ( A: in out MAT; B: in out VEC; X: out VEC);
end VIR_GEF;
```

```
with GEF_A; use GEF_A;
package body VIR_GEF is
   procedure LINLSQ ( A: in out MAT; B: in out VEC;
                      X: out VEC) is
      M: constant INTEGER := A'LENGTH(1);
      N: constant INTEGER := A'LENGTH(2);
      W: VEC( 1..2*(M+1)*N);
   begin
      LINLSQF ( A, X, B, M, N, W);
   end LINLSQ;
end VIR_GEF; -- body
```

3.2 Coupling the BLAS collection

Coupling the BLAS illustrates how to deal with generic procedures in the situation that actual counterparts of the generic formal procedures are already available via FORTRAN and implemented efficiently on various computer series, a CRAY and CYBER 205, and will hopefully be implemented on distributed architectures. How to exploit generics facilities in general for numerical programming is dealt with by Delves and Pursglove(1984). In Van der Laan (1984) the coupling of the BLAS is worked out in detail.

3.3 Coupling the intrinsic functions

The elementary mathematical functions are not included in the Ada language. Symm et al.(1984) have specified a generic package to deliver among other things the elementary mathematical functions to an 'arbitrary' number of decimal digits where some routines also allow default parameters. In Van der Laan(1984) we have worked out the use in Ada of REAL, DOUBLE PRECISION and COMPLEX (intrinsic FORTRAN) mathematical functions. The difference with the coupling of the BLAS concerns the generic names of FORTRAN (and the overloaded counterparts in Ada) and the handling of default parameters in the Ada level.

3.4 Coupling general available numerical program libraries

Roughly 100 routines (of roughly 500 user-callable routines) of the NAG FORTRAN mark 10 library, and roughly 25 routines(of roughly 600 user-callable routines of the IMSL edition 10 library, take subprograms as dummy arguments. In order to use these routines in Ada either the use of the INTERFACE pragma must be relieved from restrictions with respect to generic subprograms, or the routines must be rewritten with reverse communication facilities. The few routines from NAG which require a global function cannot be used via the INTERFACE pragma either. When the function is included in the parameter list, which is a trivial modification, then these routines can also be used via mixed language programming provided a less restricted interface facility than the INTERFACE pragma, e.g. the FORTRAN pragma (see section 4) is available. Again examples are given in Van der Laan(1984).

Interfacing Ada to Fortran

4 THE FORTRAN PRAGMA

In order to make use in Ada of FORTRAN routines with Ada subprograms as parameters, we propose a FORTRAN pragma.

```
pragma FORTRAN (NAMEF [,( A1 [ ,( B1, aggregate
                                {,BM, aggregate})]
                    {,AR [ ,( BR1, aggregate
                                {,BRM, aggregate})]}
                    )
                ]
                )
```

where A1,..., AR correspond to the dummy arguments of NAMEF, and B1,...,BM, and BR1,...,BRM correspond to arrays of a dummy subprogram, with bounds given in the subsequent aggregate (for each dimension lower and upper bounds must be given, all separated by commas), of the formal generic subprograms. NAMEF denotes the name of the coupled FORTRAN subprogram. Name restrictions are imposed by those of FORTRAN. The FORTRAN pragma is an extension of the INTERFACE pragma and aimed at generic subprograms with only procedures or functions as generic formal parameters; as extension of the INTERFACE pragma it may also be used for the cases treated in section 3, by substitution of

pragma INTERFACE(FORTRAN, NAME)   by   pragma FORTRAN(NAME).

5 EXAMPLES WITH THE FORTRAN PRAGMA

As examples we consider the FORTRAN routines ZEROINF and DIFSYSF from GEF. (LINLSQF and others are omitted for conciseness reasons.)

```
      REAL FUNCTION ZEROINF( AX, BX, F, TOL)
      REAL AX, BX, F, TOL
      EXTERNAL F
C Purpose: A zero of the function F in the interval ( AX, BX)
C          is delivered in ZEROINF.
C Input: AX, BX REAL constants: the interval which contains a
C          zero.
C        F REAL FUNCTION with REAL constant argument.
C        TOL REAL constant: desired length of the interval of
C          uncertainty of the final result.
C Remark. It is assumed that F( AX)*F( BX) .LE. 0.0 .

      SUBROUTINE DIFSYSF( T, TFINAL, N, Y, F, RELERR, ABSERR,
     +                    W, IW)
      INTEGER N, IW(5)
      REAL T, TFINAL, Y( N), RELERR, ABSERR, W( 6*N+3)
      EXTERNAL F
```

```
C Purpose: Y( TFINAL) is calculated from the system of
C          differential equations DY/DX = F( X, Y), Y( T) given.
C Input: N INTEGER constant: number of differential equations.
C        Y REAL array: the initial values.
C        T, TFINAL REAL constants: begin and end values of the
C           interval of the independent variable.
C        RELERR, ABSERR REAL constants: relative and absolute
C           error tolerances for the following local error
C           test at each step
C              ABS( local error) .LE.  RELERR*ABS( Y)+ ABSERR
C           for each component of the solution and local
C           error vector.
C        F SUBROUTINE F( T, Y, YP)
C          REAL T, Y(*), YP(*)
C          Purpose: the derivatives YP( K) = DY( K)/DT are
C                   delivered, K=1,...,N.
C        W REAL work array.
C        IW INTEGER work array.
C Output: Y REAL array: the solution vector in the point TFINAL.
C Remark. In the FORTRAN level error situations are handled.

with VECMAT; use VECMAT;
package GEF_A is
   generic
      with function F ( X:  FLOAT) return FLOAT;
   function ZEROINF( A, B, TOL:  FLOAT) return FLOAT;
   generic
      with procedure FXY ( X:  FLOAT; Y:  VEC; YPRIME: out VEC);
   procedure DIFSYSF ( XB, XE:  FLOAT;  --initial and end point
                       N:  INTEGER;    --number of coupled ODE's
                       Y: in out VEC;  --initial and solution
                                       --values
                       RELERR, ABSERR:  FLOAT;
                                       --error tolerances
                       W: in out VEC;  --work array
                       IW: in out INDEX);
private                                --work array
   pragma FORTRAN ( ZEROINF, (A, B, F, T));
   pragma FORTRAN ( DIFSYSF, ( XB, XE, N, Y,
                    FXY, ( Y, ( 1, N), YPRIME, ( 1, N)),
                    RELERR, ABSERR, W, IW) );
end GEF_A;
```

Part of the virtual Ada GEF collection: the package VIR_GEF.

```
with VECMAT; use VECMAT;
package VIR_GEF is
   generic
      with procedure RHS ( X:  FLOAT; Y:  VEC; YPRIME: out VEC);
   procedure DIFSYS ( XB, XE:  FLOAT; Y: in out VEC; RELERR,
                      ABSERR:  FLOAT);
end VIR_GEF;
```

Interfacing Ada to Fortran

```
with GEF_A; use GEF_A;
package body VIR_GEF is
-- Procedure DIFSYS is introduced above DIFSYSF in order to
-- illustrate how to abstract from details imposed by the
-- coupled FORTRAN routine while dealing with a formal
-- generic subprogram parameter.
    procedure DIFSYS ( XB, XE:   FLOAT; Y: in out VEC; RELERR,
                       ABSERR:   FLOAT) is
       N : constant INTEGER := Y'LENGTH;
       W : VEC (1..3+6*N);
       IW: INDEX (1..5);
       procedure DIFSYS_RHS is new DIFSYSF ( RHS);
    begin
       DIFSYS_RHS ( XB, XE, N, Y, RELERR, ABSERR, W, IW);
    end DIFSYS;
end VIR_GEF; -- body
```

6 NESTED USAGE

Below the finding of a zero of a function defined by a differential equation is worked out. Although this does not illustrate mixed language programming per se, it indicates the inconvenience for numerical work of parameterization over a function via generic units, because of the intermediate instantiation.

```
-- Exercise P9-3 of Forsythe et al.(1977) simplified (a
-- complete elaboration is given in Van der Laan(1984)).
with TEXT_IO, VIR_GEF; use TEXT_IO, VIR_GEF;
procedure ZERDIF is
-- Zero finding of a function defined by the differential
-- equation:     dy/dx = f(x,y) = 1/(1+x),    y(0)=0.
    function F ( X:  FLOAT) return FLOAT is
       RELERR: constant FLOAT := 1.0E-6;
       ABSERR: constant FLOAT := 1.0E-6;
       FX:   VEC (1..1);
       procedure RHS ( X:  FLOAT; Y:  VEC; YPRIME: out VEC) is
       begin YPRIME (1) := 1.0/(1.0+X); end RHS;
       procedure DIFSYS_RHS is new DIFSYS ( RHS);
    begin FX (1) := 0.0;
       DIFSYS_RHS ( 0.0, X, FX, RELERR, ABSERR);
       return FX (1);
    end F;
    function ZEROINF_F is new ZEROINF( F);
    package REAL_IO is new FLOAT_IO(FLOAT);
    use REAL_IO;
begin
    PUT ("Zero of function given by: dy/dx= 1/(1+x), y(0)=0:");
    PUT ( ZEROINF_F ( -0.5, 1.0, 1.0E-3));
end ZERDIV; -- body
```

7 I/O

A problem in relation to using FORTRAN routine collections in a host language is the handling of error messages generated by FORTRAN routines. A simple approach to overcome this difficulty is to separate the FORTRAN output from the host language output and to make them both available to the user. The more general problem is the sharing of a file by FORTRAN and the host language. Furthermore, exception handling could be extended to taking care of e.g. all arithmetic errors independent of whether they occured in FORTRAN or Ada. These latter aspects deserve further attention.

CONCLUSION

The use of FORTRAN program libraries in Ada via the INTERFACE pragma is restricted to those subroutines or functions which don't take a subroutine or function as dummy argument. In order to make full use of FORTRAN program libraries, we have extended, with respect to FORTRAN library usage, the functionality of the INTERFACE pragma by proposing a FORTRAN pragma. The INTERFACE and FORTRAN pragmas have been illustrated via representative examples. The inconvenience, for numerical work, in Ada of parameterization over a procedure or function via generic formal parameters is also indicated by examples of nested usage of a program library.
Furthermore, it is interesting to realize that providing an interface between Ada and FORTRAN (FORTRAN pragma) is estimated to cost .5 manyear for each Ada compiler, while providing a portable Ada numerical program library is estimated to cost 100 manyears, which does not include the research with respect to parallel algorithms.

ACKNOWLEDGEMENTS

The author is grateful to J.Ph. Kelders and D.D. de Vries of our computing centre and computer science department respectively, for fruitful discussions, and to the Ada Europe Numerics Working Group, especially Prof. dr. Th. J. Dekker, drs. J. Kok, D. T. Winter, G.T. Symm and dr. R. P. Wehrum, for stimulating contacts and discussions.

LITERATURE

ARM: Ada reference manual, jan. 1983. ANSI/MIL-STD 1815A.

De Bruin, R. & C.G. van der Laan (1983). The creation of a virtual NAG-ALGOL68 program library. RC-Rapport 10. Rekencentrum Universiteit Groningen.

Delves, L. M.& C. Pursglove (in preparation). Ada Generic facilities in scientific subroutine libraries.

Einarsson, B.& W.M. Gentleman (1984). Mixed language programming. Software-Practice and Experience, 14, 4, 383-395.

Forsythe, G.E., M.A. Malcolm, C.B. Moler (1977). Computer methods for mathematical computations. Prentice Hall.

Fox, P.A. A.D. Hall, N.L. Schryer (1978). The PORT Mathematical subroutine library. TOMS, 4, 2, 104-126.

FRM: FORTRAN reference manual, November 1978. ANSI X3.9-1978.

IMSL: International Mathematical Statistical Libraries Inc., Houston.

Lawson, C.L., R.J. Hanson, D.R. Kincaid, F.T. Krogh (1979). Basic Linear Algebra Subprograms for FORTRAN usage. TOMS, 5, 3, 308-323.

NAG: Numerical Algorithms Group, Oxford.

Symm, G.T., B.A. Wichmann, J. Kok, D.T. Winter (1984). Guidelines for the design of large modular scientific libraries in Ada. NPL report DITC 37/84.

Van der Laan, C.G. (1981). Programming in ALGOL 68 (as a host) and the usage of FORTRAN (program libraries). In The relationship between numerical computation and programming languages, ed. J.K. Reid, 305-314. North Holland.

Van der Laan, C.G. (1983a). Necessary conditions for graceful mixed language programming. (Submitted for publication).

Van der Laan, C.G. (1983b). From TORRIX to BLAS. RC-Rapport 9. Rekencentrum Universiteit Groningen.

Van der Laan, C.G. (1984). Interfacing Ada to FORTRAN. RC-Rapport 13. Rekencentrum Universiteit Groningen.

Van der Meulen, S.G.& M. Veldhorst (1978). TORRIX, Mathematical Centre Tracts 86.

PART IV ADA - EDUCATION NEEDS

THE DEPENDENCE OF ADA* EDUCATION ON THE SUPPORT ENVIRONMENT

I H Richmond
Edinburgh Regional Computing Centre, Edinburgh, EH8 9JU

Abstract Much consideration has been given to the introduction
of sensible Software Engineering methodologies into industry with
Ada as the Program Design and/or Implementation Language; Ada
provides a focus for attaining the suggested benefits of economy
and maintainability of software. The adoption of Ada as a standard
on both sides of the Atlantic has resulted in a greater emphasis
being placed on environmental issues than ever before. The work in
this area must however go hand in hand with its gradual
implementation in the market place. For this reason it is
important to bring an awareness in a controlled fashion to all
areas of the industrial community, not just those who are
presently involved.

1. Introduction

It is accepted fact that with new techniques and requirements
being introduced to the workplace at an ever increasing rate an employees
education must continue throughout his/her working life. It is no longer the
case that one single set of skills will maintain their usefulness until
retirement.
Throughout commercial and government organisations (which will be
termed USERS henceforth) this education is often thought to be the
responsibility of a unique body (to be termed EDUCATORS henceforth) which
relieves the others of the necessity to be concerned with its operation and
effectiveness. These EDUCATORS are in the main part operating external to the
USERS' environments due to the inability of any but the largest organisation
to be able to respond to a requirement cost effectively. As a result the
EDUCATORS are often accused of being out of touch with the USERS' real
requirements while the EDUCATORS accuse the USERS of not using their products
properly.
Each is to blame for the presumptions that are made of the other's
responsibilities. The USERS expect immediate advantage with less than minimum
commitment and the EDUCATORS supply a product that USERS will buy knowing that
insufficient time is being applied to expect anything but a cursory
appreciation. They know that the major part of the learning will be done in
the work place if appropriate conditions exist and hence there is little point
in offering any more than a generalised introduction.
Some EDUCATORS will offer a superb presentation while others look
at it as a money spinner and pay scant attention to the methodologies required
for effective information assimilation. USERS however will see little
practical advantage in either if they do not allow their employees to utilise

* Ada is a registered trademark of the U.S. Government, Ada Joint Program
  Office

their newly acquired skills immediately. It is not difficult to see therefore that the idea of "on the job training" will appeal as being the best solution of all. Not only does it obviate the need for a training budget but it also keeps employees in the workplace and therefore available at all times to use their present skills. The real cost to the USER of adopting this technique is horrendous but masked by the lack of a measurable formality.

Having generalised about the problems surrounding education itself we now turn our attention to the specific task of introducing Ada to the workplace with its associated Software Engineering (S.E.) principles. The majority of the potential benefits of Ada will be lost if these S.E. principles are not carried through. Ada will be just another computing language that a particular buyer requires as part of the contract. If this were the case then there would be little concern as to which countries used it.

It is clear however that it is not looked upon this way since the Department of Defense (DoD) in the USA is particularily worried as to how many other countries obtain it and its forseen advantages. These advantages are however currently only theoretical since its usage is not widespread. Widespread usage is where the advantage really will tell and it is on this that our major effort should be concentrated. Education in the appropriate usage is therefore the key and a major programme is necessary to produce the technology quantum jump desired. The programme must however understand the hurdles that presently face it and be applied in a methodical way. It is not sufficient to say that it is necessary and carry on blindly in the present fashion. It must be geared to produce an active requirement on the part of the USERS and be able to satisfy it.

2. Education

To understand how this educational program should be approached requires an understanding of education itself. If we are educating somebody we are trying to impart an awareness and an expertise. This expertise is more than just a skill it is really an expertise in a particular methodology of function. The important ideas are enclosed in an awareness of their application so that they can b applied effectively in a real situation and become practical in the real world.

Education usually encompasses three different methods of assimilation of information. Each of these in turn is complementary to the others and is relatively ineffective in isolation. It is also important that there is an appropriate mix so that each important point is exercised in each phase with little time lapse in between.

a) There is the lecturing or teaching phase which allows the student to become aware of but not proficient in the use of a particular bundle of collected facts. If exercised properly it should take into account the particular background of the students and their attention span. Various methods of increasing the assimilation of awareness include using audio visual effects, demonstrations and changes of speaker. No technically involved lecture that expects to have the attention of its audience should exceed thirty minutes and often should be much less. If the student cannot maintain attention then the lecture is a wasted exercise on the part of both parties.

b) While the lecturing or teaching phase is the direct introduction of facts the tuition or counselling phase is the repeat of them in an unstructured manner. This allows the information to be properly understood and suited to the knowledge base that the student has already acquired. Since the student can only be expected to remember less than 10%, vital parts of the facts are reinforced and misconceptions corrected. The practical phase is the most important of all since it is the proof that the knowledge is relevant. By putting the facts into a real environment the students memory is reinforced and all those presumptions that the lecturer made about prior knowledge are corrected if found to be wanting. The practical phase is also important because it gets past the theoretical stage to the point where the student gains confidence and builds real applications. It is now that the student is able to use what has been learnt. It is therefore vital that this can be carried out otherwise doubt and disillusionment creep in.

3. Educational Practise

While these educational phases are important they are all wasted unless the method of introduction is effective. Unless the student participates the job is much harder and less fruitful. Obtaining willing participation therefore requires that the student enjoys the system. To enjoy it there are a number of points that need to be satisfied.

Success therefore requires that education should be approached in the same way as any other product which is to be brought to the market place. It must be sold. Since a selling approach is to be adopted then it must be approached in the conventional structured manner.

In selling any product it is first necessary to establish the need for it. If the customer does not see a need for it it will not be sold. Often it is necessary to develop this need since the customer may not initially see the requirement. In education therefore it is necessary to persuade the potential student of the reason for entering the educational process. Often this is done by external factors, with educational organisations soaking up the demand. In the case of Ada however this is required due to the extensive bad publicity that it has received to date. We will cover this point in greater detail later.

Once the need has been established it requires a product to meet it. In other words we need to develop the solution in relation to the now existing need. It must be stressed that until the need has been firmly established the relevance of and hence the demand for the solution will not be clear.

Finally having developed the solution we must present it in a form that is immediately useful. Promises of what will come in the future should only be used to underline the reason for using the proposed solution. No customer buys a car with promises of the wheels in the future but they will buy a car knowing that they can put the radio of their choice in at a later date. It would be foolish however to be demonstrate a vehicle that the user has to learn to drive only to be told at a later date that they will require to use a completely different method of steering in the next model. This only serves to increase the resistance to change and develops a suspicion that the makers will change their minds once again with the next model.

4. The Educational Aim

Without a goal all this discussion of methodology is worthless. The first thing to establish therefore is the aim of Ada and S.E. education. It is probably easier to establish what it is not . In the first place it is not about the development of software tools, whether practical or not. Learning to use any of these tools in isolation is not an end in itself. The environment is a very important issue but the educational process, while very dependent on it, is not aimed at producing it. Neither is this educational process about producing isolated pieces of software as part of demonstrator projects, although these provide the basis for the proof of the practicality of the available S.E. practices.

The final aim of the educational process should be a vast body of highly proficient men and women who can use the tools, the environments and the results of the demonstrator projects. To do this their employers must be prepared to accept that the educational process must be continuous. If we are to ask them to accept this financial penalty we must provide the neccessary incentive. This is easily said but must also be demostrable, hence the requirement for demonstrator projects.

The employing organisation should be able to see a large quantity of high quality users. This will improve the economy of his production process. Rarity of expertise both drives the price up and increases the vulnerability to loss of key personnel. If the quality is high then productivity can be expected to be similarily high. This means that more of the smaller one-off jobs that were being undertaken by inexperienced personnel due to lack of response from the experts can be tackled. This increases the efficiency overall since less wheels are reinvented.

5. The Present Position

The SALTIRE (Scottish Ada Language Training and Information Resource) is a collaborative project between the Edinburgh Regional Computing Centre and MEL (Dunfermline) Ltd, who are part of the Phillips Group. In the SALTIRE project that we are currently running in Edinburgh we are meeting a degree of resistance to Ada. This effectively is a large measure of disillusionment on a number of fronts. If we examine these in turn we can illustrate the present position from which we are moving.

In the first place the whole Ada effort caught the imagination of a large number of our potential customers. Unfortunately that means that we developed a need at least five years ago without fulfilling it. It is only now that we have a small set of validated compilers available and few have even dared to define except, in the loosest possible terms, what the environment and its basic methodologies will look like. Promises have been made but we have no proof of their validity except that a compiler can be produced after five years.

Because we have had such a high visibility during the compiler design and implementation stages wild exaggerations about the language have been rife. These vary from its ability to supercede Basic to its uselessness due to its size. Neither of these claims are true but to the uninitiated they are believable and make the educational process more difficult to start, except in selected quarters such as military contractors.

Another point that is often brought to task is the subject of the "right" methodology. In S.E. it is a necessity but the proof of the effectiveness of one over the other in particular situations is not there, either due to lack of implementation or lack of communication.

As far as the potential users of Ada are concerned there is widespread agreement that adoption will not take place until the environment can do what their present environments offer. Anything less would be a step backward unless a contract is at stake. In other words until we can provide an equally useful working position from which to expand they are reluctant to make the commitment for productivity and financial reasons. This understandable reluctance must be countered effectively with a practical starting point.

The DoD's resistance to subsets or supersets is to be commended but it has still led to the early introduction and usage of subsets which have marred many potential users attitudes. Using compilers which are incomplete and not properly debugged has often proved how "difficult" the language will be to use! When offered a language which is supposed to provide easily produced and maintained software it has been easy to "prove" how right the opponents have been.

As to this environment which should be so wonderful and practical the suggestions of some vendors to use the basic operating system until something better turns up casts a dark shadow of doubt.

6. Educational Requirements

It is a requirement of education that the construction of the environment be attacked more practically. It requires that grandiose schemes with collaborators that have too many conflicting vested interests should take a less visible position. They often have too long a development time and are too susceptible to collapse. The environment should be developed gradually, to first meet the standards of other available language-specific environments simulating their capabilities in the first instance. When a particular tool is completed it should be released as the basis for others. If a steady flow of packages starts the potential users can build faith in the future of the industry and plan accordingly. The acceptability of the packages will also indicate their usefullness and indicate the practicality of further development. In short the environmental development should be by small, simple, sure steps. This will make the path more manageable for both the producers and the users, since massive potential serious changes in production methodology will not be necessary. It will also lead to the acceptability of change and take us toward the acceptability of continuous education. There is nothing quite as acceptable as a successful toe in the water test with a small but workable tool. Look at how acceptable UNIX[+] is to those who dare tread the unexpected command structures. The ability to use and integrate small tools leads to their acceptance and usage. I would also point to the acceptability of Basic, which with all its drawbacks has one thing to offer initially - simplicity and immediate usability.

7. Introducing Ada

Introducing the concept of using Ada and the S.E. principles it supports requires in the first place that the appropriate management be persuaded of its neccessity. This leads us to the type of course that is offered by an increasing number of organisations; namely the management overview. The importance of this is however still not fully comprehended and hence too fast and simplistic an approach results. How many of those attending leave thinking 'that it's a good idea but will it ever get off the ground?' or 'it's all very well for the military contractors but what use is it in a commercial establishment?'. These are the people in whom the first interests must be awakened and they must be completely convinced or we are lost before we get to first base. All too often we are so keen to get down the syntax of Ada that we forget about the project managers. Without their conviction and understanding their programmers will just produce the same Fortran style in the Ada language. This will show little benefit and high retraining costs. They must understand that both the design and the execution of the design will need higher management involvement until the appropriate tools arrive.

+ UNIX is a registered trademark of Bell Laboratories

Execution of these principles will give better results and hence easier acceptability of the tools when they arrive. It will also result in easier definition of the requirements of the support environment. Finally, when introducing the language to novices or professionals alike it is neccessary to introduce it in the correct context. The educational process should extend beyond the adoptation of the syntax alone, which will lead to Ada being written in the style of the previously known language whether it be Fortran, Cobol or even Assembler. The education of the software engineer requires that he/she is taught to use the appropriate structures in a structured fashion, not necessarily by the easiest routes. It will be the responsibility of the project manager to ensure that this practise is enforced.

8. A Plan of Action

In the current situation we therefore would encourage a potential user to adopt a relevant methodology. This should be based on what another user who has similar requirements is using successfully. Ada is an obvious recommendation since the language is so practical in most situations and offers a route into the future. The two should then be evaluated in a non-critical project which will produce some guidelines for scheduling of work, how design should be tackled, what degree of supervision is required for effective and confident time and budget planning, and evaluation of the effectiveness of the new practices before being used in more critical projects. To support this approach we therfore have established a three pronged attack on the problem. In the first place we have established a bureau facility which users can access interactively, either locally or long distance. In this way we have given our potential users the ability to evaluate what is currently available and therefore taste and try before they buy. We are presently involved in producing a software package as a demonstrator project for a local military contractor, giving us first hand experience of the difficulties of introducing it to the workplace. Above all this we are producing a set of courseware, both general and specific, which will also involve some Computer Aided Instruction. We have based our education centre round the Data General M4000 with associated development environment. Based on o,r first hand knowledge of this through our project work we expect to be able to offer an effective consultancy and advisory service to the USER community. The practical acquisition of S.E. priciples is currently based on being able to offer courseware on the management requirements, benefits and usage of the particular principles involved, a number of different levels of courses in Ada and usage and benefits of the UNIX environment which is the basis for the UK's S.E. program. These courses would be incomplete without offering an aftersales service in the form of an advisory centre which could offer consultancy based on experience with other users and our current projects, and keep members informed by maintaining an Information Resource. The aftersales service also requires that users be able to access a machine as quickly as possible, and this has been enabled by setting up a bureau service which anybody can access through the national and international PSS network.

9. Summary

To offer a successful educational package that will lead to the rapid uptake of sound S.E. practices in as large a body of the user community as possible we require a practical route towards their appropriate implementation. The environment has now become the sticking point as far as potential users of Ada are concerned. It has been talked about too long

Ada Education Support Environment

without any result. Potential users require access to it immediately, and they are not prepared to start a real educational exercise without the availability of some form of access. This we have partially met by making a service available on our local Ada host to both local and long distance users. They can now start the evaluation process and plan for its usage inhouse. Developers however should be looking at small simple packages which will meet the immediate requirements and making them available as quickly as possible.

Those readers interested in using our educational and/or bureau services should contact Iain Richmond at E.R.C.C., 59 George Square, Edinburgh, EH8 9JU. Telephone 031-667 1011 ext 6518 or 2300.

SOME EDUCATIONAL PRINCIPLES RELATING TO THE TEACHING AND USE OF Ada [R]

M. Mac an Airchinnigh
Department of Computer Science, University of Dublin,
Trinity College, Dublin, Ireland

Abstract. The package is the principal building block of the Ada programming language. In this paper I propose a coherent educational philosophy based on the Socratic approach within the context of a master/disciple relationship for the teaching of Ada. In particular, I show that, by starting with the package, a good sound strong programming discipline in Ada is fostered and encouraged. Three basic educational principles are presented. Moreover, an Ada Software Methodology based on the abstract data type approach is thereby engendered. To support this methodology, a corresponding Ada Programming Support Environment is outlined.

Key Words. abstract data type, aesthetics, Ada Programming Support Environment, Ada Software Methodology, education, package, structure, user's conceptual model

Ada is a registered trademark of the U.S. Government, ALO

1 INTRODUCTION

The development of a conceptual model for understanding Ada would facilitate the learning process' - Many reviewers have been misled into thinking that the conceptual model for Pascal applies to Ada. This has led them to conclude that Ada is too complex." (Wichmann 1984). Ada programmers acquire and continuously update, in an incremental way, conceptual models not only of a specific application domain and computer system but also of the Ada programming language itself. This latter conceptual model is fashioned as a direct consequence of the programmer's (Ada) education and experience. One may single out certain factors that strongly influence the acquisition and structure of such a conceptual model. Apart from the contribution of the actual reference manual (ALRM 1983), and derivative text books, such as (Barnes 1982), to the construction of a conceptual model, the factors of prior programming language knowledge and experience and instruction/education in Ada, must be taken into consideration. Moreover, since Ada is to be used in the wider context of a specific Ada Software Methodology and matching Ada Programming Support Environment, then these too are important.

The package is the principal building block of the Ada language. It may be considered to consist of three logically distinct units - the package specification, visible part only (PSV), the package specification, private part only (PSP), and the package body (PB) (Mac an Airchinnigh 1984 a). The PSV and PSP form a compilation unit. The PSP and PB form an implementation unit. With respect to the package one may readily identify three separate roles that an Ada programmer may play - designer, implementor, and end-user. The relation between these roles and corresponding conceptual models of the application domain is outlined in (Mac an Airchinnigh 1984 a). The package may be considered to be an encoding of the representation of part of the designer's conceptual model of the application domain. End-users of the package who also have their own respective conceptual models of the same application domain, will find the package useful only in so far as it expresses that which they expect. If the package has the property of "conceptual invariance", that is to say, it conserves conceptual models, then it is a clear candidate for inclusion in a universal standard Ada software library. This primacy of the package dictates the kind of educational approach presented herein.

In a paper of this size it is not possible to present a complete strategy for the education, instruction, and training of Ada programmers. Therefore, only a brief sketch of the proposed educational methodology is attempted. Nor is it possible to include fragments of actual code. These are left to the oral presentation. I adopt, as a basic premise, the master/disciple relationship that ought to exist between teacher and student. Within this framework, a kind of Socratic approach may be employed whereby the teacher extracts from her students (educare: "to lead out") the Ada text which is the expression of the concepts and conceptual relations possessed by the students as a result of their perception of the specific application domain in question. Of course, a purely Socratic approach is impossible, since the students must already have some knowledge of Ada package structure and syntax before they can develop their own packages. Hence a certain amount of exposition is also called for at different stages in the students' development. Naturally, it is expected that each teacher will develop her own particular educational philosophy. Using the approach that I have adopted, I have already shown that there is no need for the enumeration type in Ada, since the Ada package is a higher level data type modelling construct than it, analogous to the primacy of the loop control construct over the goto statement (Mac an Airchinnigh 1984 b).

Section 2 deals with the concept of Ada as a language and presents three educational principles that are particularly relevant for language teaching. In section 3, I sketch very briefly the Ada Software Methodology that is implied by, and supports, the educational methodology of section 2. Finally, section 4 presents an outline of the interactive Ada Programming Support Environment, called INTERAda, that provides the tools needed to support the methodology of section 3.

2 EDUCATIONAL PRINCIPLES

"A structure contains, in the first place, certain unifying elements and connections, but these elements cannot be singled out or defined independently of the connections involved ... structures (defined in this way) may be considered independently of the elements that go to make them up." (Piaget 1971). Ada is a language. Therefore, psychological and educational principles that are relevant, in general, to the teaching and learning of (natural) native/foreign languages, are pertinent. Since Ada is only a written language, then the focus of attention may be restricted to that aspect of language education - ability to read and write well. However, Ada is deemed to be a written language, more in the way that Mathematics is, rather than, say, Latin. I present here just three educational principles. It must be borne in mind, however, that these principles are not mutually exclusive.

2.1 *Structure acquisition*

We learn by imitation and analogy. The teaching of the grammar of Ada ought to be done via the use of well chosen examples. As a result of rote learning, drill, and practice, the would-be Ada programmer will assimilate the basic structures of the language and, at the same time, accumulate significant templates for her own creative work. The teacher of Ada must be careful in the selection of the basic material. For example, it is essential that the Ada material chosen should conform to a well defined and agreed upon set of guidelines such as those set out in the Ada-Europe Style Guide (Nissen 1984).

The package, viewed as the Ada "incarnation" of an abstract data type, is the primary structure of the language. One of the key examples, often cited in the literature, is that of COMPLEX NUMBER (Mac an Airchinnigh 1984 a). Having acquired this structure, the Ada programmer may readily be led to develop analogous packages, such as, for example, packages for the different kinds of colour models that are commonly used in the domain of (interactive) computer graphics applications (Mac an Airchinnigh 1984 c). Other simple examples which inculcate this structural approach are the abstract data types BOOLEAN (Mac an Airchinnigh 1984 b), and WEEKDAY. In this way, a particular method of thinking about how Ada may be used for the encoding of representations of "real world" objects, is firmly established, and becomes a key stone in the programmer's conceptual model of the language. This is, of course, the so-called "object oriented" approach. It is worth noting here that the function subprogram (and to a certain extent the procedure subprogram) is seen to belong to the package structure and not viewed as a separate entity in its own right. However, "real world functions" as distinct from "Ada functions" may also be subjected to the object oriented approach (Mac an Airchinnigh 1984 d). Functions represented by Ada packages may be passed to other Ada packages in a clean and consistent manner.

I would like to make two simple observations on the structure of the PSV. First, for those programmers with prior experience of the assignment statement, the teacher may wish to provide the Ada package incarnations in the context of the private type only, leaving the concept of limited private type to a later point in the course (Mac an Airchinnigh 1984 c). Ideally, only limited private types would be employed in order to attain full realization of the incarnation of the abstract data type concept. Second, the concept of deferred constant may be replaced by the concept of a constant function of the private type. The choice and number of such constant functions is also very important.

Before I consider the second educational principle I wish to indicate the place of second level Ada language structures in the context of the primary structure, the Ada package. It is at the level of implementation, PSP and PB, that secondary structures such as the "innate" data types and corresponding control constructs make their appearance. The first of these to be introduced are the array and record data types. Each of these structures has its own constructor and selector operations which

are part of the Ada language itself. These are the things of relevance
to the Ada programmers in the role of implementor.

2.2 *Concrete-to-abstract*

A basic educational principle is to start with those things
with which the students are familiar - those things which are conrete.
For a child, objects such as pebbles, buttons, pieces of wood, etc., form
the concrete stuff out of which the mathematical abstraction of number may
be formed. In the case of language, the concrete stuff may be itself
abstract. We have already seen how the package as incarnation of abstract
data type is just such a concrete-to-abstract mapping. However, there is
another higher level of abstraction. Considering existing Ada packages
themselves as concrete stuff, one then develops the abstraction of generic
package. For this to be realisable in practice, the students must already
have knowledge of different packages that may be viewed as instantiations
of some generic package, i.e. they must exhibit the same structure!
Finding examples of such packages from the domain of computer science is
simple, cf. (Barnes 1982). The STACK_OF_(...), QUEUE_OF_(...),
SET_OF_(...) package incarnations are typical.

Another application domain that supplies an abundant store of
examples is that of mathematics. The mathematical principle of
"isomorphism" is, of course, of particular relevance to the development
and use of generic packages. Typical examples are the different kinds of
cartesian coordinate systems required for the Graphics Kernel System (GKS)
(Mac an Airchinnigh 1984 c). Also, in the area of (interactive) computer
graphics, the RGB, CMY, and YIQ colour models may be treated as instantiations of a 3-dimensional cartesian coordinate based generic colour model
(ibid.). Finally, let me consider the third educational principle.

2.3 *Aesthetics*

With respect to written (natural) language, the educated reader
easily detects the quality of a piece of writing. The choice of words,
the turn of phrase, together add to, or subtract from, that quality. Some
written work is beautiful, some is ugly. In the words of Donald Knuth
(1968), the "process of preparing programs ... can be an aesthetic experience much like composing poetry or music". But, of course, such an
aesthetic sense must be acquired.

Aesthetics is very difficult to define. I believe that it entails notions such as beauty, elegance, order, symmetry, and harmony. Inevitably, subjectivity plays a major role. Finding suitable examples in Ada is not easy due to the newness of the language. In the computational geometry facet of computer-aided design, I have shown that a Bezier cubic function may readily be expressed as the package incarnation of an abstract data type. Furthermore, in developing the package for the Bézier bicubic surface patch, the Tensor Product method gives rise to an Ada structure that is of the same order of complexity as that of the original cubic function! (Mac an Airchinnigh 1984 d). Moreover, the concept of Tensor Product is mirrored exactly by the Ada textual structure.

One way in which to capture the notion of aesthetics in Ada is to develop the packages in such a way that the aesthetics of mathematics is invariant under the modelling operation. This has been the case for the Bézier cubic and bicubic surface patch mentioned above. The derived type feature of Ada allows one to construct a mathematical lattice of abstract data types that are tightly coupled. For example, instead of treating the colour models mentioned above as instantiations of a generic colour model, one may use the derived type to build them into a lattice. In other words, we can use Ada to reflect the fact that both CMY and YIQ colour models may be derived from the RGB colour model (Mac an Airchinnigh 1984 c). Similarly, I have shown how a Bézier cubic and a Hermite cubic may be considered to be derived from a canonical cubic (Mac an Airchinnigh 1984 d).

3 *Ada SOFTWARE METHODOLOGY*

"The emergence of several widely used methods for analysis, specification, and design, combined with compatible APSEs, should lead to a small set of technical approaches to the specification, design, development, and validation of Ada programs, yielding standardized forms of work products" - Methodman (Wasserman & Freeman 1983). Ada is more than a programming language. Adoption of the educational approach outlined above, leads naturally to a simple Ada Software Methodology (ASM) based on the abstract data type approach. We have called our ASM, AdaM. According to this ASM, Ada programmers work with packages and generic packages only! In other words, a given Ada software assemblage consists entirely of packages. It is envisaged that, due to lack of experience on the programmer's part or to the state of the art in abstract data type theory, not all of the packages in an assemblage will conform to the notion of package as incarnation of abstract data type. Such non-conforming packages are called amorphous packages. All other packages are called ADT packages.

Let U denote the universe of packages in a given software assemblage. Let K denote the set of ADT packages. K is called the kernel of U. Then $\bar{K} = U - K$ is the set of all amorphous packages in U. In essence, the ASM AdaM involves (1) extending the kernel K, and (2) re-organising the kernel K. In general, that part of K which consists of generic packages will belong to the universal standard Ada software library. Other non-generic packages in K will belong to the local standard Ada software library.

3.1 *Extending the kernel*

The ADT packages in K will be formally specified and verified. Currently, Anna, a language for annotating Ada programs (Krieg-Brueckner et al. 1982), is used for this purpose. In our terminology, Anna plays the role of canonical semantics. We also envisage the use of native semantics particular to different classes of user. One such native semantics is a form of extended Vienna Development Method (VDM) (Mac an Airchinnigh 1983). In addition to semantics, we propose the use of a formal notation for the specification of that part of the user's conceptual model for which the ADT package is an expression. In the software life-cycle peculiar to AdaM, one of the major tasks will be to construct other ADT packages from the existing set of amorphous packages $\bar{K}$ in the software assemblage. This task is called "extending the kernel".

3.2 *Reorganising the kernel*

A second major task of the life-cycle peculiar to AdaM is concerned with the restructuring of the kernel. Given a set of ADT packages (non-generic) that are (almost) structurally isomorphic, we will replace them with instantiations of single generic ADT packages that are formally specified and verified. Other clusters of ADT packages that are related via a "derivative" relation will be reorganised to conform to a mathematical lattice of ADT packages.

4 *Ada PROGRAMMING SUPPORT ENVIRONMENT*

"A more general approach is to regard the user interaction as being expressed entirely within Ada program segments which are executed or interpreted as necessary in the context of relevant points in the APSE database, thus providing a total Ada environment similar, for example, to an Interlisp environment" (STONEMAN 1980). Tools are needed to support AdaM. A year's experience in the use of AdaM in the domain of interactive computer graphics using GKS and in the domain of computer-aided design has enabled us to identify special purpose tools that are essential for the package-only approach. A very brief outline of some of these tools is given here. The tools are incorporated in a highly interactive programming support environment (under development) which is called INTERAda. Like Interlisp, these tools are integrated within the environment. To manage the different categories of Ada programmers we require a user interface management system (Mac an Airchinnigh 1983). INTERAda allows not only the traditional style of imperative programming in Ada, but also an applicative style and an assertive style of programming. The package-only approach implies the need for a special kind of package manager which caters for the ADT packages. Its main purpose is to handle the extension and re-organisation of the kernel of a software assemblage. It relies on the particular structure of the ADT packages to carry out these tasks. Either as part of the package manager, or as a separate tool in its own right, we require a security/protection manager. Its main function is to lock out the PSP and PB from unauthorised access by designers and end-users. An implementation manager is another tool that matches PSP and PB units with a corresponding PSV unit for differing applications. Typical uses are for (1) prototyping, (2) highly efficient executable code, and (3) multi-processor and distributed environments. Finally, a naming manager is essential for the different entities of an Ada package that are visible to end-users. The names used must correspond with the concepts and conceptual relations of the end-users with respect to a specific application domain. These tools have already been described in more detail in (Mac an Airchinnigh 1984 c,d,e). As well as the usual database for the Ada packages, we also require a knowledge base for the knowledge representation encodings used by both the user interface management system and the naming manager.

5 CONCLUSIONS

"The apparently singular fact becomes known, understood and conceptually grasped only in so far as it is 'subsumed' under a general idea, recognised as a 'case' of a law or as a member of a manifold or a series" (Cassirer 1953). Realisation of the fact that the package is the principal building block of the Ada language and that it is a good linguistic structure for the incarnation of abstract data types has led to the development of a specific educational methodology for the teaching of Ada. Since Ada is a written language, one may draw on those principles relevant to language education in general. Three such principles have been identified as basic: "structure acquisition", "concrete-to-abstract", and "aesthetics". One immediate consequence of the educational methodology adopted is a very strong programming discipline based on a package-only approach. This methodology inevitably leads on to a corresponding Ada Software Methodology, AdaM. It is another consequence of the educational approach taken. Finally, tools to support this ASM are readily identified on a "need-to-have" basis.

6 ACKNOWLEDGEMENTS

Many thanks are due to my colleague Hans-Juergen Kugler for discussion on the finer points of the Ada language. His cooperation has led to the crystallisation of the ideas expressed herein. My thanks are due also to the many members of the Ada-Europe working groups who have acted as a sounding board for these ideas, the Education WG, the Computer Integrated Manufacturing WG, and the Environment WG. I wish also to acknowledge the financial support given by the CEC to Ada-Europe which made all of this possible.

7 REFERENCES

ALRM (1983). Reference Manual for the Ada Programming Language. ANSI/MIL-STD 1815A. La Celle-Saint-Cloud, France: Alsys.
Barnes, J.G.P. (1982). Programming in Ada. International Computer Science Series. London: Addison-Wesley Publishing Company.
Cassirer, E. (1953). Language and Myth. trans. S.K. Langer. New York: Dover Publications Inc.
Knuth, D. (1968). The Art of Computer Programming, vol. 1, Fundamental Algorithms. Reading, Massachusetts: Addison-Wesley Publishing Company.
Krieg-Brueckner, B., Luckham, D.C., von Henke, F.W. & Owe, O. (1982). Draft Reference Manual for ANNA - A Language for Annotating Ada Programs. Universitaet Bremen & Stanford University.
Mac an Airchinnigh, M. (1983). The Model of the User's Conceptual Model of ..., Proc. of the IFIP WG. 5.2/EUROGRAPHICS Workshop on User Interface Management Systems. Seeheim, FR Germany, November 1983, to be published.
Mac an Airchinnigh, M. (1984 a). Ada Packages and the User's Conceptual Model. ACM SIGPLAN AdaTEC Ada Letters, III, no. 4, III-4.70 - III-4.77

Mac an Airchinnigh, M. (1984 b). Les Modèles Conceptuels des Programmeurs Ada. unpublished manuscript.
Mac an Airchinnigh, M. (1984 c). The Specification and Implementation of GKS Application Software in Ada. to be published in the Computer Graphics Forum, the Journal of the European Association for Computer Graphics.
Mac an Airchinnigh, M. (1984 d). CAD, GKS, and Ada. Proc. of the EUROGRAPHICS Workshop on Graphics Programming. Wenschdorf, FR Germany, January 1984, to be published.
Mac an Airchinnigh, M. (1984 e). CAD, KE, and Ada. submitted to the IFIP WG 5.2 Working Conference on Knowledge Engineering in Computer-Aided Design. Budapest, Hungary, September 1984.
Nissen, J. (1984). Ada Style Guide. The Companion Series. Cambridge: Cambridge University Press, to be published.
Piaget, J. (1971). Biology and Knowledge - An Essay on the Relations between Organic Regulations and Cognitive Processes. Edinburgh: Edinburgh University Press.
STONEMAN (1980). Requirements for Ada Programming Support Environments. U.S. Department of Defense.
Wasserman, A.I. & Freeman, P. (1983). "METHODMAN", Ada Methodologies - Concepts and Requirements. ACM SIGSOFT Software Engineering Notes, *8*, no. 1, 33-50.
Wichmann, B.A. (1984). Is Ada Too Big? A Designer Answers the Critics. Comm. of the ACM, *27*, no. 2, 98-103.

TRAINING CONCEPT FOR THE COST-EFFECTIVE DEVELOPMENT OF RELIABLE SOFTWARE USING THE PROGRAMMING LANGUAGE Ada

H. Hummel, M. Nast, E. Uthke
Industrieanlagen-Betriebsgesellschaft m.b.H.,
Einsteinstrasse 20, D-8012 Ottobrunn, Germany

1 INTRODUCTION

This study is a joint project involving
- Ferranti Computer Systems Ltd. (FCSL), UK,
- Imperial College of Science and Technology (IC), UK, and
- Industrieanlagen-Betriebsgesellschaft m.b.H. (IABG), FRG (prime contractor)

financed by the Commission of the European Communities (CEC) under the Multi-Annual Data Processing Programme.

1.1 Problem Definition

Good quality software is functionally adequate, reliable, and easy to maintain. Achieving these properties necessitates consistent adherence to properly integrated software engineering principles and methods throughout the software life-cycle. In the past, most programming languages contained few features to support or reflect such principles and methods. However, the programming language Ada developed on US DoD finance incorporates more of these required features.

Numerous projects have begun implementing Ada compilers and APSEs. However, the full benefits of the APSE tools and of the modern Ada language concepts can be realised only if the people who use the language understand their purpose and value, take advantage of them, and use them responsibly. The possibility of realising the full potential of Ada's modern features could be lost if trainees are allowed to gain the habit of using a subset of Ada in the style with which they are familiar in other languages. It is therefore necessary to acquaint the trainees not only with an understanding of the language, but also - and more importantly - with software engineering principles that Ada supports.

The trainees identified in the study are expected to be already in the software industry and thus the course units specified are geared towards retraining in an evolutionary way. This retraining will provide the foundation for further development of software engineering courses based on Ada. The study is not directed towards universities, however it is hoped that any conclusions will assist in course formulation.

1.2 Objectives

The objectives of the project are:

(a) To provide the basis for the development of course units for Ada

   (i) by considering software engineering goals and principles as well as methods and Ada language features supporting them,

   (ii) by specifying teaching requirements for all life-cycle phases and for all areas of a software project model.

(b) To establish guidelines for programming in Ada that facilitate software maintenance and enhancement.

(c) To set up a basis for additional work:

   (i) Specification of APSE tools assisting the user in applying or enforcing these guidelines.

Ada Training Concept

(ii) Enable full use of the CEC funded work on Ada.

(iii) Provide the European data processing industry with a suitably educated mobile workforce and with a decisive edge in competitive markets through the cost-effectiveness and high quality of its software.

The project exploits proven principles and methods applicable to the life-cycle of all languages, with special consideration given to Ada and its environment.

1.3 Project outline

The project consists of two phases with the possibility to continue with a third phase upon approval by the CEC. Phases 1 and 2 are subject of this report.

A project and a life-cycle are defined; both models serve as a base throughout this study. An Ada course survey was performed. The categories of personnel for whom Ada training is required are identified taking the project and life-cycle models into account. The survey did not show new categories. Then, software engineering goals and principles are identified with their relationships to the supporting Ada language features. References to methods applying these principles are mode. Course units are specified which cover both the Ada language and Ada-related topics (e.g., life-cycle model, APSEs). Their relationships with principles and categories are shown. The general outline of a complete course closes Phase 2.

2 THE PROJECT MODEL

The project model includes all management, documentation, review, and production techniques that are necessary to coordinate and support the efforts of the members of the project team. Such a model guarantees a cost-effective software development taking advantage of all available resources and resulting in reliable and modifiable software. The essential part of the project model is the software development life-cycle.

3 THE LIFE-CYCLE MODEL

Software development is a process which consists of different phases and activities, including the generation of documents.

The completion of a phase is determined by the satisfactory review of the products developed during the phase. Products are defined by their corresponding documents. They form the baseline for the work in the next phase. The products/documents of the next phase again are then checked against the previous baseline before they themselves form a new baseline.

The software development life-cycle shown in Fig. 1 is the result of a selection process from different models used in various companies and published in several papers. As none of these models seemed to be <u>directly</u> acceptable for this study, another model was necessary for the intended purposes.

Components design and module design result in components specifications and module specifications, respectively. These specifications describe the behaviour of the components and modules, respectively, from an external viewpoint.

The box "Code" is the actual implementation phase ("programming") of the aforementioned specifications. The resulting modules can now be verified against their specifications. Following, they are integrated to form components.

Fig. 1: Software Development Life-Cycle

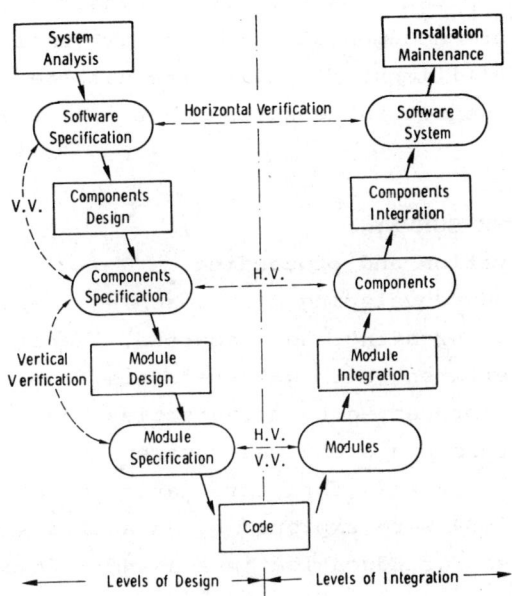

The analogous process applies to the components: verification and then integration into the software system that itself can now be verified.

The installation/maintenance "phase" is represented only by a single box, but it includes different phases and activities.

Quality assurance/control of a software product has to ensure, that the software system is documented consistently, completely, and unambiguously and meets its specifications.

Validation and verification together constitute the quality assurance/control activities.

<u>Validation</u> of a representation is the establishment that the system behaves as stated in earlier requirements. A validated representation ensures that the team builds the "right system".

Verification of a representation is a proof both of its internal correctness (i.e. having no contradictions, no ambiguities, preserving the given standards, a complete and sufficient documentation) and external correctness resulting in fulfillment of all external requirements. A verified representation ensures that the team builds the "system right".

4 COURSE SURVEY
4.1 Motivation and proceeding

A study developing Ada teaching packages cannot ignore already existing Ada courses. Therefore, a course survey was undertaken which gathered data from Ada courses being developed/presented by universities and companies.

The European scene was covered by sending a questionnaire which asked for information about Ada courses. Courses in the USA were explored by an analysis of the Catalog of Resources for Education in Ada and Software Engineering (CREASE).

4.2 Conclusions

1. Both surveys do not identify new categories of trainees.

2. In general, there are no great differences between the European and the US's scene.

3. European courses seem to primarily address managers by a language overview, whereas in the USA more technical details for development people are taught.

4. According to available computing facilities, more hands-on experience in Ada can be acquired in the United States than in Europe at present.

The course survey was not very conclusive.

5 THE CATEGORIES OF TRAINEE

Identification of the classes of person for whom training is required has been achieved by examining the project and life-cycle models. The project model identified four main activities. These are associated with corresponding categories of personnel.

Similarly, the life-cycle phases enable to derive categories of the software production team.

The following list includes the categories identified:

- Senior Manager (SM)
- Project Manager (PM)
- Configuration Manager (CM)
- Quality Controller (QC)
- Problem Analyst (PA)
- System Designer (SD)
- Component Designer (CD)
- Module Designer (MD)
- Coder (CO)
- Component Integrator (CI)
- System Integrator (SI)
- Maintenance Programmer (MP)

As a working hypothesis, it is suggested that module designers and component integrators are the same, or at least have identical skills; similarly, for component designers and system integrators.

Each category is characterised by

- phase(s) of the life-cycle relevant for the category,
- activities performed,
- applicable methods,
- results obtained, and
- knowledge and skills required.

6 SOFTWARE ENGINEERING GOALS, PRINCIPLES, AND Ada LANGUAGE FEATURES

6.1 Goals, principles, and methods

In the course of the analysis of the software engineering principles underlying the features of the Ada language, an understanding emerged of the relationship between project goals and methods of achieving them, and the principles which underlie the methods. Such methods are used to construct software having certain qualities. These qualities are the abstract goals of software engineering.

The fundamental relationships are recognised in terms of a commuting diagram, involving abstract and concrete goals and principles (Fig. 2).

Fig. 2: Relationships among Goals, Principles, Methods, and Ada Features

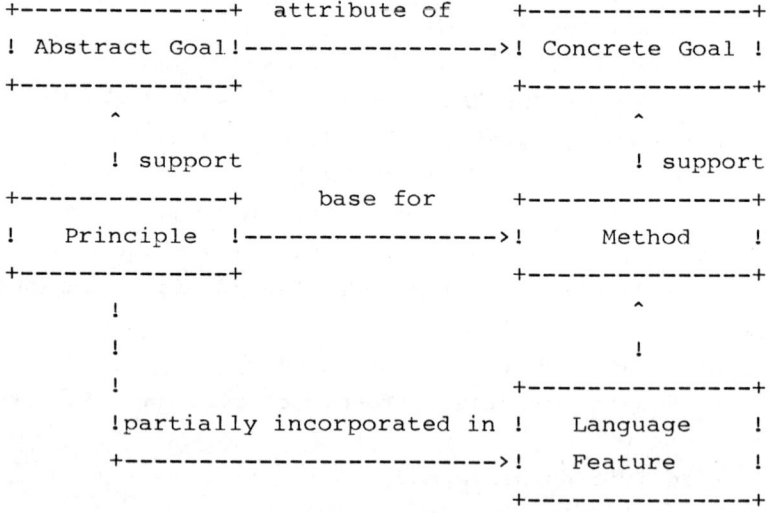

One of the tools used in the software engineering process is a compiler for a language; when the language is

an advanced language such as Ada, many of the principles are already supported by the language. It is therefore convenient to distinguish between Ada language features and methods.

6.2 Goals of software engineering

The concrete goal of software development is a well engineered software product. Depending on the particular product certain objectives are more important than others. For example, consider the software to control a nuclear power plant as opposed to that to control a telephone exchange.

The varying properties or qualities of the software product are the abstract goals, typically

- Reliability,
- Understandability,
- Modifiability,
- Portability,
- Usability,
- Integrity, and
- Efficiency.

6.3 Principles of software engineering

For the purpose of the study the principles considered to be of main interest are:

1. Hierarchy,
2. Modularity,
3. Decision Postponement,
4. Abstraction,
5. Information Hiding,
6. Simplicity,
7. Structured Programming,
8. Semantic Consistency,
9. Concurrency, and
10. Faithful Modelling.

Ada Training Concept

This list does not claim to be comprehensive, however it contains the most important principles. Apart from concurrency the remaining principles should guide all software developments resulting in a well engineered product. The principle of concurrency is essential for software systems requiring concurrent processes.

6.4 Relationship between goals and principles

The use of each software engineering principle leads to achievement of the abstract goals. The following matrix "Goals vs. Principles" details what abstract goals are achieved by what principles.

```
Reliability
!  Understandability
!  !  Modifiability                Goals
!  !  !  Portability
!  !  !  !  Usability
!  !  !  !  !  Integrity                            Principles
!  !  !  !  !  !  Efficiency
!  !  !  !  !  !  !
   x  x                       Hierarchy
x  x  x  x                    Modularity
      x  x                    Decision Postponement
   x  x  x                    Abstraction
x  x        x                 Information Hiding
x  x  x  x                    Simplicity
x  x  x                       Structured Programming
x           x                 Semantic Consistency
   x              x           Concurrency
x  x  x     x                 Faithful Modelling
```

6.5 Relationship between principles and Ada language features

Another important relationship is that between principles and Ada language features. A complete description is omitted here.

7 METHODS

As explained previously, a method is the means by which a principle is applied to achieve a goal. In some cases the method is little more than the application of relevant Ada language features; in others the use of the features may be guided by recommendations concerning style and technique, while in yet others software tools may be available to aid the designer/programmer.

Methods refer to procedures, techniques and tools which are considered as aspects of the same kind of object. A procedure is a way of doing something. A technique is considered to be a formalised method, while a tool is an automated one. This notion of method should not be confused with a proprietary method.

It is assumed that any relevant method of applying the principles involved will be taught as part of the course unit, but identifying which methods to teach will be the prerogative of the teacher. The most appropriate method will depend on considerations such as the application area, the preferences of the management, the available hardware, cost and availability.

8 COURSE UNITS
8.1 Language features and software engineering principles

The following broad groupings of Ada features may be identified as basic course units:

    Introduction to the Ada language   IAL
    Types and declarations   TYP

Ada Training Concept

Expressions	EXP
Control structures and subprograms	STR
Packages	PAC
Visibility	VIS
Tasks	TAS
Separate compilation	SEP
Exceptions	EXC
Generics	GEN
Low level features	LLF
Input/Output	IO
User control of compilation	UC

It can be seen that these groupings correspond closely to the ARM chapters, but there is not an exact correspondence and detailed contents also differ from those in the ARM. The groupings used here correspond more closely than does the ARM to the general approach adopted in the study (e.g. the emphasis on software engineering support).

The support for software engineering principles is summarised in the following matrix.

Principle						Unit						
	IAL	TYP	EXP	STR	PAC	VIS	TAS	SEP	EXC	GEN	LLF	IO	UC
HIER			x	x			x	x					
MOD			x	x			x	x					
DECPOST	x			x				x	x	x	x		
DATABS	x			x						x			
PROCABS			x				x			x			
INFHID	x			x	x								
SIMP	x	x	x	x	x	x		x	x		x		
STRUCT				x									
SEMCON	x	x	x						x				
CONCUR	x					x							
FAITH	x			x	x		x		x				x

Ada Training Concept

The following units complete the Ada related ones:

Life-cycle/project model	LCM
SE goals and principles	SE
APSEs	APS
Human factors	HUF
Ada culture	CUL

8.2 Course unit levels

For each unit, three "levels" may be identified, based on the requirements of various categories of staff. These levels do not simply correspond to different depths of coverage of detail (syntax, etc.), but rather reflect the differing roles of staff categories. The module levels proposed are:

<u>Appreciation</u> (A). Provides a broad overview of the language feature, with no details of syntax, etc. Emphasis is on the software engineering aspects of the feature, but at a fairly superficial level.

<u>Use</u> (U). Essentially covers how to use an Ada feature. Emphasis is thus on syntax.

<u>Exploitation</u> (E). Covers when an Ada feature should be used. The emphasis here is clearly on the software engineering aspects and style. Topics from the appreciation unit are covered to a greater depth, together with some new ones.

The units appropriate for each category of staff are shown in the matrix below, together with an indication of the level of unit (A, U or E).

													Unit				
Category	IAL	TYP	EXP	STR	PAC	VIS	TAS	SEP	EXC	GEN	LLF	IO	UC	LCM	SE	APS	HUF	CUL
SM	A	A			A		A	A	A					A	A	A		A
PM	A	A			A		A	A	A					E	A	A		A
CM	A				A			E		A				U	A	A		
QC	U	E	E	E	E	E	E	E	E	E	E	E	E	U	A	A	A	
PA	A				A		A		A					A	A	A	A	
SD	A				A		A	A	A		A			A	A	A	A	
CD	U	A	A	A	E	E	E	E	E	A	E	A	A	A	A	A	A	
MD	U	E	E	E	E	E	E	E	E	E	E	E	E	A	A	A	A	
CO	U	U	U	U	U	U	U	U	U	U	U	U	U	A	A	A		
CI	U	E	E	E	E	E	E	E	E	E	E	E	E	A	A	A	A	
SI	U	A	A	A	E	E	E	E	E	A	E	A	A	A	A	A	A	
MP	U	E	E	E	E	E	E	E	E	E	E	E	E	A	A	A	A	

8.3 A complete course

The above matrix indicates the major constituents of each course. However, the needs of each category will differ, and the course will not be complete without a final unit to put the goals, principles, and language features learnt about into perspective.

Thus the final unit for each course should be a category-dependent "concluding" unit doing just this, called WHY.

To summarise, the course for each staff category is as defined in the matrix above, together with the relevant concluding unit.

9 LITERATURE

Booch, G. (1983). Software Engineering with Ada. Menlo Park, California: The Benjamin/Cummings Publishing Company, Inc.

Budde, R. et al. (1980). Untersuchung über Maßnahmen zur Verbesserung der Software-Produktion, Teil 1: Theoretische Ansätze auf dem Gebiet der Software-Produktion. Bericht Nr. 130 der GMD. München, Wien: R. Oldenbourg Verlag.

CREASE (1983). Catalog of Resources for Education in Ada and Software Engineering. Ada Information Clearinghouse, IIT Research Institute, Rome, NY.

Druffel, L.A. (1982). The Potential Effect of Ada on Software Engineering in the 1980's. ACM SIGSOFT Vol. 7, No 3.

Freeman, P. & Wassermann, A.I. (1982). Software Development Methodologies and Ada ("Methodman"). Ada Joint Program Office, Department of Defense, Washington, D.C.

Reference Manual for the Ada Programming Language (1983). ANSI/MIL-STD 1815A. Ada Joint Program Office, Department of Defense, Washington, D.C.

Ripken, K. & McDermid, J. (1983). Life Cycle Support in the Ada Environment. Management Summary and Final Technical Report. TECSI-Software, Paris & Systems Designers Limited, Fleet.

Ross, D.T. et al. (1977). Software Engineering: Process, Principles, and Goals. In Tutorial on Software Design Techniques, ed. P. Freeman & A.I. Wasserman, pp. 62 - 72. IEEE Computer Society, Long Beach, California.

Softech (1982). Ada Software Design Methods Formulation. Final Report. Waltham, Mass.: Softech, Inc.

The Augusta Consortium (1981). Ada-based System Development Methodology. Study Report, British Department of Industry, London.

Tily, C.N.J. (1982). The Impact of Ada on the Ministry of Defence in the 1980's. Fellowship Thesis, Imperial College, London.

NEEDS IN ADA(*) EDUCATION: EXPERIENCES AND OBSERVATIONS

Michael B. Feldman
Department of Electrical Engineering and Computer Science
The George Washington University
Washington, DC 20052 U.S.A.

Abstract. Over the last several years the author has become increasingly involved in Ada educational activities. These have included three for-credit courses: one in data structures and two in comparative programming languages; a number of directed research projects; and a number of five-day non-credit seminars at the University and various industrial sites. Details of programming projects in the different contexts are presented. Observations and recommendations regarding the Ada education process are offered. These relate to the differences in background and motivation between industry programmers and university students; issues in designing re-training courses for the former and integrating Ada into curricula serving the latter; and the need for a mature, balanced, and objective presentation of Ada's strengths and weaknesses in the textbook literature.

INTRODUCTION

Over the last several years the author has become increasingly involved with Ada education. At this stage our involvement is in four areas:

o A data structures course, required of undergraduates and most M.S. candidates, in which Ada is the primary design language and an optional coding language;

o Two graduate seminars in comparative languages, one emphasizing support for data structures and modularization, the other concentrating on concurrency primitives;

o Directed projects in program design and implementation, using Ada as design and coding language;

o Five-day short courses, mostly involving hands-on experience, both on-site at GWU and at industry workplaces.

Programming is done on a DEC VAX/11-780, mostly using the TeleSoft Ada compiler under VMS; some directed projects use the NYU Ada/Ed system where they need language facilities not yet supported by TeleSoft. We shall discuss each of these activities in some detail, then offer some observations and recommendations on the Ada education process. Because programming cannot be learned passively, programming courses are characterized strongly by their "hands-on" projects. Thus our discussion will concentrate in that area.

ADA IN A MODERN DATA STRUCTURES COURSE

Computer Science 159 (CSci 159), <u>Programming and Data Structures</u>, is required for undergraduate Computer Science and Computer Engineering majors. The course is also taken by a large population of graduate students, mainly those starting an M.S. program in Computer Science who come from less-recent computer science undergraduate programs or other undergraduate disciplines.

The current "official" textbook is that of Aho, Hopcroft and Ullman (1983), where the design language used is Pascal; this is augmented by pre-publication notes for this author's forthcoming text (Feldman 1985), in which the design language is Ada. The Ada Language Reference Manual (LRM) (U.S. Department of Defense 1983) is used as a reference.

Lectures emphasize the abstract data type (ADT) idea, as implemented in the Ada package facility. There is also concentration on the tradeoffs between abstraction and performance and some material on algorithm performance.

Typically three or four programming projects are assigned; the general philosophy of each is to require a package of some kind. The emphasis is on thoughtful design and documentation of a software component.

The student must demonstrate the correctness of the package by providing a rudimentary main program to serve as a test harness. The sole purpose of this main program is to drive the package through its paces; input and output are allowed to be quite primitive, and handwritten annotation of the test output is tolerated.

Coding of these projects is done in Pascal or Ada; typically one-third or so of the students opt for Ada.

Project Series 1 - Fractions and Vectors

We have used with success a series of projects with a "mathematical software" flavor.

Project 1. Design an implementation of the ADT "fractions" or "rational numbers". This should provide the same level of arithmetic support, relational operations, and input/output as the base programming language provides for the primitive numeric types. A "sketch" of such a package is given in the LRM and in many texts; the task here is to turn the sketch into a complete, viable package. The specification for the package is given; the students are required to the supply the package body.

The operator and procedure-name overloading usually "makes a hit" with the students; it turns out to be one of the things they really wish they had in other languages.

Project 2. Design an implementation for vector arithmetic, where the vectors are to be considered "sparse" and thus implemented as linear lists. The sparse vector setting provides an excuse for the students to come to understand linked allocation and pointers.

This package is to be tested first using _integers_ as the vector elements, then revised and re-tested to use _fractions_. The student learns here about the advantages of localizing type declarations and other references to type as much as possible, so that the fraction package and the vector package can be integrated without heavily rewriting either one. Such integration is not easy in standard Pascal; that's just the point.

Project 3. Revise Project 2 as though the implementation language had no support for records or pointers. Do this with a minimum amount of re-coding, i.e. hide the implementation change in a small number of storage-allocation operations.

This requires "cursor" or array implementation of a storage pool for fractions and another for vector elements. A storage pool of fractions, then, becomes an array of numerators, an array of denominators, and an array of pointers.

The goal is to emulate the data structures of a weak language like Fortran or Basic. Most students see very readily, after completing this project, the advantages of designing in a powerful language like Ada, and then coding in a weaker language only where one must.

Project Series 2 - Text-Handler

Series 2 is similar in philosophy to Series 1, except that the intended application is text-handling rather than mathematical software.

Project 1. Design and implement a package for handling text using quasi-variable-length strings. A text object is a record consisting of a fixed-length array (of course) and a length field to indicate the current logical length of the string. Routines are to be provided for conversion of these text objects to and from Pascal or Ada standard strings; concatenation of text objects; relational comparisons (<,>,=,<>) between text objects; and substring search.

This package is fairly well specified in the Ada Language Reference Manual; students are given this specification, and those coding in Pascal need to decide how best to handle the overloaded-operator question.

Project 2. Convert the package from Project 1 so that a text object is implemented as a linear list of four-character nodes. Leave the user interface essentially unchanged, except that text objects are now essentially unlimited in length.

Project 3. As in Series 1, recode Project 2 to use array-based storage pools and no records.

Further details on the history and structure of this course have been previously reported by the author (Feldman 1984).

Comments

Others, particularly Augenstein et al. (1983), have conjectured that Ada has considerable promise as a language for teaching data structures.

Our experience is bearing out these conjectures. Students with previous programming experience in Pascal find learning Ada to be not only reasonably easy, but actually fun. This is, they report, because they appreciate the ways in which Ada extends Pascal, particularly in the operator-overloading and packaging areas.

Pascal programmers also notice the many syntactic and semantic idiosyncracies of Pascal that are corrected in the Ada design. These include:

- a more flexible order of declaration of types and objects;
- a less cluttered way of dereferencing pointers;
- a handier structured programming syntax (fewer begin-end pairs, etc.);
- automatic garbage collection where Pascal provides none;
- the ability to pass structures as function results where Pascal allows only scalars.

Students doing their coding in Pascal are aided in the translation process by the fact that examples in Ada from the Feldman textbook are often coded in lecture in Pascal, and by the implementation hints given in the text.

Students coding in TeleSoft Ada are able to complete and turn in their projects at the same time as the Pascal coders, even though they are learning a new language. The difficulties they encounter stem most often from a misunderstanding of just how strict the strong-typing scheme is. Semantic errors caused by the incomplete implementation of the language are a source of frustration, but will disappear with the emergence of full-language compilers.

ADA IN COMPARATIVE-LANGUAGES COURSES

Ada is one of several languages studied comparatively in CSci 258, <u>Comparative Programming Languages</u>, a graduate-level course. In recent years, the comparison has been chiefly with Snobol4 and C. In this course attention is given to the primitive and definable data structures supported by the languages, the inner syntax, and the modularization or partitioning capabilities. The main references for Ada are the LRM and the text by Booch (1983).

In a project series all students must complete, the same application program is developed in all the languages. The application is a cross-reference listing generator for programs written in the same language, and the program must be shown to work on itself.

Students get ample exposure to most of the language constructs; they must also understand the lexical structure of the language in order to write a scanner which can detect identifiers and keywords. The table of identifiers and line numbers is maintained either in a binary search tree or a hash table.

This project series serves as a good starting point for "compare-and-contract" discussions. In addition, each student must design a term project; in recent years about half the projects have turned out to be Ada-related.

In a follow-on course, CSci 358, <u>Concurrency and Parallelism in Programming Languages</u>, attention is focused on issues of concurrency and language primitives for supporting it. The Ada tasking model is compared with alternative designs like Modula-2's coroutines and monitors.

The project series here consists of implementing, in both Ada and Modula-2, a visualization of concurrently executing sort programs on a character-oriented terminal. Each of several sort programs controls a window on the screen, making the CRT device driver a critical resource. The sort programs are thus made to "race" each other, writing to the screen whenever two values are interchanged in their respective arrays.

As in CSci 258, individual projects are required. Some of these are discussed below.

<u>Comments</u>

The comparative projects provoke useful and interesting debates on the merits of language features. In the concurrency area particularly, the virtues of the powerful but inflexible Ada tasking model stands in contrast to the merits of the "small is beautiful" philosophy in languages like Modula-2. Although implementing compilers and run-time systems is not the primary focus of the seminar, the sophistication of many of our students has stimulated some animated discussion in this area. Indeed the "sort race" project focuses attention on just how tasks exchange control on a single processor. Moreover, the project provokes curiosity about algorithm visualization and graphics-based debugging, a current research area.

<u>DIRECTED GRADUATE PROJECTS</u>

A number of students have developed individual projects involving Ada. Some of these have been done as term projects in the language courses, others as independent research courses. Some of these projects are:

    o an implementation of concurrent operations on B-trees, using Ada task types for readers and writers;

Needs in Ada Education 233

- o studies of concurrent tasks as an alternative to recursion in implementing divide-and-conquer algorithms;

- o an interpreter for a subset of Prolog;

- o a discrete simulation system;

- o a spelling checker that runs concurrently with data input;

- o a study of "on-the-fly" garbage collection using tasks;

- o an implementation of the Bic data-protrection model;

- o a graphics sublanguage using Ada´s overloaded operators to support operations on graphics primitives;

- o a device driver for the GIGI graphics terminal;

- o a "smart" menu handler, using enumeration input/output, as a component of a user interface management system.

We have through these projects gained some experience in the application of Ada in several areas: language processors, simulation, data base, graphics and user interfaces. We expect to be reporting a number of these in the literature.

ADA IN THE "SHORT COURSE" CONTEXT

We have organized several five-day "short courses", offered at the University and at several military or military-industrial sites. These courses have, for the most part, incorporated a fair amount of "hands-on" experience, using the TeleSoft system on the VAX.

The lectures have roughly followed the development in the Booch book, but we have designed our own workshop projects. These are adaptations of programming assignments from the various university courses, suitably modified to take the time constraints into account. The projects have been met with approval, and most students are able to finish them in the time allowed.

In each project students are allowed to use portions of the application already provided in hard-copy or in a library. There are two chief advantages to this approach: first, the amount of program coding is kept to a minimum so that students can concentrate on the important things and not the keying; second, the students see the benefits of Ada packaging and the ease of integration of different parts of a system.

Workshop 1 - Fractions

The student is given, in hard-copy form, the specification of a package for dealing with fractions, as described above. The program library contains the full code for the package. Also distributed in hard-copy is the <u>output</u> of a test driver. The assignment is to provide a test driver which will give that output.

The student must then compile the package, write the code for the test routine, then compile and test it. This is relatively easy, and serves to give the student experience with the inner syntax of Ada and with the compilation environment.

Two or three hours is sufficient to accomplish this task; students see almost immediate results and feel connected to the real world in which they often have to write code to test someone else's program.

Workshop 2 - Vectors and Matrices

Here the goal is to become acquainted with how Ada's functions and procedures work, with one- and two-dimensional arrays and their attributes, and with exceptions.

The student is given the specification of a package to do addition and inner-product multiplication of vectors, and one to do addition, multiplication and transposition of matrices. Routines to GET and PUT vectors and matrices are also required. A test program is also provided in the library; its output from a test run is distributed. The student must provide the package bodies; the code for matrix transposition is supplied as an example.

Again, keying is kept to a minimum but the student sees and writes a lot of interesting Ada. Exceptions are introduced to report cases where vectors or matrices aren't conformable; attributes are introduced to interrogate the dimensions; overloaded operators are used for addition and multiplication and examples of operator composition (nesting) are given in the test program. Also, the Ada input/output philosophy is introduced and the students have a chance to write their own I/O routines.

Workshop 3 - Cross-Reference Listing Generator

The goal of this project is to teach recursion and recursive data types, pointers, and integration of packages.

An introductory lecture on recursion and binary search trees is given, and lexical scanners based on finite-state machines are discussed. The student is given a package which uses a lexical scanner to read text and return Ada identifiers, and a specification for a search-tree update and traversal package. A main program is shown which loops through an Ada source file inserting identifiers into a tree, then prints out the tree in a legible form to give a cross-reference listing. The student must write the body of the tree handler.

The packaging process is illustrated well here; it is clear that an arbitrary language could be treated just by re-writing the scanner; no change to the tree handler would be needed. Also, binary search trees are useful in other applications.

Workshop 4 - Tasking Demonstration

This program is an adaptation of a program which comes with the TeleSoft demonstration library. Four programs execute concurrently: two counters whose outputs are continuously displayed, a box-drawing program, and a main program which puts a character in the center of the box. Each task controls its own window; a semaphore is used to control access to the CRT device driver, which is a critical resource.

This program is demonstrated and the code is discussed. The students are then directed to modify the program: change the number of tasks by adding or removing counters; and remove the semaphore to see what happens. Changing the number of tasks is straightforward; removing the semaphore creates chaos on the screen because each task moves the cursor to its own window but another task gets to write the output (now at the wrong place).

We would prefer a more interesting tasking exercise, but since TeleSoft does not yet support task types and objects, the number of choices is limited. This project works well, as far as it goes.

Comments

An important discovery we have made in building these workshop problems is that since, in short courses, time is of the essence, it really pays to design carefully partitioned projects to keep coding and typing time to a minimum while still teaching an important number of concepts. Also, the package notion is taught in this way, by showing good examples of partially completed systems. This seems very realistic.

OBSERVATIONS ON ADA EDUCATION

University students are different from industry programmers. An important difference these days seems to be that upperclassmen and graduate students are usually somewhat fluent in Pascal or some other "structured" language before trying to learn software engineering with Ada.

Students with some experience in a modern language find little difficulty picking up the data structures and inner syntax of Ada. They do find the relentless type checking a bit intimidating at first, and tasking of course is a wholly new idea. A data structures course has been an ideal place to introduce Ada as an abstract-data-type implementation language, concentrating on packages and overloading issues. Students in our course find the improvements over Pascal, in this area especially, very appealing.

In contrast, industry programmers without recent university training, particularly those working mainly in Fortran or assembly language, find Ada rather foreign. This seems to be due as much to their lack of understanding of data structures, particularly record and pointer types, as to the "structured" inner syntax of Pascal-like languages. They are often a bit baffled as well by the notion of an enumeration type in which the compiler carries out the external/internal binding; they are too used to doing it themselves to feel comfortable delegating it.

One thing industry programmers, especially those working on defense contracts, do have is a good feel for what concurrency is all about. This stems from their experience in building real-world real-time systems; university students seem to find concurrency and real-time efficiency problems as foreign as Fortran programmers find records, pointers, and recursive programs and types.

Another difference which always seems to be lurking in the background is that university students tend to be in "learning mode", treating new and different things as an intellectual challenge, but working programmers are often learning Ada because their employer (or their country's defense establishment) has told them they must. Thus their mandate to learn Ada represents, at best, time away from their daily responsibilities; at worst, it represents an outright threat.

RECOMMENDATIONS

One of the challenges of upgrading industry programmers to Ada is that if they are going to use it well, they often need to learn some computer science along with the language. In particular, assembler and Fortran programmers need to learn structured programming and data structures. For those designing "conversion" courses, then, a one- or two-week course in <u>just</u> Ada isn't enough. We recommend showing sensitivity to these programmers' unfamiliarity with the "advanced" data structures so familiar to current university students. We have found that several "mini-courses" of an hour or two each, embedded at the right points in a short course, and devoted to concepts of types and data structures <u>per se</u>, is time well invested.

Due regard needs to be shown for the very real misgivings about efficiency expressed by programmers familiar with the issues of real-time programming. It may be that Ada compilers indeed will provide enough run-time performance to do the job, but this fact is not obvious to people who have spent years of their career "bit-fiddling" for time and space efficiency in critical systems. Without good full-language compilers available, our response must finally be "learn the language, benchmark, wait and see what the compiler can do for you." But we can certainly also recognize that it is a genuine issue.

This leads to the subject of educational materials. Many of the current textbooks are rather defensive about Ada, adopting a partisan pro-Ada position and concentrating on the languages features and what can be done with them, while avoiding unbiased consideration of those things that cannot be easily expressed. Experienced programmers recognize "hype" when they see it, and this recognition understandably leads to skepticism. Ada will truly have arrived when the textbooks don't just teach Ada feature-by-feature, but rather approach the software engineering problem objectively, showing due respect for Ada's considerable power while pointing out how best to cope with her imperfections. We will be really credible when we can admit Ada has faults!

CONCLUSIONS

In the final analysis, Ada will be most successful when it has been "mainstreamed" into the university computer-science and software-engineering curricula. In the short term, this will probably be done using Ada as a second language, presumably following on the heels of Pascal, in courses devoted to data structures and concurrency. Our experience in the data structures course certainly shows the viability of Ada as a design language for such courses. Ada's viability as a coding language will become evident as compilers become widely available.

When the time is ripe to begin teaching Ada as a first language, it is essential that Ada's "interesting" attributes, especially concurrency and packaging, be introduced very early in the education process. Ada provides an opportunity to train new professionals to think in terms of concurrent rather than sequential designs, and to develop a fluency with modularization and information hiding as well as the inner-syntax issues we call "structured coding". If Ada is taught to beginners as though it were just Pascal -- or just Fortran -- this opportunity will be lost.

REFERENCES

Aho, A.V., Hopcroft, J.E., and Ullman, J.D. (1983).
  Data Structures and Algorithms.
  Reading, Massachusetts: Addison-Wesley.
Augenstein, M. et al (1983).
  Selecting a Primary Programming Language for a Computer Science Curriculum: PL/1, Pascal, and Ada.
  In Proc. 14th SIGCSE Technical Symposium on Computer Science Education, pp. 148-153.
  New York: Association for Computing Machinery.
Booch, G. (1983). Software Engineering with Ada.
  Menlo Park, California: Benjamin Cummings.
Feldman, M.B. (1984). Abstract Types, Ada Packages, and the Teaching of Data Structures. In Proc. 15th SIGCSE Technical Symposium on Computer Science Education, pp. 183-189.
  New York: Association for Computing Machinery.
Feldman, M.B. (1985). Data Structures with Ada. (to appear)
  Reston, Virginia: Reston Publishing Company, Inc.
United States Department of Defense (1983). Ada Programming Language.
  ANSI/MIL-STD-1815A, January 1983.

PART V ADA AND SOFTWARE ENGINEERING METHODOLOGY

A MASCOT APPROACH USING ADA

A.P. Hill
Plessey Defence Systems, Christchurch, Dorset BH23 4JE

J.K. Slape
Plessey Defence Systems, Christchurch, Dorset BH23 4JE

ABSTRACT

MASCOT (Modular Approach to Software Construction, Operation and Test) is a widely used UK MOD Standard Method for the development of real-time systems.

This paper investigates the implementation of MASCOT designs in Ada and makes comparisons between the Ada features used and the standard facilities that are currently required and provided to support the MASCOT approach when used with other implementation languages such as CORAL and Pascal. APSE facilities for supporting the MASCOT approach are also considered.

1. INTRODUCTION

MASCOT (Modular Approach to Software Construction, Operation and Test) [MASCOT80] is a language independent approach to software design, construction, operation and test, widely used in UK Industry for the development of real-time systems. Since the introduction of MASCOT in 1972 a standard integrated toolset has evolved for supporting the MASCOT approach; this includes a process scheduling kernel, facilities for constructing independent modules into a system, and monitoring facilities for testing and optimizing the system. Toolsets are currently available for use with the languages CORAL [CONTEXT] and Pascal [PERSPECTIVE].

The Ada language [ADA83] was specifically designed for developing real-time systems and directly supports many of the features required for supporting a MASCOT approach thus alleviating the need for the standard MASCOT kernel and toolset. In the remainder of this paper we describe how MASCOT designs may be implemented in Ada, and make comparisons between the Ada language facilities used and those standard facilities that have evolved to support the MASCOT approach. Consideration is also given to the additional facilities that would be required of an APSE to fully support a MASCOT approach.

A MASCOT Approach Using Ada

The work is partly based on practical experiments implementing an existing MASCOT design in Ada. The work is being done using the Telesoft Ada Compiler on a VAX 11/780 and Callan MC68000 based Workstation.

2. INTRODUCTION TO MASCOT

The concept of co-operating parallel processes is the starting point for the derivation of modularity in MASCOT. In MASCOT there are two major kinds of component - 'activities' which are separately schedulable processes that conceptually run simultaneously with all other activities and 'inter communication data areas' (IDA's) that satisfy all the data communication requirements between activities. An important aspect of a MASCOT design is that the total external data communication requirement of all activities is well defined and controlled.

There are two particular classes of IDA in MASCOT, the 'channel' and the 'pool'. A channel is such that the flow of data through it is transient, being placed there by an activity and subsequently removed by another in a destructive reading operation (i.e. a first in, first out buffer). Pools on the other hand are generally used as a repository of data for reference purposes. All data is local to the IDA's and may only be manipulated by activities through calls to the 'access procedures' of the channel or pool which contain code to ensure their mutual exclusion during critical accesses to shared data structures.

The design process in MASCOT consists of considering data flows from input devices to output devices, and at the same time postulating an Activity Channel Pool (ACP) Diagram (see Fig. I for example). Development is then evolutionary and proceeds by implementing all the different types of module that exist in the system and gradually integrating objects of these module types into subsystems (which are groups of related activities, channels and pools) and finally a system. Systematic testing and monitoring is performed at each stage of the integration in an environment such as that shown in Fig. II.

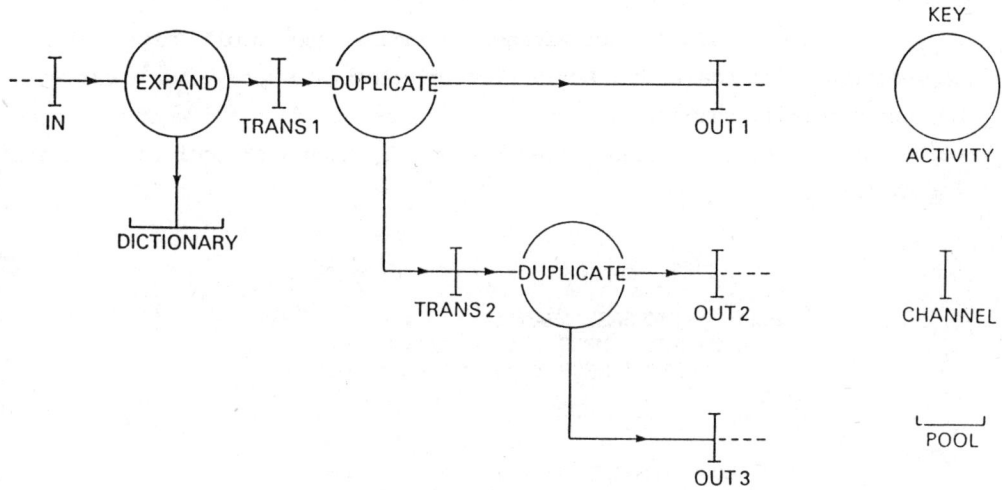

Fig. I - Example Activity Channel Pool Diagram

```
┌─────────────────────────────────┐
│ Test  Interface                 │
│         ┌──────────┬──────────┐ │
│         │ Software │ Simulated│ │
│         │ Under    │Environment│ │
│         │ Test     │          │ │
│         ├──────────┴──────────┤ │
│         │ Test Mode Kernel    │ │
│         │ Facilities          │ │
│         └─────────────────────┘ │
└─────────────────────────────────┘
```

Fig. II - Test Environment

3. ADA IMPLEMENTATION OF A MASCOT DESIGN

We consider the implementation of MASCOT designs in Ada in two parts. Firstly, we consider the general mapping between the MASCOT activity, channel and pool features and secondly, the implementation of the MASCOT design structure into an Ada program structure.

3.1 General Mapping of MASCOT Features onto Ada

The MASCOT activities, channels and pools may all be implemented using Ada tasks. Activities correspond to active Ada tasks with no entry points, channels and pools correspond to Ada tasks with an entry point for each of the access procedures of the channel or pool (see Fig III for example).

```
task type MESSAGE_CHAN is
   entry PUT ( MESS : in  MESSAGE );
   entry GET ( MESS : out MESSAGE );
end;

task body MESSAGE_CHAN is
   BUFFER : array ( BUFFER_LIMITS ) of MESSAGE;
   INP,
   OUTP   : BUFFER_LIMITS := 1;
   COUNT  : INTEGER       := 0;
begin
   loop
      select
         when COUNT < BUFFER_SIZE =>
            accept PUT ( MESS : in MESSAGE ) do
               BUFFER(INP) := MESS;
            end PUT;
            INP := INP mod BUFFER_SIZE + 1;
            COUNT := COUNT + 1;
      or
         when COUNT > 0 =>
            accept GET ( MESS : out MESSAGE ) do
               MESS := BUFFER(OUTP);
            end GET;
            OUTP := OUTP mod BUFFER_SIZE + 1;
            COUNT := COUNT - 1;
      end select;
   end loop;
end MESSAGE_CHAN;
```

Fig III - Ada Implementation of a Simple MASCOT Channel

A MASCOT Approach Using Ada

On comparison of the Ada implementation of channels and pools with a solution using the 'control queue' mechanism [SIMPSON79] that is provided by the standard MASCOT toolset, we found the Ada solution using a rendezvous mechanism far easier to use; however it should be pointed out that the Ada solution does incur certain overheads -

Firstly, the Ada solution increases the interaction between channel input and output operations by only allowing one of these operations to take place at any one time where as the control queue solution only enforces mutual exclusion when the channel buffer is either empty or full.

Secondly, the use of the Ada rendezvous mechanism for implementing such message passing systems incurs additional scheduling overheads that could well prove to be unacceptable in MASCOT type systems that rely on the extensive use of loosely coupled processes.

The problem of the additional scheduling overheads introduced by the Ada solution is discussed in detail in Roberts et al. [ROBERTS81]. Here they also discuss compiler optimisation techniques that eliminate the rendezvous by replacing each accept statement linkage with a procedure that implements the required mutual exclusion and synchronisation with some internal primitive such as a semaphore. A similar compile time optimisation is described in KIRCH83; this also reduces the number of processes in the system and thus the cost for storage management.

3.2 Implementing the MASCOT Design Structure in Ada

When considering the mapping from a MASCOT design structure (ACP Diagram) to an Ada program structure there are many possible approaches for packaging the task types; these may take into account the management of visibility, amount of recompilation etc. (see [DOI81]). From our practical point of view however, we were slightly constrained by the fact that the compiler did not provide task types or generics. In view of this, the approach we took was to declare each activity, channel and pool as a task, each in a separate package; the task specification in the package specification and the task body in the package body. In addition to these packages, additional package specifications were also used for specifying data types that were common across component and subsystem boundaries.

The ability in Ada to provide separate specification and implementation parts was found particularly useful in that it allowed the MASCOT design structure - the package specifications, to be written and compiled early in the design process, thus enforcing the design upon the programmers and ensuring the consistency of the design.

4. APSE REQUIREMENTS FOR MASCOT

The development and test environment will be required to support the evolutionary system approach to development and test. Here we compare this to what can be expected from an APSE and discuss the implications on the run-time kernel.

4.1 Evolutionary System Construction and Test

Considering the implications of the evolutionary system approach on Ada we find that the difference between separate and independent compilation effect the way the approach can be followed. With an independent compilation system there is no checking of interfaces and no check that a system is complete whereas with Ada's separate compilation system these checks are enforced. So where previously partial systems could be tested without being complete programs we must now test a complete Ada program. To form a complete Ada program from a partial system we must provide simulated software to replace called software. e.g. Where an entry call is made to a task not yet included a simulation of that task is required. Although this is also required for independently compiled software there is no check and it could be provided by the test environment using a generalised harness. During the evolution of the system this simulated software will be replaced with real software.

This involves supporting simulation software (generation of simulated software and configuration control aspects of keeping the source of both simulated and real versions of packages), build facilities, test facilities, monitor facilities etc. The configuration control here is source control and not the Ada library unit configuration control required by [ADA83]. Further, to fully test software for embedded systems a target test facility including target loading and target control is required. Here we concentrate on the host facilities (figure IV). Target testing can be considered as an extension of this. The MASCOT commands

START(subsystem,p), TERMINATE(subsystem), HALT(subsystem) and RESUME(subsystem) [SIMPSON79] are expected to have parallels in Ada debug/test environments. The p in START(subsystem,p) indicates a priority which, in Ada is a compile time parameter. Logically this dynamic allocation of priority can not be achieved in Ada although it may be possible (and useful) in a specialised host debug/test environment. Another point worth mentioning here is that the Ada equivalent debug/test commands would probably apply to Ada TASKS rather than groups of tasks (or subsystems). So a reasonable Ada debug/test environment should be sufficient to follow the MASCOT approach. It is also expected that trace facilities for Ada will provide an equivalent to the MASCOT monitor. The MASCOT monitor facility gives visibility of and the ability to record the interaction of MASCOT systems with the kernel.

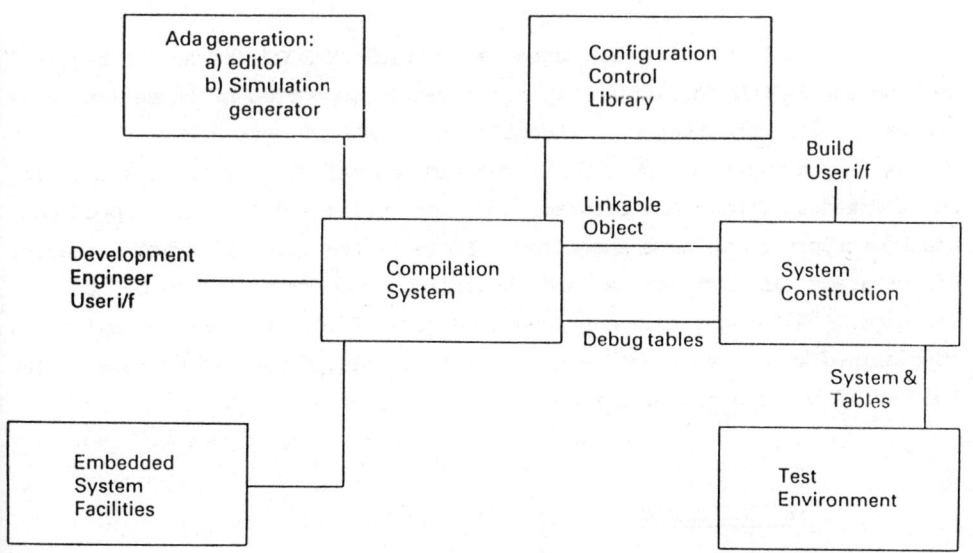

Fig. IV - Development and Test Environment

Construction facilities to enable the replacement of simulated packages are required. The specification part of simulated packages would be the real specification part, thus the inclusion of real bodies would not necessitate the recompilation of the complete system but rather the relinking. Whether this relinking extends to replacing parts of a linked system or requires the linking of a new system from constituent packages is not relevant here as the effect is the same (considerations of configuration control and efficiency would determine this).

4.2 Simulation Software Generation

The generation of simulation software could simply be via the same means as real software; an engineer creating Ada source using an editor or be achieved using a tool generating Ada source (or linkable object code even) from the package specification part (which could access test tables for responses). Clearly the second is more costly and would take time to develop. However in the absence of this the first is adequate and enables a valid approach to the MASCOT evolutionary system using Ada.

4.3 Ada Kernel Aspects

With existing languages a special MASCOT kernel is required because the MASCOT facilities are not directly supported by those languages (in particular concurrency). Adoption of a MASCOT approach with Ada puts no extra requirements on the Ada run-time kernel so long as systems are represented as single Ada programs and Activities and IDAs are mapped onto Ada constructs as we have suggested. There is the possibility of treating Ada programs as Activities and providing concurrency outside of the language. Although this may lead to a more efficient run-time system a specialised kernel would be required. It is also not known to what extent this would be accepted by the DoD.

5. CONCLUSIONS

The Ada language is very suitable for expressing a MASCOT design, however, concerns about the efficiency of the concurrency features of the language have still to be answered.

The facilities that can be expected from an APSE (particularly symbolic debug) would be sufficient to support the MASCOT test and monitor requirements.

REFERENCES

ADA83 - "Reference Manual for The Ada Programming Language". ANSI/MIL-STD 1815 A. United States Department of Defence, January 1983.

CONTEXT - "CONTEXT Microprocessor Development System". System Designers Ltd., 1 Pembroke Broadway, Camberley, Surrey GU15 3XH, UK.

DOI81 - Department of Industry. "Ada-Based System Development Methodology". Study Report Volume 1, September 1981.

KIRCH83 - Kirch et al. (1983). "Optimization in Ada". ACM Ada Letters 3(3), 45-57.

MASCOT80 - "The Official Handbook of MASCOT". Mascot Suppliers Association, Dec 1980.

PERSPECTIVE - "PERSPECTIVE The Integrated Programming Support Environment". System Designers Ltd., 1 Pembroke Broadway, Camberley, Surrey GU15 3XH, UK.

ROBERTS81 - Roberts ES et al. (1980). "Task Management in Ada - A Critical Evaluation for Real-Time Multiprocessors". Software Practice and Experience, 11, 1019-1051.

SIMPSON79 - Simpson HR & Jackson K. (1979). "Process Synchronisation in MASCOT". The Computer Journal, 22(4), 332-345.

LIMITS ON THE USE OF ADA FOR SPECIFICATIONS

I.C. Pyle
Computing Service, University of York,
Heslington, York YO1 5DD, England.

ABSTRACT

Much recent work on the frontiers of applicability of Ada has emphasised its importance as a Program Design Language. Ada has a major role in expressing software design, i.e. in stating with some degree of formality the interfaces and constituents in a software system, which will eventually lead to executable code. Work in the CEC Study on Ada for Specifications has shown that Ada has an important but limited role in expressing software specifications. Beyond this, Ada can be used to describe the morphology of a system (software and hardware) before and after it is designed, particularly the interfaces between components; it can also (with appropriate conventions) describe the functionality of constituent subsystems, including hardware components. However, Ada cannot describe practical constraints (performance, reliability, quality). Nor is it good for expressing the initial requirements for a system.

1 Introduction

This paper explores limits on the use of Ada, concentrating on its ability to describe information systems (rather than prescribing code to be executed), and bearing in mind the crucial passage from informal to formal modes of expression. It reports work on the use of Ada for a purpose that was not (explicitly) intended when it was designed. Nevertheless, the exploration is felt justified as it helps to clarify the proper range of applicability of Ada, by discovering why it can not be used for certain purposes in software development, before ordinary programming. We need aids for specifying systems, so let us see how far Ada can help.

The initial requirements for a system are always expressed informally, but the eventual code is formal, produced by mechanical translation from a formal language. The most difficult transition we have to make is from an informal mode to a formal statement, whether of specification or design. This is the stage in the software life-cycle that we now examine.

Ada strikes a middle path between the highly formal and the completely informal modes of expression. While Ada's linguistic structure imposes structural and surface formality (which permit a number of automatic checks for consistency), there is sufficient informality in the freedom of choice of identifiers and the use of strings and comments to permit parts of a specification to be left informal (or omitted) within a formal Ada framework. Most methods of incorporating semantic specifications in Ada programs rely on this technique. (It follows the view that programming consists of specifying and designing, presented in Pyle (1984), which holds that during the design phase a program is necessarily incomplete, as some parts that are eventually needed have not yet been considered.)

2 CEC Study on Ada for Specifications

The Commission of the European Communities has sponsored a study on the use of Ada as a specification language, as reported at EWICS (Goldsack 1983). The study is now complete, and is expected to be published later this year. The present paper is based on work done during the study, but is not part of it.

The CEC study shows how Ada may be used for describing system structures, in terms of objects they contain, by naming the parts. This principle is applicable to the hardware of systems as well as to software. It is important to realise that, used in this way, Ada allows the designer to describe structure but not behaviour. The nature of the constituents identified is not expressed formally, but is left to the interpretation of the reader, through the use of identifiers, supplemented by strings and comments. In the case of hardware components, one can use Ada to describe their interfaces, and inner structure if appropriate.

Ada is also well established as a Program Design Language (Booch 1981, Sammet et al 1981, Privitera 1982, Softech 1982, Lindley 1983) as it can show an intended program design as a compilation unit without having to provide declarations for all its constituents. Thus the design of a program to control a filtration plant can be written

```
with MAJOR_PHASES; use MAJOR_PHASES;
procedure SINGLE_UNIT is
begin
  loop
    DELIVER_WATER;
    CLEAN_FILTER;
  end loop;
exception
  when others =>
    CLOSE_DOWN;
end SINGLE_UNIT;
```

needing only the "specifications" of the constituent procedures:

```
package MAJOR_PHASES is
  procedure DELIVER_WATER;
  procedure CLEAN_FILTER;
  procedure CLOSE_DOWN;
end MAJOR_PHASES;
```

to ensure that the identifiers are properly defined.

The same principle can be used for hardware descriptions, writing Ada text that is never intended to be compiled into code, but is directly performed by the hardware.

Limits on the use of Ada for specifications   253

The major problem confronting the designer at this stage is how to express behaviour, or semantics. The above example shows that Ada can express the sequential behaviour in terms of elementary actions (and its tasking notation allows actions that occur simultaneously to be also described, but less conveniently), but there is an essential deficiency: Ada focusses attention on the transitions between states, not on the states themselves. We can regard the semantics of an action as the relationship between the states before and after it; Ada gives us the notation for describing the transition, but not the relationship, between the states. This issue is taken up again in the next section.

Another fundamental issue that has to be addressed is the domain transition from an informal expression of requirements to a specification in a formal notation, from which a program can be derived, and in comparison with which an eventual program can be validated. Crossing this domain gap is a harder and deeper problem than progressing from a formal specification to a formal program. Ada can be used in this area, by a technique of progressive increase in formality at each level in a program design. This technique is described in the CEC study; it consists of replacing program units (as Ada expects, using the recompilation rule) with progressively more formal and detailed units having the same name, or by providing bodies for units that previously had only "specifications". (Note that what Ada calls specifications are purely syntactic: they define calling sequences and contexts where the specified item may legitimately be used, but give no semantics.) This style is particularly appropriate with 'object-oriented' programming, using Ada packages and program-defined types. At some level of design, for example, we could identify application types, such as VALVE and VALVE_STATUS, with related operators such as TURN(V: VALVE; TO_BECOME: VALVE_STATUS). We can express them in a valid Ada program unit by notations such as

```
package VALVE_HANDLING is
   type VALVE is private;
   type VALVE_STATUS is private;
   procedure TURN(V: VALVE; TO_BECOME: VALVE_STATUS);
   -- etc.
end VALVE_HANDLING;
```

The only irritant is that Ada requires further information about private types. This can be provided by adding a private part or expanding the original declaration with

```
type VALVE is new ENTITY;   -- or
type VALVE_STATUS is (NOT_DEFINED, YET);
```

using notations and conventions from package SPECIFICATIONS (Pyle 1983).

Notice how the properties of the application concepts are defined: although only specified syntactically, there is a higher degree of formalism than in a natural language, permitting a syntactic check that is well worth having. All the interpretation is left to the reader knowing what valves are, and guessing what valve status might be. (As the program is developed, these concepts get refined and expressed formally, but one cannot do everything at the beginning.)

This style of programming is intermediate between informal and fully formal. Imagine what would have been written by a designer whose natural language was not English, or imagine the identical program structure written with arbitrary identifiers. It would be nowhere near as useful as an intermediate program design specification. The structure and the syntactic checks made possible by Ada's degree of formalism are valuable aids at this stage in programming.

This is the limit of pure Ada: it can describe the structure of a system (using packages and other program units), and ensure structural compatibility, but that is all. The important Ada separation between "specification" and "body" of a package may suggest that there is more, but that is not so. The specification part gives the syntactic specification, but no semantic information.

3 Introducing Semantics

Several authors have investigated the possibility of adding semantics to Ada programs by using annotations (Krieg-Brueckner 1980, Gordon 1982, Hill 1983), using what amounts to a major extension to the programming language. They use all of Ada apart from the comment rule, which is replaced by a whole new set of production rules, not particularly like the rest of Ada. This amounts to introducing a new language, making the program a multilingual text (in the style of Mentor: Donzeau-Gouge et al 1984). The fact that this has been found necessary reinforces the above view on the limit of Ada.

An alternative approach, also mentioned in the CEC study, is to use more of Ada's notations in expressing semantics. Specifically, it is commonly require to state predicates or relations between data items: Ada can do this quite well. We can define the semantics of a procedure by giving the predicate that it causes to hold when it is completed (and the predicate it assumes to hold when it is entered) using the ideas of pre-condition and post-condition introduced by Hoare(1969). Now we see some much more subtle limits on the use of Ada for specifications.

The predicates can be written as functions returning Boolean values, whose bodies consist of the expression concerned, which might involve the procedure parameters and possibly other non-local objects. These are all in scope in the declarative part of the procedure, so that is a natural place to put the predicate specification. Unfortunately, if the procedure is introduced in a package (as it should be), the rules of Ada prevent this from going in the specification part: it must go in the procedure body in the package body. Hill (1983) points out the value of having a semantic specification in the specification part _as well as_ the implementation semantics in the body.

The predicate on entry involves the values of data items at that instant. They must all be in scope at the procedure call, and can be written as a Boolean expression. But we cannot properly state that this Boolean expression _is_ the precondition. The best we can do is to fall

Limits on the use of Ada for specifications

back on informality (by choice of identifier). There can be only one precondition in each procedure, so we use the name PRE_CONDITION to express what it is:

```
function PRE_CONDITION return BOOLEAN is
begin
  return A < B;
end PRE_CONDITION;
```

to say that the procedure containing this declaration assumes that A < B on entry. The function is never called inside the procedure (so an optimising compiler, or one with pragma INLINE(PRE_CONDITION)) would not generate any code for it; however, the program could be systematically modified to insert

```
ASSERT(PRE_CONDITION);
```

before the first statement of its executable part as a run-time check that the pre-condition actually holds.

A further problem arises with the predicate on completion. This normally (in Hoare's style) involves the values of data items not only at that instant, but also some data values from entry time. We can use the above technique to describe relations between values at the same time:

```
function POST_CONDITION return BOOLEAN;
```

but we cannot in legal Ada express a relationship between values of the same variable at different times. This will be necessary when a procedure parameter is of mode *in out*, and may be necessary when a procedure parameter has an access type, or when the procedure uses non-local variables. McGettrick (1982) uses the attribute notation: X'IN for the entry value and X'OUT for the exit value. This emphasizes the difference between a specification and an algorithm: we can specify whatever relation we like between X'IN and X'OUT, but to obtain an algorithm, the relations must be manipulated to express X'IN in terms of X'OUT.

The above methods work in simple cases, but not further. We need universal and existential quantifiers, to assert that for all (or some) values in a subtype, a certain predicate holds: particularly when we want to express an invariant. For example, there is an array of VALVE_DETAILS holding among other things the STATUS for each VALVE, of type VALVE_STATUS. It is detected by two micro-switches, expressed as

```
type VALVE_STATUS is
record
  OPEN: BOOLEAN;
  CLOSED: BOOLEAN;
end record;
```

and there is a predicate that for all valves, the status cannot be both open and closed (but it may be neither). We can say

```
function INVARIANT return BOOLEAN is
begin
  for V in VALVE loop
    if VALVE_DETAILS(V).STATUS.OPEN
       and VALVE_DETAILS(V).STATUS.CLOSED then
      return FALSE;
    end if;
  end loop;
  return TRUE;
end INVARIANT;
```

or, by using a generic function to express the universal quantifier,

```
function CHECK(V: VALVE) return BOOLEAN is
begin
  return not ( VALVE_DETAILS(V).STATUS.OPEN
       and VALVE_DETAILS(V).STATUS.CLOSED );
end CHECK;
function INVARIANT is new FOR_ALL(VALVE, CHECK);
```

As can be seen even in this simple case, the notation is clumsy. There is also a serious limit: Ada's insistence that a loop parameter must be a scalar. This makes sense in the context of generating code, but it does not in the context of specifications.

My conclusion is that Ada can be taken a little beyond the obvious limit, but a number of problems arise, and the notation using Ada becomes far too clumsy and difficult to read (contrary to Ada's intention).

4 Diagrams

The work also sheds light on the respective merits of diagrams and text for expressing specifications. Diagrams allow relationships to be expressed in terms of pre-defined types of component, as does a text form such as Ada, after such relationships and types have been defined. The difference is essentially in the order of decisions in a design. A system can be sketched as an ACP diagram in MASCOT (Jackson & Simpson 1974),

Fig 1. Mascot ACP diagram.

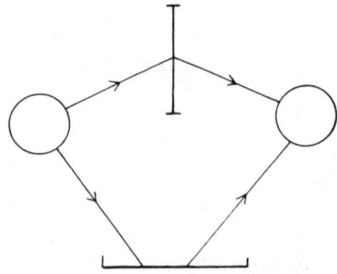

Limits on the use of Ada for specifications

using symbol shapes to show the component types and directed lines to show the relationships, but no identifiers (although names would almost certainly be used, perhaps orally, when the diagram is drawn). The nearest corresponding information in Ada (assuming package MASCOT.ACP that defines the same concepts of Activity, Channel and Pool), cannot be written without identifiers because we cannot use positions on the page to distinguish the entities involved in relationships. So we must name the activities, channels and pools before we can say how they are connected:

```
package EXAMPLE is
   task A1;
   task A2;
   type M is (NOT_DEFINED, YET);
   type D is (NOT_DEFINED, YET);
   type K is (NOT_DEFINED, YET);
   package C is new CHANNEL(M);
   package P is new POOL(K,D);
end EXAMPLE;
```

Note that Ada also requires us to specify the types of the data carried over the channel and held in the pool at the time they are introduced; with the diagrams, this decision can be left until much later. The connections can only be expressed inelegantly:

```
package body EXAMPLE is
   task body A1 is
     M1: M;
     K1: K;
     D1: D;
   begin
     --
     C.GIVE(M1);
     P.WRITE(K1,D1);
     --
   end A1;
   task body A2 is
     M2: M;
     K2: K;
     D2: D;
   begin
     --
     C.TAKE(M2);
     P.READ(K2,D2);
     --
   end A2;
end EXAMPLE;
```

The statements in the task bodies indicate possible calls, not the actual order: we cannot say this in Ada. (We would like to have a "sub-type" of a package, to say that only specified elements in it are visible in a particular context.)

Limits on the use of Ada for specifications

Thus Ada, by requiring identifiers at the outset, makes it more difficult to express the structural information about data flow.

Diagrams are easier for most people to assimilate, and more compact in expressing a set of relations (provided they are not too complicated), but they require more powerful computer support to handle their maintenance. With modern work-stations, it will be possible to handle diagrams expressing relationships within a system that is programmed in Ada. Particular kinds of diagram (e.g. Mascot ACP diagrams, DIN 40719 function charts, ladder diagrams, SADT diagrams, Nassi-Schneiderman diagrams) use different kinds of component and express different relationships, usually using the same pictorial shapes (annotated rectangles linked by directed lines); the distinctions can conveniently be made in Ada by defining packages that express the types and relationships required for the diagram, and using the Ada context specification to state which is needed for a given text.

5 Methodology

An important feature of programming methodology is the order in which decisions are taken, and the guidance it gives on what to leave out as well as what to put in, as information is being acquired during a project. An analysis of the information eventually produced in a software engineering project shows that the majority of information about the actual product can be expressed in Ada, and identifies what kinds of information are beyond the expressive power of Ada, so need other notations or linguistic frameworks.

Much of the specification consists of morphological information, naming parts of the system and expressing their structure; also a great deal concerns the data to be handled - its types, sources, destinations and representations. There are also computational relationships, and (quite often) sequential relationships between actions, all of which can be adequately expressed in Ada.

What can not be expressed are the quantitative aspects of the specification: performance and reliability figures, data flow rates and volumes. These are the aspects that most formal methods also omit, and include (surprisingly) the specifically real-time characteristic: response times. Ada cannot express a real-time requirement.

A further category of requirements that cannot be specified in Ada can be grouped as "quality" attributes: user friendliness, maintainability etc. These can best be regarded as meta-attributes, expressing general desirable qualities that are not specific to the particular system (i.e. not <u>specific</u> ation), but attributes we would like the specification to imply.

In addition to the information about the product, there is information about the project of producing it, for which Ada is also unsuitable. This includes project constraints (time-scales and budgets) and any particular restrictions applicable to development or operation of the system. These require facilities in the support environment,' but are outside the scope of Ada.

The notation used has a strong influence on the decision-making order. One of the arguments against using Ada for specifications is that it encourages programmers to work in too great detail too early: it is difficult to avoid the temptation to write executable programs when using a programming language. The fact that Ada includes executable statements provides a great temptation to use them early! Strangely, the fact that most of the linguistic structure is about non-executable parts (declarations, name visibility, representations) is often overlooked: Ada is considered to be a 'procedural' language because it contains procedures (even though procedure declarations in the same declarative part can be written in any order). If we refrain from using 'sequence_of_statements' it becomes non-procedural.

The method of using Ada non-procedurally, with emphasis on specifications rather than on sequences of statements takes advantage of its comprehensive power: its ability to express structure by program units and subunits, and particularly of program design by the use of such conventions as (NOT_DEFINED, YET) and NOT_DESIGNED_YET in package SPECIFICATIONS. The price to pay for an easy transition from design to actual program is that the programmer may find the transition so easy as to be imperceptible. Should we try to put an artificial barrier in the way?

6 Conclusion

Much has been written about what Ada can be used for, and how it will assist the software engineering process. This paper has sought to shed light on the process and on the programming language by pushing Ada way beyond the use it was designed for, in order to establish confidently its proper area. A test flight takes an aircraft to the limits of its performance to ensure that there is a good margin beyond normal use. Similarly by demonstrating how far out we can use Ada before reaching its limits, we confirm that it is more than adequate for programming and design. The results show how easy it is for practical system designers and programmers to take advantage of its power.

References

Booch G (1981). Describing software design in Ada; ACM Sigplan notices.
Donzeau-Gouge V, Kahn G, Lang B & Melese B (1984). Document structure and
 modularity in Mentor; ACM 0-89791-131-8/84/0400/041
Goldsack S G (1983).
 Ada for specifications; Proceedings EWICS 1983, Imperial College, London.
Gordon M (1982). Byron: A Program Design Language and Documentation Tool;
 Intemetrics' Ada Update vol 5 pp 1..5 (Oct 1982)
Hill A (1983). Towards an Ada-based specification and design language;
 Ada UK News vol 4 no 4 pp 16..32 (Oct 1983).
Hoare C A R (1969). An axiomatic basis for computer programming; CACM vol
 12 no 10 pp 576.80 (Oct 1969).
Jackson K & Simpson H R (1974). MASCOT, a modular approach to software

construction operation and test; RRE Technical Note 778; RSRE Malvern, England.
Krieg-Brueckner B & Luckham D C (1980). Anna : Towards a Language for Annotating Ada Programs; ACM Sigplan notices vol 15 pp 128..138.
Lindley L M (1983). Ada Program Design Language Survey; Ada Letters II-3.32..33 (1982) updated in II-1.61..63 (1983).
McGettrick A D (1982). Program Verification using Ada; Cambridge University Press.
Privitera J P (1982). Ada design language for the structured design methodology; Proceedings of the AdaTEC conference on Ada, pp 76..90 (Oct 1982).
Pyle I C (1983). Using Ada for specification of requirements and design; University of York YCS.63.
Pyle I C (1984). Programming equals specifying plus designing; Proceedings Real-Time Data82, INRIA, France.
Softech (1982). Survey of Ada PDLs; Softech report.
Sammet Jean E, Waugh D W & Reiter R W Jnr (1981). PDL/Ada -- A Design Language based on Ada; ACM81 Conference Proceedings pp 217..229.

ASPHODEL - AN ADA COMPATIBLE SPECIFICATION AND DESIGN LANGUAGE

A.D. Hill
Central Electricity Generating Board,
Computing and Information Systems Department, Laud House,
20 Newgate Street, London EC1A 7AX, U.K.

Abstract: Asphodel is a language for the formal specification and design of software. Its structure and syntactic style are similar to those of Ada and it may be used in an annotational form to add formal descriptions of behaviour to Ada programs.

INTRODUCTION

The importance of specification and design

There is much evidence to suggest that the most critical phases in the development part of the lifecycle of large software systems are the earliest ones, namely those of system specification and design. Various surveys, e.g. Boehm (1980), have shown that in such systems most errors typically occur during these phases rather than during coding, also that the earlier in the lifecycle an error occurs, the later it is likely to be detected, and that the later it is detected, the more expensive it will be to fix. It may thus be 100 times more expensive to remove an error which is discovered operationally than if it had been found during requirements analysis. Whilst most errors in coding are likely to be detected during module testing, errors in design are unlikely to be found until acceptance testing, or worse, during operation.

What kind of language?

Clearly a greater emphasis upon the specification and design phases should produce not only more reliable systems but, in the long term, cheaper ones (poorly designed systems are never cheap!). The ability to reason about and to manipulate the design is the key. How should we record our designs? What kind of language is most appropriate? Traditionally this has been natural language (e.g. English, German, etc.). The problem is that natural languages are informal and often ambiguous, are not appropriately structured, and are not machine processable. An alternative approach which has become popular recently is to derive program design languages (PDL) from existing programming languages. The drawback with this is that programming languages are essentially imperative notations and relatively weak on description (i.e. are concerned with <u>how</u> rather than <u>what</u>). The descriptive content of PDL's is thus often informal whilst the structure is formal.

A third approach is to employ formal languages especially designed for specification and design purposes. Formal languages have several advantages over natural languages. They are unambiguous and are capable of producing machine checkable documents. Thus it should be possible to create support tools which can aid in the mechanical verification of an implementation in a programming language against a formal specification.

On the other hand it is often claimed that natural language is easier to read, that it is something we all understand, and that it is difficult to master a new notation , especially one that embodies new principles. However, though we may all understand it, unfortunately we often "understand" something rather different from each other. Secondly, once one has become accustomed to using a formal language, at least from personal experience, it is actually easier to read than English. Most technical and legal disciplines find it desirable to invent their own special notations in preference to English for reasons of convenience and precision. After all, we already employ formal languages for the coding stage (and have done so for 3 decades!).

The adoption of formal methods

Why should there be any resistance to the adoption of formal languages for specification (as opposed to coding)? Partly, perhaps, because these have until recently been mainly in the domain of the mathematician and often employ what appears to the average programmer to be rather esoteric mathematical notations. There is a serious lack of extensive published examples of the use of formal techniques in a notation that programmers (and their managers) can readily comprehend. On the other hand, industry's traditional methods of educating new trainees are also to blame. Formal training often goes little further than courses in the chosen programming language and on the operating system of the chosen implementation machine. New graduate programmers are constrained to follow the existing methods of their team, the coding standards laid down a decade ago and still regarded as holy writ. They will quickly forget what they have been taught at university. In the eyes of their employers, unless particularly enlightened, all that academic stuff may be fine for toy systems, but when it comes to "real" software it's far too speculative and risky. All this results in an inbuilt resistance to change.

Tools are another critical factor. Many formal specification methods used so far have been essentially pencil and paper affairs. This is tolerable for small pieces of software, but for large systems the clerical overheads can make this impractical. Formal specifications can still be an aid to rigorous analysis, but if we cannot record them mechanically and verify that the transformations of specifications which typically occur during the design process are at least compatible, then the sheer volume of transcription errors which can occur may annul many of the benefits of this approach.

The relationship of specifications to programs

In a sense a specification is not fundamentally different from a program. A specification may imply an executional behaviour, even though it might not contain any clues as to how to realise it. A program explicitly states how to achieve that behaviour, and is usually concerned to do it efficiently. Thus the primary quality of a specification language should be its expressiveness, of a programming language its efficiency. Both should of course be easily readable and both should be formally definable. The development process may be regarded as a sequence of transformations or "refinements" from a highly abstract specification to a concrete program. If these transformations are to be mechanically checkable (ideally provable) it is necessary that the notations chosen for specification and implementation should match. In the intermediate stages of development it may indeed be desirable to combine them.

System maintenance

We have been concerned so far with the development part of the software lifecycle. Many systems are extremely long lived, and the effort expended upon their maintenance, and continued development after delivery, will consequently often greatly outweigh that spent upon their development. Errors can often creep in at this stage because precise and accurate details of subtleties of coding, implicit assumptions, etc., may not be easily available. All too often documentation is insufficiently detailed, or not reliably kept up to date, and the only reliable "description" of the system may be the code itself. Enhancement of functionality is often accompanied by gradual degradation of reliability. It is highly desirable that the specification language chosen should enable us to annotate the program code in a formal manner, to make the job of maintenance less error prone. Such annotations could serve a second purpose : to assist in the verification of the code, either by formal proof, or by suggesting critical tests.

ASPHODEL

Choice of method

The specification and design language Asphodel (accent on the first syllable) is an attempt to fulfil some of the needs expressed above. It may be used alone during the early specification and design. It may also be used in an annotational form to embellish the program text for use in the maintenance phase. For instance a package specification may be extended with a semantic description of its subprograms. It is complementary to Ada in that it is primarily concerned with the specification of behaviour, while Ada is primarily concerned with implementing that behaviour. It has the same package structure as Ada and has a similar syntactic style. It is also strongly indebted to ANNA (Annotated Ada) (Krieg-Brueckner et al, 1982) for much of its concrete syntax, particularly as used to annotate Ada programs, but contains a number of additional features. Whereas ANNA favours the algebraic style of specification, Asphodel additionally supports the Vienna Development Method (VDM) - Bjorner & Jones (1978), Jones (1980).

The choice of VDM was made mainly for pragmatic reasons. The concept of describing behaviour by building abstract models, and of gradually transforming these until one ends up with an executable program, is an easy and natural one for the average programmer to grasp. In addition, VDM is well documented and many published examples of its use exist; training courses are also available. VDM would appear therefore to stand a better chance than most other formal methods of bridging the gap between academic theory and industrial practice. The implicit techniques of algebraic specification can be quite difficult to apply in practice and the lack of adequate tutorial material would seem to make their widespread industrial adoption somewhat premature. They do have certain advantages however and sometimes it may even be useful to mix the two methods. For example, in the specification of a circuit diagram abstraction, the circuit topology was best expressed in VDM, whilst the expression of the circuit flow (i.e. Kirchhoff's laws) was most simply expressed in an algebraic, implicit manner. Our approach is thus eclectic rather than sectarian!

Asphodel employs the Ada concepts of package and subprogram specifications but extended with descriptive parts. The action of a subprogram would typically be specified by pre- and post-conditions. Basically a <u>postcondition</u> is a Boolean expression which defines the relationship between the values of the relevant program state immediately before and after a call to that subprogram. However this relationship is only guaranteed to hold provided that the state value before the call satisfied the <u>precondition</u> - another Boolean expression. This "relevant" state comprises that collection of program variables upon which the subprogram behaviour depends, or which it affects: parameters, returned value of a function, global variables. The interesting problem arises - how can we describe the behaviour of a package subprogram when part of the relevant state may not be visible in the package specification, but is hidden within the package body? The algebraic approach manages to avoid any mention of the hidden state, defining behaviour by a set of equations, e.g. the famous STACK equation

POP (PUSH (X)) = X

We choose here to follow the more explicit approach of VDM by instead <u>modelling</u> the hidden state within the specification, which thus enables us to use pre- and post-conditions, based upon this model rather than the real package state. In constructing these models we employ sets, mappings and sequences since these result in simpler and more mathematically tractable expressions than would be possible if we were to use the standard data structures of Ada.

<u>Example: a file handling system</u>

We shall illustrate some aspects of the specification language Asphodel by means of a few extracts from a design for a file handling system. See Hill (1984) for more details. This proceeds through a series of progressive refinements, or elaborations, starting from a highly abstract specification, which gradually transform the model and the operations upon it, reflecting the desire to produce an efficient and reliable means of storing files and pages (their contents) on disk-like devices. The example is based upon Chapter 11 of Bjorner & Jones (1982).

The system is represented by an Ada package, and operations upon it are represented as procedures and functions. Files are identified by parameters of type FILE_NAME. Within each file, pages are identified by a parameter of type PAGE_NAME. The value of each page is of type PAGE.

The operations defined are quite conventional: CREATE and ERASE to add or remove a file to or from the system; PUT, GET and DELETE to manipulate individual pages within a file. Note that the operations OPEN and CLOSE do not appear in the top level abstract specification, but only in a later development stage where they are clearly seen as concessions to hardware limitations (e.g. the relative inefficiency of disk accesses over core storage accesses).

In the early stages of development, explicit error handling is ignored. Invalid requests are defined by preconditions. Later refinements replace these by <u>exception</u> <u>clauses</u> defining the exact system behaviour upon receiving an invalid request.

The abstract specification

The filing handling system is first specified in a highly abstract manner, which does not concern itself with any actual representation of file structure, in particular with considerations of efficiency.

The declaration of the model variables and types are included within the package specification along with the subprogram declarations. Note that, however, names appearing in model declarations cannot be exported outside the specification and represent the "hidden state" of the system.

The model

The semantic model of the system is given by a model variable FILES, which is a <u>mapping</u> from a set of FILE_NAME values (called the <u>domain</u> of the mapping) to a set of values of model type FILE (called the <u>range</u> of the mapping). Each FILE value is a mapping from a set of PAGE_NAME values to a set of values of type PAGE.

```
model FILES : map of FILE_NAME -> FILE := {->} ;
model type FILE is map of PAGE_NAME -> PAGE ;
```

The initial value {->} of the variable FILES is an empty mapping which indicates that the system initially contains no files. Each file in the system is uniquely identified by a value of type FILE_NAME and each file consists of a set of uniquely named (by "PAGE_NAME") pages (of value type "PAGE").

To help illustrate the concept further, consider the following example of a possible value of the system model variable FILES

```
FILES = { FN1 -> FILE´{ PN11->PG11, PN12->PG12 },
          FN2 -> FILE´{ PN21->PG21 },
          FN3 -> FILE´{ -> } }
```

The braces { } denote a mapping constructor - an extension of the Ada aggregate notation. E.g. { A->X, B->Y } would indicate a mapping with domain set { A, B } and range set { X, Y } in which A maps to X and B maps to Y. The qualification FILE´ has the same significance as in Ada and is optional but included here for clarity. The interpretation of the above value is as follows: the system contains just three files named FN1, FN2 and FN3; the first file contains two pages named PN11 and PN12, which contain data values PG11 and PG12, respectively, the second contains only one page, whilst the third is an empty file.

The operations

File operations may now be defined in terms of pre- and post-conditions upon the model variable FILES. One such definition will be given as example.

```
       procedure CREATE ( FN : in FILE_NAME ) ;
       where
           global  ( FILES : in out ) ;
           in      FN not in dom FILES^ ;
                   --  cannot create a file with an existing name
           out     FILES = FILES^ mrg { FN -> FILE´{->} } ;
                   --  the system is extended with a new mapping
                   --  from FN to an empty file value
       end CREATE ;
```

In the above procedure specification, the keyword "where" introduces a <u>descriptive part</u> which is terminated by the keyword "end". This description may contain a number of clauses, each introduced by a distinct keyword and terminated with a semicolon. The keyword "global" introduces a <u>global clause</u> which defines (in addition to any parameters and returned value) that portion of the total program state upon which execution of the subprogram may depend (i.e. the relevant state). Asphodel employs a <u>closed</u> form of scoping in that variables from an enclosing unit are not visible unless they are explicitly imported by such a global clause. (This also applies to a compilation unit which names a separate library unit by means of a context clause.) This contrasts with the <u>open</u> form of scoping employed within Ada. The form of the list of imported variables is identical to a parameter list but omitting the type marks.

The keyword "in" introduces the <u>precondition clause</u>, the keyword "out" the <u>postcondition clause</u> (see above). A variable name marked with ^ represents the value of that variable on input. Any name not so marked represents its value on output. The unary operator "dom" extracts the domain set of a mapping, the binary operator "mrg" (merge) combines two mappings.

<u>Model refinement</u>

The next stage of refinement introduces the concepts of file catalogue and directories, although still in a very abstract manner.

The semantic model is now represented by three model variables: (i) CATALOGUE which records the name of each file (of type FILE_NAME) within the system and associates with it a unique DIRECTORY_ADDRESS value, (ii) DIRECTORIES which contains the file directories (of model type DIRECTORY) accessible via the DIRECTORY_ADDRESS and (iii) PAGES which is a page location directory, allowing access to each PAGE value via its PAGE_ADDRESS.

```
model CATALOGUE    : map of FILE_NAME <-> DIRECTORY_ADDRESS := {->} ;
model DIRECTORIES  : map of DIRECTORY_ADDRESS <-> DIRECTORY := {->} ;
model PAGES        : map of PAGE_ADDRESS -> PAGE := {->} ;
model type DIRECTORY is map of PAGE_NAME <-> PAGE_ADDRESS ;
```

The use of the special symbol <-> above denotes a one-to-one mapping. A consequence of this is that no two files can share the same directory and that no two directories are identical. (Use of the normal symbol -> would denote a many to one mapping, i.e. different members of the domain set could map onto the same member of the range set.) Note that all three system components are initially empty. Each DIRECTORY value records the location of a set of pages, accessed by a PAGE_NAME value. No two page names within each directory value can map to the same physical page. A directory value exists for each file in the system.

PAGE_ADDRESS and DIRECTORY_ADDRESS just represent sets of unique values. Their actual representation is not significant at this stage.

We can show that the model variables CATALOGUE, DIRECTORIES and PAGES are adequate to represent all possible values of the abstract state FILES (by defining a retrieve function - see below). However the converse is not true: not all possible combinations of values of CATALOGUE, DIRECTORIES and PAGES are valid representations of some value of that abstract state. They must additionally conform to certain internal consistency constraints, as defined by the invariant clause below

```
invariant
    rng CATALOGUE = dom DIRECTORIES
    and dom PAGES = union { rng DIR for DIR in rng DIRECTORIES }
    and ( for all PA in dom PAGES :>
                for unique DA in dom DIRECTORIES :>
                        PA in rng DIRECTORIES(DA) ) ;
```

The above is a Boolean expression which must be TRUE before and on completion of all operations upon the filing system. It expresses the requirements that there will be a distinct directory for each file in the catalogue, that every page addressed in PAGES will be recorded somewhere in a directory, and that every page in PAGES will belong to a unique file. (The unary operator "rng" returns the range set of a mapping, "union" is the distributed union of a set of sets, the notation { A for X } is an implicit constructor denoting the set of all values of A for which X is TRUE, and :> should be read as "it is true that")

As before, we shall illustrate the structure of the refined state by means of an example, which corresponds to the same system value as shown previously.

```
CATALOGUE   = { FN1->DA1, FN2->DA2, FN3->DA3 }
DIRECTORIES = { DA1 -> DIRECTORY'{ PN11->PA11, PN12->PA12 },
                DA2 -> DIRECTORY'{ PN21->PA21 },
                DA3 -> DIRECTORY'{ -> }  }
PAGES       = { PA11->PG11, PA12->PG12, PA21->PG21 }
```

We are now in a position to redefine the filing operations for the refined model, using pre- and post-conditions as before.

One other important ingredient of model refinement is the _retrieve_ function which enables the construction, from each refined state value, of each corresponding state value in the abstract specification. The existence of such a function provides the necessary demonstration that the refinement is adequate. Further, it provides information required to prove that the operations defined for the refined value are adequate representations of those of the abstract specification. This topic is addressed at greater length in Hill (1983).

Later levels of refinement of the design are concerned with such things as efficiency of access, i.e. by keeping a copy of the directory of any currently accessed file in core. This necessitates additional operations OPEN and CLOSE. Security, i.e. reliable recovery from system failure, is considered in yet another stage. Explicit error recovery is included by replacing all preconditions by exception clauses. A separate storage management module is introduced to deal with allocation of core storage as required - this can lead to exception propagation if insufficient storage is available. This module would be named in the global clause of any subprogram which used it and the corresponding postcondition would include the state change of that module.

e.g. CORE_MANAGER = CORE_MANAGER^[call ALLOCATE]

would indicate that the state of CORE_MANAGER had been changed as a result of a call to its ALLOCATE procedure.

Note that the abstract specification as first presented is a <u>stage</u> in the design process. It will not necessarily describe the behaviour of the completed system (i.e. OPEN, CLOSE, error handling), but should be readily updated to do so, with fairly minor changes.

CONCLUSION

Asphodel is an evolving language. As yet it has limited capacity for describing tasking (safety, but not liveness). It has been tried out on a number of small pieces of software (including the text formatter used to produce this paper). The results are encouraging but it is clear that further progress in applying it demands the creation of support tools and this will be the next stage of development. At the very least it should be possible to perform syntax checking and type checking. Sets, mappings and sequences could possibly be simulated as Ada generic types (thus allowing early prototyping). Pre- and post-conditions and invariants could be used to generate run-time checks.

I should like to acknowledge the influence of many helpful discussions with my colleague Dr Stephen Bear during the course of this work; also of many fruitful interchanges within the Ada Europe and Ada UK Formal Methods groups of which I am a member.

REFERENCES

Boehm, B. (1980). Software Engineering : R & D Trends and Defense Needs. In Research Directions in Software Technology, ed. P. Wegner, pp.44-86. Cambridge, Mass.:MIT Press

Bjorner, D. & Jones, C.B. (1978). The Vienna Develoment Method : The Meta Language. Lecture Notes in Computer Science no.61

Bjorner, D. & Jones, C.B. (1982). Formal Specification and Software Development. Prentice-Hall International

Hill, A.D. (1983). Towards an Ada based specification and design language. Ada UK News, <u>4</u>, no.4,16-32

Hill, A.D. (1984). Design of a filing system using Asphodel. CEGB report in preparation

Jones, C.B. (1980). Software Development - a Rigorous Approach. Prentice-Hall International

Krieg-Brueckner, B., Luckham, D.C., von Henke, F.W. & Owe O. (1982). Draft Reference Manual for Anna. Stanford University.

EXPERIENCE WITH AN OBJECT ORIENTED METHOD OF SOFTWARE DESIGN

S.B. Mickel
General Electric Company, 1277 Orleans Drive, Sunnyvale, CA. 94086

Abstract. This paper documents practical experience in applying an object oriented design method to the production of Ada (Ada is a registered trademark of the U.S. government) software. The object oriented method is described together with the procedures by which it was applied to the development of a simulation language capability. Lessons learned concerning the method applied, the procedures by which it was applied, and the Ada language itself are reported.

1.0 INTRODUCTION

Development of the Ada language was intended to facilitate the development of systems that are more reliable, modifiable, efficient and understandable. To ensure that these benefits are realized in Ada systems, however, requires more than just a programming language. A coherent software engineering methodology that guides the structuring of systems in a disciplined manner is needed.

Previous experiments have demonstrated that improved software quality is not an automatic by-product of the use of Ada. In a 1982 case study a traditional, top-down functional design methodology was used in re-designing a software system in Ada. The software had initially been implemented in FORTRAN. Although the Ada programmers were unaware of the FORTRAN design, the finished Ada system was remarkably similar to the original FORTRAN system. It was concluded that few of the potential benefits of Ada (e.g., increased reliability) has been realized. It was recommended that application of a design technique supporting information hiding would have been more successful.

In 1983 the design of a simulation language capability in Ada was undertaken. Given the results of the case study, an alternative design technique was sought. Available literature was surveyed and the object oriented method described by Grady Booch in his book, Software Engineering with Ada, selected (Booch 1983). There were several reasons for the selection. First, the technique supports an information hiding approach. Second, it provides a method for specifying packages and tasks, something rarely addressed in other methodologies. Finally, objected oriented design was considered mature enough to be applied to a real software development problem in 1983.

2.0 OBJECT ORIENTED DESIGN TECHNIQUE

The following overview of Booch's object oriented technique is necessarily brief. Those interested in more detail are referred to Booch (1983).

The steps of Booch's object oriented technique are simply:

o Define the problem
o Develop an informal strategy
o Formalize the strategy
   - Identify objects and their attributes
   - Identify operations on the objects
   - Establish the interfaces
   - Implement the operations

The goal of the first step is to gain an understanding of the structure of the problem space. The problem definition is usually documented in a formal requirements specification. The next step is to create an informal strategy that parallels our view of the world. The strategy is expressed using natural language (e.g. English) descriptions in terms of concepts from the problem space. To formalize the strategy, objects and their attributes are identified with nouns and adjectives extracted from the informal strategy. Operations are identified with verbs extracted from the strategy. Each operation is associated with a particular object identified previously. To complete the formalization, relationships among objects are established by describing the scope and visibility of each object using Ada package specifications. Operations are implemented by implementing the corresponding package bodies.

3.0 APPLICATION TO SOFTWARE DEVELOPMENT PROBLEM

In the paragraphs which follow, the manner in which Booch object oriented technique was applied to a simulator development project is described.

3.1 Define The Problem

This application is intended to be a general purpose process-oriented discrete event simulation language in which special simulation capabilities have been added to the Ada language. The user

Object Oriented Method of Software Design   273

will develop and instantiate process objects to represent the behavior of the system being modeled, and instantiate resource objects to represent entities of the system being modeled. The user will not need to be an expert Ada programmer.

3.2 Develop an Informal Strategy

The second step creates an informal strategy that parallels our view of the world. A discrete event simulation model can be decomposed into three components: The workload component, the resource component, and the process component (Wong 1984). The workload component represents the stimuli from the environment external to the system. The resource component represents the system capabilities which are utilized to perform the work of the system. The process component represents the patterns of resource utilization and process interaction present in the system. The workload defines when certain processes are externally activated. Processes compete with each other to utilize resources. The unavailability of a resource will cause a process execution to be blocked until the resource is available. Processes interact with other processes by activating new processes and by synchronizing with processes that have already been activated. System behavior is recorded through resource utilization and contention statistics, and process throughput and response time statistics.

3.3 Formalize the Strategy.

The strategy statement yielded several objects: processes, resources, and statistics. The remaining objects were selected in a bottom-up fashion. Queues and random variate distributions are objects of general utility in simulation systems.

Following selection of the simulation objects, the operations to be permitted upon those objects were determined. The entire list of objects and operations is too lengthy for inclusion here. However, for illustration, a subset follows:

OBJECTS	OPERATIONS
process	create
	activate
	suspend

resource	resume
	terminate
	create
	request
	release
queue	create
	insert
	empty
	length

The object definitions and their operations were encapsulated within Ada packages and documented as compilable Ada package specifications. All objects defined above are what Booch calls "common nouns" defining classes of entities. They do not identify specific objects, but rather imply abstract data types. Thus, in the package specifications they appear as data types, not object declarations. All operations were transformed into Ada procedures or functions.

In developing package specifications (or interfaces), the recommendations of Parnas with respect to information hiding (Britton & Parnas 1981) were applied:

o system details that are likely to change independently should be the secrets of separate modules
o the only assumptions that should appear in the interfaces between modules are those that are unlikely to change.
o every data structure is private to one module.

Although Parnas uses the term "module", his definition of that term fits quite well the definition of an Ada package.

Each of the seven packages composing the system was reviewed three times. For the package being reviewed, the designer delivered three items to all reviewers at least 3 days in advance: a compilable Ada package specification, a scenario for use of the package, and a graphical description of data structure (where applicable) showing organization and relationships.

At each review three questions were asked regarding the package:

1. Does the package satisfy its requirements?
2. Has an information hiding approach been taken?
3. Is the scenario for use reasonable and present a simple and effective interface?

Reviewers evaluated the materials presented with respect to these questions. Changes were requested as necessary and documented in a memo following the review meeting. Packages were thus released to the next level of design.

4.0 LESSONS LEARNED

This section summarizes the lessons learned regarding the technique applied, the procedures by which it was applied, and the Ada language itself.

4.1 Object Oriented Technique

While Booch's book provides a good description of the object oriented process, it does not provide rigorous, repeatable procedures by which it can be applied to an actual software development project. For example, Presentation materials appropriate to design reviews are not addressed.

Despite this lack of specificity, we concluded that object oriented design had generally worked well. A major advantage in employing this approach is its emphasis on information hiding and its use of packaging from the very beginning. Packages are not just convenient ways of collecting pieces of the system, such as collections of mathematical routines. Packages are integral parts of the system architecture. Decisions concerning how the parts of the system interact are made early and documented in package specifications.

There were two significant difficulties in applying the object oriented technique. First, no set of design quality measures to apply to the selection of packages was available. Parnas' decomposition recommendations (which were used in this project) are very general guidelines subject to wide interpretation.

The second difficulty relates to the use of Ada as the design language. The designers tended to consider the package specifications as code rather than design. Typically, attention was directed towards obtaining a clear compilation rather than to satisfaction of requirements and clean package interfaces. Part of this was undoubtedly due to lack of experience and confidence with the Ada language.

4.2 Design Reviews

At each design review, a scenario for use was presented for each package being reviewed. The scenario consisted of 1-2 page(s) of Ada code utilizing the resources of the package under review. Figure 1 illustrates a sample scenario.

These scenarios were an important part of the review process. It put the designer in the user's position, resulting in a tendency to make the interface simpler and more effective. It also displayed the designer's understanding of the requirements in a very concise and visible manner. It was much easier for reviewers to determine whether all requirements had been met.

Compilable package specifications were also presented at design reviews. The private section of most packages is extensive. We soon realized that at preliminary design reviews, private sections should not be presented. Private sections provide information needed by the Ada compiler, but not needed, indeed prohibited from, the package user. It is implementation and not appropriate at preliminary design reviews. Without private clauses, however, package specifications are not compilable.

Each package was reviewed three times, at increasingly detailed design levels. Frequent and comprehensive reviews ensured that the entire system progressed at the same rate. Experience has shown that a functional decomposition technique can result in increasingly detailed threads of functionality. Use of an object oriented technique and regular design reviews produced complete system descriptions at each level of abstraction. As a result, changes were easier and less expensive to make and interfaces between packages remained consistent.

```ada
with ada_simulation; use ada_simulation;
procedure BANK_SIMULATION is
-- Entities are a teller and a sequence of customers
-- Customer arrival times use exponential distribution
-- Simulation terminates after a specified duration
-- Simulation report is histogram of customer service times

    NEW_CUSTOMER: process;
    TELLER: facility;
    CUSTOMER_ARRIVAL_TIME: exponential_random;
    END_SIMULATION_TIME: float;

    task type CUSTOMER_PROCESS;
    package CUSTOMER is new process_creator (CUSTOMER_PROCESS);
    task body CUSTOMER_PROCESS is separate;

begin
    create_facility (facility_ref => TELLER,
        facility_title => "TELLER");
    create_exponential (exponential_ref => CUSTOMER ARRIVAL TIME,
                        exponential_title => "CUSTOMER ARRIVAL TIME",
                        exponential_seed => 123456,
                        mean_value => 2.0);
        .
        .
        .

    END_SIMULATION_TIME := 1000.0;
    start_simulation (simulation_duration=>END_SIMULATION_TIME);
    report_histogram (histogram_ref=> SERVICE_TIME_HISTOGRAM);

end BANK_SIMULATION;

separate(BANK_SIMULATION);
task body CUSTOMER_PROCESS is
    NEW_CUSTOMER: process;
    SERVICE: facility_unit;
    ARRIVAL_TIME, SERVICE_TIME: float;
begin
    ARRIVAL_TIME := exponential (exponential_ref =>
                    CUSTOMER_ARRIVAL_TIME);
    if current_simulation_time <= END_SIMULATION_TIME then
        CUSTOMER.create_process (process_ref => NEW_CUSTOMER,
                process_title => "CUSTOMER_PROCESS",
                activation_time => current_simulation_time
                                                + ARRIVAL_TIME,
                process_priority => 0);
    end if;
        .
        .
        .
end CUSTOMER_PROCESS;
```

Figure 1 Example of an Ada-Based Simulation Language Program

4.3 Ada Style Issues

The following is a summary of the types of statements found in the seven package specifications.

Statement type	Number of packages including statements
Type declarations	1
Private declarations	5
Object declarations	0
Procedures	6
Functions	6
Exceptions	5

Note that there are no object declarations in any of the package specifications. This is a measure of success of the object oriented technique in promoting information hiding: there is no common or shared data between packages. Consider the simulation clock. It could have been declared a common object. Instead it is accessed via a visible function, CURRENT_SIMULATION_TIME. This function reads the clock and returns the current value. It also ensures that users are unable to modify the clock time in any way, thus increasing reliability.

All type declarations in the package specifications are private. The vast majority of them are limited private. This is another measure of information hiding. To promote reliable performance, user access to anything that should not be modified by the user is restricted. The random stream types are examples of this. NORMAL_RANDOM, POISSON_RANDOM, etc. are private types so that the user cannot interfere with each random stream of values. This is important since each random value is used recursively to generate the next value in the stream.

In all but two of the packages, exceptions have been declared. This indicates that exceptional conditions have been identified and handled properly. Exception names such as QUEUE_EMPTY_ERROR were chosen to indicate exactly what condition gave rise to the exception.

Finally, Ada functions (as opposed to procedures) are specified primarily in two cases: for mathematical functions and for logical conditions. Mathematical functions include LN, EXP, "**", etc. Functions such as QUEUE_IS_EMPTY, CURRENT_PROCESS_NAME, and CURRENT_SIMULATION_TIME determine the state of some value or the truth of a condition. Names were selected to read naturally where used, as in "if QUEUE_IS_EMPTY then . . ."

All WITH and USE clauses currently appear on the package specifications. To comply with information hiding principles, visibility should be restricted to the smallest possible scope. Therefore, where possible these clauses will be moved to the corresponding package bodies as they are implemented. This will also reduce the amount of recompilation required when used packages change.

4.4 Rapid Prototyping In Ada

Prototyping was used to investigate the best method of implementing simulation processes. Our application made fairly sophisticated use of Ada tasks and task types. It was impossible, given the concurrency requirements of simulation, to divorce the package specification from the tasking structure that would be required to implement them. Given the limited Ada experience of the designers, it was difficult to tell if their schemes were feasible. Ada tasking features were not being used in a straightforward manner. A quick prototype of package bodies was the best verification of implementability and at times resulted in adjustments to the specifications which led to a simpler and more efficient system. Prototyping was, therefore, essential to the development of this application.

In addition, a large portion of the package bodies is already implemented. Since the prototype was done in Ada, the prototype need not be thrown away. Development will continue as enhancements to the existing package bodies until full functionality has been achieved. This process parallels the prototyping process described by Duncan (1983).

5.0 SUMMARY

This project has demonstrated that an object oriented design technique can be used successfully to design Ada systems exhibiting enhanced modifiability, efficiency, reliability, and understandability. At this time, however, object oriented design is more an approach than a comprehensive methodology. It must be supplemented with design metrics to guide the wise selection and packaging of objects. This project has identified a few of these metrics. Further experience is needed to complete the list. Further attention to documentation methods for Ada designs is also needed.

While much was learned in the course of this project, it must be the first of many such projects. We have only begun to find was of dealing with Ada and to improve the quality of our software. Only by monitoring our increasing experience with Ada on larger and more complex systems can we eventually develop a comprehensive methodology and fully supportive APSE that will lead to reliable and maintainable systems.

6.0 REFERENCES

Booch, G. (1983). Software Engineering with Ada. Menlo Park, CA: Benjamin Cummings.

Britton, K.H. & Parnas, D.L. (1981) A-7E Software Module Guide, NRL Memorandum Report 4702.

Duncan, A.G. (1982) Prototyping in Ada: A Case Study, ACM Software Engineering Notes, Vol #7, NO#5.

Wong, G. (1984) Ada-Based Distributed Computer System Modeling Language. In proceedings of the Conference on Simulation in Strongly Typed Languages, 1984.

FORMAL SPECIFICATION TECHNIQUES FOR PARALLEL AND DISTRIBUTED SYSTEMS
A Short Review

presented on behalf of the
Ada-Europe Working Group on Formal Methods for Specification and Development
by
Dr. Howard Barringer
Department of Computer Science
University of Manchester
Oxford Road
Manchester M13 9PL

Abstract. Criteria for the classification of formal methods for specification and development of parallel and distributed programs are presented. Specification techniques based upon Petri nets, path expressions and temporal logics are then surveyed and reviewed with reference to the given criteria.

INTRODUCTION

Inadequate specification of computer software and hardware has long been quoted as a root cause of software failure, software failing to meet expectations, and the very high software maintenance costs. For the past decade much research effort, directed at resolving this and related issues, has concentrated on the development and application of techniques for formal specification and verification of computer programs, in particular the advancement of denotational semantic, axiomatic semantic and algebraic semantic techniques (Lucas 1978). Some of these specification techniques, see for example (Prehn et al. 1983), have been developed to such a degree that they now form the basis of well-proven system specification, design and documentation methods; the application of those approaches is at present largely restricted to the development of sequential programs. With the dramatic growth in the production and use of distributed and parallel computing systems, it is imperative that similar formal design methods are also employed in the construction of distributed and parallel software.

Unfortunately, the transfer of specification and verification techniques from sequential to parallel programs is, however, far from straightforward. There is an explosion in the number of different techniques available, each appearing to be adequate for certain aspects of the system construction. For example, there are approaches based on path expressions (Campbell & Habermann 1974, Goldsack & Morton 1982), Petri and predicate transition nets (Genrich & Lautenbach 1979, de Bondeli 1984), relational semantics (Jones 1983), temporal logic (Lamport 1983; Barringer & Kuiper 1983; Barringer et al. 1984), interval logic (Schwartz et al. 1983), CCS (Milner 1980), CSP and communication histories (Hoare 1981) to name but a few.

In the following section, criteria are presented which can be used as a basis for classifying and comparing some of the above-mentioned approaches to formal specification. Such a classification is part of preliminary work undertaken by the Ada-Europe Working Group on Formal Methods for Specifications and Development in order to expose and/or develop formal specification techniques applicable to Ada and its tasking aspects. The specification techniques considered below are those which have either been presented and discussed at Working Group meetings, or are being used-cum-researched by some of the members of the Working Group; this brief survey is *not* intended to be a Which? guide to formal methods for parallel systems!

CLASSIFICATION CRITERIA

As indicated above, formal specification and development of parallel and distributed systems is still very much an open problem and hence, as yet, no general consensus has been reached amongst researchers as to what features a "good" specification technique should possess. The list of criteria presented below may, therefore, be viewed with some scepticism as to its realism; however, it does appear to provide a useful basis for comparison of techniques.

Clearly, the criteria should include the usual motherhood about formal methods (carried over from sequential program development), that is, that they *are* formal, understandable to the non-mathematician, teachable, free of implementation bias, applicable to programming in the large, etc. Other criteria used are discussed under the following sub-headings; it is felt that these together with the motherhood form a sound basis for comparison and classification.

Applicability

The applicability of a specification technique is a useful starting point for classification. The questions 1 and 2 below are typical for applicability.

1. Where does the technique fit into the software life cycle? Does it cover requirements specification, the whole development process, or does it just directly model the (concrete) implementation and is therefore intended for analysis purposes?

2. What model of concurrency is employed? Is it suitable for specification of Ada tasking? For example, is it an interleaved model supporting shared variables and synchronous message passing, or is it "real" concurrency which is modelled?

Modularity and compositionality

For a specification technique to be successfully used in a hierarchical system development framework it should possess an "independence principle". That is to say a valid decomposition of some specification into some combination (sequential, parallel, conditional, etc.) of specifications of sub-components must guarantee that each of the sub-specifications can be developed independently of the other sub-components. In sequential system development this can be easily obtained as specifications are usually functions (or relations) from input to output values, and sequential composition is simply functional (relational) composition. However, for parallel system development, this is one of the key research areas. Specifications of (parallel) components should express, somehow, environmental constraints, e.g. one might require that on certain shared variables interference can not be tolerated while on others only to some limited extent, thus restricting the environment of the component in its particular behaviour with respect to those variables.

Expressiveness

The specification language should be sufficiently expressive for its desired application. Thus, for example, do specifications directly express both liveness (responsiveness, fairness, etc.) properties, i.e. stating that something good will happen (Owicki & Lamport 1982), and safety properties, i.e. stating that nothing bad happens, or do such properties have to be derived from the specification? For real-time applications the technique, naturally, should allow "real" timing constraints to be expressed, for example, as in the requirement that if a process in a communications protocol does not receive a response in 20ms then it should retransmit the message.

Abstractness

It is desirable that the specification technique be capable of giving "fully abstract" specifications at each level of development. For example, for an application in a shared variable environment, is it possible to give specifications in terms of only the externally observable variables, or is it necessary to introduce some sort of auxiliary (internal) state components? Such requirements are of course necessary to avoid over-specification and/or the introduction of implementation bias.

Adaptability

The specification approach should, to a certain extent, be implementation strategy independent (a sort of abstractness requirement). For example, given a good abstract specification of a bounded buffer, it ought to be possible to develop it into a shared variable framework and also into a synchronous (or asynchronous) message passing framework. Independence of implementation language (e.g. whether Ada-oriented?) clearly falls under this heading.

Usability and practicality

Naturally, the specification technique should be practically useable. Some of the motherhood criteria indeed reflect this (understandable, teachable, etc.), however, other aspects are suggested by the following questions.

1. How easy (or difficult) is it to verify an implementation against its purported specification? Are the proof rules for the justification of development steps easy to apply?

2. What tool support for the specification language and methodology exists? For example, are there language processors, or do verification (validation) tools exist (or can they be constructed straightforwardly) to aid in the process of development?

3. Can efficient implementations be derived, by automatic transformation, from the specification?

Exercisability

It is very often desirable to be able to exercise a specification in order to discover whether it does capture what was intended (from the requirements). Ensuring that specifications are executable, or that simulations can be automatically produced, is one such technique (rapid prototyping); proving theorems from the specification is an alternative approach.

SOME SPECIFICATION TECHNIQUES

An overview and classification of specification techniques based on predicate transition nets, path expressions, temporal and interval logics is now presented. The lack of available space has made it impossible to include any worked examples in the techniques, however, for the interested reader, sufficient references to the technical literature have been included to enable deeper investigation to be made.

Petri net based techniques

Petri nets were first proposed by C.A.Petri as a model of concurrent systems in his dissertation (Petri 1962). Such nets are marked directed bipartite graphs constructed from two types of nodes, S-elements (denoting local atomic states) and T-elements (denoting transitions, i.e. local changes of state). The arcs of the graph provide the relation between the S-elements and the T-elements, and the marking of the graph is a distribution of tokens (with no internal structure) over the S-elements in the graph. Movement of the tokens is used to investigate behavioural properties of the system being modelled. Such transformation of the marking (movement of the tokens from one set of S-elements to another) of the graph is specified by a firing rule which states when and how the transitions associated with the T-elements can occur.

The major advantage of Petri net models is that they provide a simple, abstract and general framework for analysing distributed systems. They allow powerful analytic techniques to verify important properties such as freedom from deadlock, freedom from livelock, etc. For example, the computation, through linear algebraic methods, of S-invariants (giving sets of S-elements which are invariant in the number of tokens they possess) and T-invariants (corresponding to cyclic sequences of transition firings), and the computation of reachability trees (giving all possible reachable markings from an initial marking) are possible, see (Genrich et al. 1980). However, such nets have the distinct disadvantage that they produce very large, unwieldy and unstructured descriptions of the systems being modelled. For that reason tokens are allowed to possess internal structure and then a variety of powerful net models arise (Genrich & Lautenbach 1981; Jensen 1981).

Predicate transition nets (Pr/T-net), introduced in the paper (Genrich & Lautenbach 1979), are an evolution of ordinary Petri nets. An S-element of a Pr/T-net can model several S-elements of an equivalent Petri net, furthermore, tokens may be coloured by tuples of data (constants/variables). Similarly, a T-element of a Pr/T-net may model several T-elements of an equivalent Petri net. The arcs are labelled by sums of tuples of data (constants/variables) which define the set of tokens consumed or produced by that transition. The advantage that such nets have over ordinary Petri nets is clearly conciseness of representation.

De Bondeli (1983) has developed predicate transition net models for the control of concurrency in Ada. These models are principally intended for (i) designing and debugging concurrent Ada programs and (ii) teaching how Ada tasking constructs work. It is claimed that it may also be possible to use such models for (iii) formal proofs of Ada tasking programs and (iv) providing dynamic semantics for Ada tasks. We comment briefly on the application of such models in system design and then on the relation to the classification given earlier. Typical applications are considered as a collection of cooperating objects. The design process comprises essentially two phases; the first phase defines the objects and their interfaces in some hierarchical fashion using an existing methodology such as HDM (Levitt et al. 1979) or VDM (Bjoerner & Jones 1982), and the second phase consists modelling the interworking of these objects through their interfaces with predicate transition nets. Naturally, internal concurrency within an object can be handled in a similar way. The application of this net theory is limited to the control flow aspects of system design and it is necessary to resort to some other technique to handle data and data type abstraction. There exist several design methods which are based upon the above ideas but using Petri nets; two most notable methods are SARA (Campos & Estrin 1978) and GALILEO (Vidondo et al. 1980). Control flow aspects are modelled by place-transition nets and data flow models can be overlayed.

Petri nets have been used in a hierarchical fashion (although this is still an ongoing research topic) and thus the whole development from top level specification may eventually be possible for a not too restrictive class of nets; this is again frontline research for Pr/T-nets. However, net theory has in general been applied to analysing particular system models. The model of concurrency underlying the theory is true concurrency (not an interleaved model); both synchronous and asynchronous communication mechanisms can be modelled. Since models of systems are presented directly, specification of safety and certain liveness properties are indirect; it is necessary to apply heavy computations to analyse the graphs for such properties. Fairness properties in general are not treated; the theory assumes a minimal fairness requirement on choices. For predicate transition nets some of the analytic techniques from Petri nets have carried over, but, the general subject area is still very much open research. For Petri nets, production systems exist as well as research tools, e.g. as in SARA and GALILEO, and for performing static analysis of dynamic properties, albeit rather costly. GALILEO tools also support timing analysis.

Path expressions

Path expressions, introduced in the paper (Campbell & Habermann 1974), are a formalism for specifying process synchronisation. In the original exposition, path expressions describe synchronisation at the level of procedures; they describe how the execution of the body of one procedure is allowed to execute in relation to other procedures, irrespective of when invoked. The path expression notation is based on regular expressions and hence allows representation by finite state machines. The notation was restricted to enable implementation of path expressions in terms of other synchronisation primitives. As a simple example, the expressions

    path {read} , {WRITE} end and path write end

define a reading/writing policy which allows read executions to overlap each other (thus, once reading starts all processes requesting reading may proceed) but not with WRITE executions, similarly WRITE executions may only overlap with other WRITEs. Now, assuming the procedure WRITE is implemented by write, actual writing can only proceed in a sequential fashion, although all WRITEs will finish before any reading can resume.

  Path expressions have been incorporated into a path-process notation (Lauer & Campbell 1975) and given a formal semantics in terms of marked, labelled transition nets. A program is associated with such a net and should be considered as formally specifying the concurrent behaviour of the net. COSY (Lauer et al. 1979) incorporates the path-process notation and provides facilities for the iterative definition of large path-process programs. Tools for the support of COSY notation have been developed at the University of Newcastle (Lauer 1983).

  Various suggestions have been made to incorporate path expressions (informally) into Ada package specifications. Such expressions would describe the allowed concurrent behaviour of the procedures and functions provided by the package. The paper (Goldsack & Morton 1982) describes such inclusion of path expressions as formal comments and outlines a preprocessor to construct control code, in terms of Ada tasking primitives, from the path expressions. McGettrick (1982) makes similar suggestions for the specification and verification of tasks. Clearly, the automatic production of synchronisation code from path expressions has some distinct advantages over manual production of such code. A path expression is a syntactic object and a collection of path expressions thus defines a grammar and hence determines a trace language; a collection can be thus thought of as defining a set of possible histories of concurrent behaviour. Formal analysis techniques for these behaviours have been developed (Shields 1979) for properties related to freedom from deadlock.

  Now as path expressions describe complete concurrent system behaviours in terms of appropriately chosen abstract entities, their application in development is rather restricted; other techniques are required to develop the abstract entities, for example, the read, WRITE and write procedures above. The modularity and compositionality criteria do not apply as only one level (the global view) of concurrent behaviour is described. Their expressiveness is limited in that not all possible sequences of possible behaviour are describable, but for their usual application (control of synchronisation) they appear rich enough. Path expressions are both easy to use and practical in the sense that straightforward efficient translation schemes exist (Campbell & Kolstad 1979). Simulation and formal analysis techniques are also possible, as has been demonstrated in BCS (Lauer 1983).

Temporal Logics

Temporal logic is a member of the class of modal logics and was designed in order to discuss the variability of situations over time. In essence they extend the propositional and predicate calculi with operators which enable such variability to be reasoned about. In the application of temporal logics to programs, typically the situations are states of the program and the temporal operators enable one to discuss with reference to a particular state the truth of statements occurring in the state, or in states in the future (past) of that state. The use of such logics in program semantics has been extensively studied for almost a decade and hence, as one might expect, many flavours of temporal logic exist, e.g. linear (past and) future time logics, branching time logics, interval temporal logics.

The basic application of temporal logic (linear time) to concurrent computation is given in Pnueli (1981). A simple shared variable model of concurrent program execution is used; given a global state (containing all variables used by the concurrent processes) an execution sequence of the concurrent program is any sequence of state values which satisfy conditions enforcing an interleaving of process execution. Temporal formulae can be given which state properties about such execution sequences. For example, given the temporal operators $\Box$ ($\Box P$ means P holds in every future state) and $\Diamond$ ($\Diamond P$ means P holds in some future state) one can formulate various safety and liveness properties; $\Box(x>2)$ states that x is always greater than 2, $\Diamond(x=0)$ states that from this moment on x is eventually 0, $\Box((y=1) \rightarrow \Diamond(x=10))$ states the property that whenever y is 1 there will a future moment when x is 10. Thus within this single framework both invariance properties (partial correctness, clean behaviour, mutual exclusion, deadlock freedom, etc.) and liveness properties (total correctness, accessibility, responsiveness, fairness, etc.) can be handled. Now, given the temporal semantics of a particular concurrent program (a temporal formula which is satisfied by just all possible executions of that program) such properties as above can be proven within the logical framework (Manna & Pnueli 1982, 1983b). In the paper (Manna & Pnueli 1983a) it is shown how to construct temporal proof systems for your own variety of language, both shared variable and message based communication mechanisms being handled.

Such application of temporal logic can be criticised for being global, non modular and non compositional. In order to formulate and verify a temporal property as above, it is necessary to possess the complete program. Thus although the temporal language, as used here, provides an excellent global specification and verification tool, there is little or no support for hierarchical and rigorous development. To overcome such difficulties it is necessary to extend the computational model to labelled execution sequences where the labelling essentially states the owner of a transition. Allowing such labels to appear as propositions in the logic, one can capture the notion of environment and component actions. Such a distinction allows modularity and compositionality of specifications. These approaches have been followed in the papers (Lamport 1983, Barringer & Kuiper 1983, Barringer et al. 1984). Lamport gives techniques for the specification and construction of concurrent programs modules. Specifications are presented in terms of the (temporal) behaviour of state functions, hierarchical development is then handled through refinement of state functions between the different levels of specification. Barringer & Kuiper (1983) present a specification style based upon purely externally observable quantities, simple parallel composition rules for specifications of components are obtained and the "independence principle" of above is achieved. In Barringer et al. (1984) these ideas are extended and complete compositional temporal proof systems are obtained for shared variable and CSP-like languages.

Another major criticism which has been raised against such temporal logics is that the temporal operators are too low level (Schwartz & Melliar-Smith 1982). In order to describe certain behaviours or contexts solely in terms of externally visible objects and the temporal operators such as ☐, ◊, until, large complex and difficult formulae result. This is quite often avoided by allowing auxiliary state components to be used, however, this can lead to a loss of abstractness in the specification. The higher level temporal operators of interval logic (Schwartz et al. 1983) have been developed to enable context descriptions to be given without resorting to "extra state". Such a logic clearly enhances the expressiveness advantages of standard temporal logics, but at the cost of complexity in decision procedures for the language.

Temporal logic specification techniques have been developed to fit into the complete software development cycle, however not much experience has yet been gained in this application. It is now known how to obtain (crude) compositional proof systems, thus meeting some of the modularity and compositionality criteria; however proof rules for certain combinations are not as easy as desired (this is still ongoing research). Of course, temporal proofs in a non-compositional manner are far from trivial! The logics are sufficiently expressive in order to capture desired safety and liveness properties (in the same framework), and some experiments to use a real-time temporal logic in protocol applications have been made (Koymans et al. 1983). Abstract specifications can be given although sometimes this appears to be at the expense of clarity. Some decision procedures (of high complexity) exist for the logics (see the papers of Plaisted, in Schwartz et al. 1983) and thus limited verification tool support is becoming available; again this is a highly active research area (Queille & Sifakis 1981). Furthermore there is active research involved in synthesising concurrent program skeletons from temporal logic specifications (Clarke & Emerson 1981, Manna & Wolper 1981).

CONCLUSION

It is apparent that none of the reviewed specifications yet possess all our desired features. This is in some sense is to be expected. Although the application of net theory in conccurrent systems has been studied extensively for the past twenty years, it is only very recently that effort has been directed at techniques for the development of concurrent programs. Similarly, the application of temporal logics has largely taken a global view of concurrent programs (for which, like net theory, it appears a very useful tool) and research attention has only recently focussed on compositional proof systems and developmental aspects. Temporal logics have the distinct advantage of being more expressive, but the disadvantage that the formulae are sometimes very difficult to read, let alone understand and then prove. Net theory clearly has the advantage that models are usually quite comprehensible, albeit somewhat big, but lacks in analysis techniques for all desired liveness properties.

For these techniques, however, some promising results are appearing in the research literature; naturally, though, much further research is required before such formal specification techniques can be easily applied in the complete development (from requirements to implementation) of parallel and distributed systems.

This short survey has addressed only three different types of formal specification techniques and the author apologises to all those whose work has not been mentioned or referenced. However, to have incorporated every technique would have been far beyond the scope of this current presentation.

ACKNOWLEDGEMENTS

The author expresses his thanks to the CEC for having supported his attendance at several Ada-Europe Working Group meetings, to the SERC for their financial support, and, in particular, to Bernd Krieg-Bruckner and other members of the Ada-Europe Working Group on Formal Methods for interesting discussions and their patience.

REFERENCES

Barringer, H. & Kuiper, R. (1983). Towards the Hierarchical, Temporal Logic, Specification of Concurrent Systems. In Proceedings of the STL/SERC Workshop on the Analysis of Concurrent Systems. Heidelberg: Springer Verlag.
Barringer, H., Kuiper, R. & Pnueli, A. (1984). Now You May Compose Temporal Logic Specifications. In Proceedings of the 13th ACM Symposium on the Theory of Computing. Washington.
Bjoener, D. & Jones, C.B. (1982). Formal Specification and Software Development. London: Prentice Hall International.
de Bondeli, P. (1983). Models for the Control of Concurrency in Ada based on Predicate-Transition Nets. In Proceedings of the Adatec / Ada-Europe Joint Conference on Ada, Brussels, 1983.

Campbell, R.H. & Habermann, A.N. (1974). The Specification of Process Synchronisation by Path Expressions. Lecture Notes in Computer Science, Vol. 16, pp. 89-102. Heidelberg: Springer Verlag.

Campbell, R.H. & Kolstad, R.B. (1979). Path Expressions in Pascal. In Proceedings of the 4th International Conference on Software Engineering, Munich.

Campos, I.M. & Extrin, G. (1978). Sara Aided Design of Software for Concurrent Systems. In Proceedings of the National Computer Conference.

Clarke, E.M. & Emerson, E.A. (1981). Synthesis of Synchronisation Skeletons for Branching Time Temporal Logic. In Proceedings of the Workshop on Logic of Programs, Lecture Notes in Computer Science, Vol. 131. Heidelberg: Springer-Verlag.

Genrich, H.J. & Lautenbach, K. (1979). The Analysis of Distributed Systems by means of Predicate Transition Nets. Lecture Notes in Computer Science, Vol. 70, pp. 123-146. Heidelberg: Springer Verlag.

Genrich, H.J., Lautenbach, K. & Thiagarajan, P.S. (1980). Elements of General Net Theory. In Lecture Notes for Computer Science, Vol. 84. Heidelberg: Springer-Verlag.

Genrich, H.J. & Lautenbach, K. (1981). System Modelling with High-level Petri Nets. Theoretical Computer Science, Vol. 13.

Goldsack, S.J. & Morton, T. (1982). Ada package specifications: path expressions and monitors. IEE Proceedings, Vol. 129, Pt. E, No. 2, pp. 49-54.

Hoare, C.A.R. (1981). A Calculus for Total Correctness for Communicating Sequential Processes. Science of Computer Programming, *1*, pp. 49-72.

Jensen, K. (1981). Coloured Petri Nets and the Invariant Method. Theoretical Computer Science, Vol. 14.

Jones, C.B. (1980). Software Development: a rigorous approach. London: Prentice-Hall International.

Jones, C.B. (1983). Specification and Design of (Parallel) Programs. In Proceedings of IFIP 83, pp. 321-332. North Holland.

Koymans, R., Vytopil, J. & de Roever, W.-P. (1983). A Real-time Temporal Logic for Asynchronous Message Passing. In Proceedings of the 2nd ACM Symposium on the Principles of Distributed Computing.

Lamport, L. (1983). Specifying Concurrent Program Modules. ACM Transactions on Programming Languages and Systems, Vol. 5, No. 2, pp 190-222.

Lauer, P.E. & Campbell, R.H. (1975). Formal semantics fro a class of high-level primitives for co-ordinating concurrent processes. Acta Informatica 5, pp. 297-332.

Lauer, P.E., Torrigiani, P.R. & Shields, M.W. (1979). COSY: A System Specification Language Based on Paths and Processes. Acta Informatica, Vol. 12, pp. 109-158.

Lauer, P.E. (1980). Users introduction to BCS: A computer based environment for specifying, analysing and verifying concurrent systems. Report ASM/107, Computing Laboratory, University of Newcastle-upon-Tyne.

Levitt, K., Robinson, L. & Silverberg, B. (1979). The HDM Handbook. SRI International, Menlo Park, California.

Lucas, P. (1978). On the Formalisation of Programming Languages: Early History and Main Approaches. In The Vienna Development Method: The Meta Language, ed. D. Bjoerner, C.B. Jones. Lecture Notes in Computer Science, Vol. 61. Heidelberg: Springer Verlag.

McGettrick, A. (1982). Program Verification and Ada. IEE Proceedings, Vol. 129, Pt. E, No. 2, pp. 55-62.

Milner, R. (1980). A Calculus of Communicating Systems. Lecture Notes in Computer Science, Vol. 92. Heidelberg: Springer Verlag.

Manna, Z. & Pnueli, A. (1982). Verification of Concurrent Programs: The Temporal Framework. In The Correctness Problem in Computer Science, ed. R.S. Boyer & J.S. Moore, pp. 215-273. International Lecture Series in Computer Science. London: Academic Press.

Manna, Z. & Pnueli, A. (1983a). How to Cook A Temporal Proof System for your Pet Language. Proceedings of the 10th ACM Symposium on Principles of Programming Languages, Austin, Texas, pp. 101-154.

Manna, Z. & Pnueli, A. (1983b). Verification of COncurrent Programs: A Temporal Proof System. In Foundations of Computer Science IV, ed. J.W.DeBakker & J.Van Leuven, Mathematical Centre Tracts No.159, pp. 163-255.

Manna, Z. & Wolper, P. (1981). Synthesis of Communicating Processes from Temporal Logic Specifications. In Proceedings of the Workshop on Logic of Programs, Lecture Notes in Computer Science, Vol. 131. Heidelberg: Springer-Verlag.

Owicki, S.S. & Lamport, L. (1982). Proving liveness properties of concurrent programs. ACM Transactions on Programming Languages and Systems, Vol. 4, No. 3, pp. 455-495.

Petri, C.A. (1962). Kommunikation mit Automaten. Schriften des IIM 2, Institute fur Instrumentelle Mathematik, Bonn, W.Germany.

Pnueli, A. (1981). The Temporal Semantics of Concurrent Computation. Theoretical Computer Science, Vol. 13, pp. 45-60.

Prehn, S., Hansen, I.O., Palm, S.U. & Gobel, P. (1983). Final Report of an ESPRIT preparatory study "Formal Methods Appraisal". Technical Report DDC 86/1983-06-24. Dansk Datamatik Center.

Queille, J.P. & Sifakis, J. (1981). Specification and Verification of Concurrent Systems in CESAR. In Proceedings of the Fifth International Symposium in Programming.

Schwartz, R.L. & Melliar-Smith, P.M. (1982). From State Machines to Temporal Logic: Specification Methods for Protocol Standards. IEEE Transactions on Communications, Dec. 1982.

Schwartz, R.L., Melliar-Smith, P.M., Vogt, F.H. & Plaisted, D.A. (1983). An Interval Logic for Higher-Level Temporal Reasoning. NASA Contractor Report 172262, SRI International, California.

Shields, M.W. (1979). Adequate Path Expressions. Lecture Notes in Computer Science, Vol. 70, pp. 249-284. Heidelberg: Springer-Verlag.

Vidondo, F., Lopez, I. & Girod, J.J. (1980). Galileo System Design Method. Electrical Communication, Vol. 55, No. 4.

"ADAKOM"

ELECTRONIC MAIL AND CONFERENCING FACILITY FOR THE ADA COMMUNITY

A. Patel
University College of Dublin

M. W. Rogers
Commission of the European Communities

1 INTRODUCTION

One of the earliest needs identified by the Ada Europe group was the necessity of an efficient European communications facility that provided some of the functionalities supplied to the US R & D community by ARPANET. The Ada Europe Information WG formulated a set of requirements in late 1982 and submitted them to its host committee, the Working Group on Standards. By mid 1983, the pilot phase of ESPRIT had initiated a system to meet its own infrastructure needs.

2 ADAKOM

In late 1983 the Commission, having fully tested the ESPRIT facility, instantiated the identical software for the Ada community. The system installed is the KOM System from QZ University Computer Centre, Stockholm, Sweden which is currently the object of support under the community COST 11 programme. A dedicated machine operates under secure conditions in UCD Dublin, and may be accessed via IPS, Euronet or direct dial up lines. The user needs only to be able to emulate a simple teletype configuration.

Use of the system for the first year is subsidized by the Multi-Annual Programme to 50%, for the membership of Ada-Europe.

3 ADAKOM - TECHNICAL OUTLINE

The system is a series of objects (names, conferences, texts, notices) handled in a database with circular lists. Different objects have different attributes, which allows a deal of flexibility.

A <u>letter</u> is a text originating from one point to one or more points. Once received, a comment can be directed back to the point of origin (personal) or to all recipients. Comment trees are thus built up and can be retrieved in a similar sequence.

A <u>conference</u> is a collection of individuals, under an organiser, who discuss a common theme. Entries (notices) into a conference are available to all members of the open or closed conference. Outsiders can write letters into any conference.

Letters or Notices have destination lists maintained on them, and verification of receipt of text is therefore possible.

Address and contact details of users are easily accessible.

Each Ada Europe Working Group maintains a conference on itself, and users join other conferences as interests dictate (eg Ada News Headlines, Ada Companion Series).

A full database, 3RIP, is also available, with full text indexing as a default, in inverted lists.

The underlying TOPS20 system is also easily accessible.

Forwarding to other KOM systems and ARPANET are being pursued.

4 SOME OF THE ADVANTAGES OF ADAKOM

- Ada Europe membership spreads across over a dozen countries with almost as many languages. People comprehend and communicate more efficiently in a foreign language if the text is written.

- Physical meetings have critical sizes - computer conferences have no limit on effective participation. The more the better!

- Travel time is zero; saving exhaustion, time and money. For Europe, this is a major obstacle and source of inefficiency.

- It is easy to poll opinion in short timescales, independent of letter carrying services.

- Scanning allows selective reading.

- Reviewing allows comment paths to be traced automatically, allowing use as a filing system (of about 9 months retention).

- Interactive facility available.

- Multiple membership allows users to follow all lines of interest in parallel.

ADAKOM 297

- Offline text preparation is possible, then downloading at high speed (and vice versa) minimizes connect time.

- Dual password facilities give a high security level.

- Built in editor allows message editing prior to sending.

- Can be used as memo pad to oneself (marking).

5 SOME OF THE DRAWBACKS

- A telephone, modem and terminal are essentials.

- The national P.T.T. usually needs to authorize the data transfer lines, which may require a long lead time.

- The scan command has no string variable context search parameters.

- Some network nodes are less reliable than others, often needing direct international dialling if delays of up to 2 hours cannot be tolerated.

- Control characters from offline preparation will often not be implemented in the recipients terminal, as it is often a different sort.

- Access to a printer is a practical desirability.

- Texts have the legal status of telephone calls only.

6 JOINING ADAKOM

1 Enquire at your local P.T.T. for the necessary requirements.

2 Write, stating

- Your name and address

- Invoicing address, if different

- An initial 6 letter password (ASCII)

- Agreement to pay charges

to M W Rogers, A25 8/12A, CEC, 200 Rue de la Loi, B 1049 Brussels, Belgium.

3 You will receive a joining "Toolkit" and manuals from the facility in University College of Dublin (UCD), and you may then join.

4 Note : Ada Europe members receive a 50% subsidy under certain circumstances.

THE 1985 "ADA IN USE" CONFERENCE

INTRODUCTION

This will be held in Paris, France, 14-16th May 1985. It it the Ada event of 1985, and attendance is estimated at over 500 people.

The theme is a word play - the conference is to report on Ada in use in real applications, and as it is the joint initiative of Ada Europe and Ada TEC (which will be elevated to SIGADA by that time), the title reflects the union of US(A) and E(urope).

THE TECHNICAL PROGRAMME

Authors are invited to submit papers on topics relating to Ada programming language and its use. Particular areas of interest include:

"Infrastructure" for the use of Ada
- Training, both traditional and automated approaches
- Views of current and future use of Ada
- Transition to Ada
- Project Management

Compilers
- Compiler construction
- Optimization techniques
- Compiler validation
- Run-time support
- 'Mixed languages' component linkages

Design Methods
- Specification techniques
- Reusable software components
- Configuration control

Application Areas
- Embedded systems
- Special-purpose hardware support
- Telecommunications
- Database management systems
- Commercial applications
- Graphics

Ada Programming Support Environments
- Tools
- Debugging
- Transportability and interoperability

THE CONFERENCE COMMITTEE

Conference Co-Chairman   J.A.N. Lee   H. Hünke
Conference Secretary   M.W. Rogers
Programme Co-Chairman   G. Fisher   J.G.P. Barnes
Conference Coordinator   J. Ichbiah

Authors should prepare an extended abstract (no more than 6 pages), in 10 copies to each of the programme chairmen:

Dr. John Barnes
11 Albert Road
Caversham
Reading RG4 7AN
Berks
Great Britain

1985 Conference

Dr. Gerry Fisher
IBM Research
Rm 34-137
P.O. BOX 218
Yorktown Heights
NY 10598
USA

IMPORTANT DATES:

November 1, 1984:   Extended Abstracts Due
January 15, 1984:   Notification of Acceptance
   May 15, 1985:   Completed Papers Due

Proceedings to be published by September 1985.

Mike W. Rogers

LIST OF ADA EUROPE OFFICERS AND WORKING GROUPS

ADA Europe Officers

Chairman	K. Ripken	CGE F
Vice Chairman	M. Boasson	HSA NL
Secretary	G. Glynn	Ferranti UK

Working Groups and Chairmen

Environment	J. Nissen	GEC UK
Formal Spec.	B. Krieg-Brückner	U. Bremen D
Formal Def.	J. Stoy	U. Oxford UK
CIM	D. Vojnovic	Renault F
Telecomm.	C. Bjoerkvall	Telelogic Sw
Portability	J. Nissen	GEC UK
Numerics	B. Ford	NAG UK
Information	M. Jackson	STL UK
Validation	E. Wegner	GMD D
Language Review	C. Lester	Portsmouth Poly UK

List of Attendees

Ms V. Almstrum
Philips Elektronik Industry, S-17588 Jarfalla, Sweden

Mr A. Alvarez
Facultad de Informatica, CRTRA, Valencia KM 7, Madrid 31, Spain

Mr A. Ardo
University of Lund, Box 725, S-220 07 Lund, Sweden

Mr F. Arribas
Sancho Davila, 24-20E Madrid, Spain

Mr P.O. Bain
Marconi Radar Systems, Writtle Road, Chelmsford, Essex, United Kingdom

Mr C. Barkey
TNO IBBC, Delft, The Netherlands

Mr J.G.P. Barnes
Ada Group Ltd, Prestcold Building, Station Road, Theale, Berkshire, United Kingdom

Mr H. Barringer
Department of Computing, University of Manchester, Oxford Road, Manchester M13 9PL, United Kingdom

Mr B. Basdell
SPL International, The Charter, Abingdon, Oxford OX14 3UE, United Kingdom

Mr P. Baudouin
ROLM UK, Dorner House, Guildford Road, West End, Surrey GU24 9PW, United Kingdom

Mr M. Bidoit
Laboratoire de Recherche en Informatique, 490 Universite Paris-Sud, F-91405 Orsay Cedex, France

Mr C. Bjoerkvall
Telelogic AB, S-12386 Farsta, Sweden

Mr S. Bjornson
Telelogic, Box 1001, S-14901 Nunashamn, Sweden

List of Attendees

Mr M. Boasson
Vice Chairman Ada Europe, Hollandes Signaal Apparaten, Dpt SEAT,
Box 42, NL-7550 GD Hangelo, The Netherlands

Ms S.K. Boestad-Nilsson
Research Institute of National Defence, Box 27322, S-10254 Stockholm, Sweden

Mr N. Bogstad
Digital Equipment SA, 1 Rue de l'Aeronef, B-1140 Brussels, Belgium

Mr P. de Bondeli
14 Boulevard Jean Mermoz, Neuilly-sur-Seine, France

Mr C. Bonnet
TECSI Software, 29 Rue des Pyramides, F-75001 Paris, France

Mr H.J. Bos
National Aerospace Laboratory, Box 90502, NL-1006 BM Amsterdam, The Netherlands

Mr P. Boulle
Thomson-VSF/Laboratoire Central de Recherche, BP 10, F-91401 Orsay Cedex, France

Mr Branquart
Philips Research Laboratory, 2 Avenue van Becelaere - Bte 8, 9-1170 Brussels
Belgium

Mr R.K. Brewer
GEC Computer Ltd, Boreham Wood, Hertfordshire, United Kingdom

Mr B.M. Brosgol
ALSYS Inc., 400-1 Totten Pond Road, Waltham, Massachussetts 02154, United States

Mr J. Bruin
PHL-TNO, Box 96864, NL-2509 YG den Hague, The Netherlands

Dr A. Burns
Computer Science Department, University of Bradford, Bradford BD7 DP,
West Yorkshire, United Kingdom

Mr A.J. Burton
Department of Industry, 29 Bressenden Place, London SW1E 5DT, United Kingdom

Mr A. Camici
CSELT, 274 Via G. Reiss Romoli, I-10148 Torino, Italy

Mr G. Canevet
Informatique Int., 20 Rue Saarinen SILIC 232, F-94578 Rungis-Cedex, France

Mr I. Carlsson
Forsvarets Materielverk, Kameralbyran, Stockholm, Sweden

Mr U Cederling
Rotvagen 4, S-360 51 Hovmantorp, Sweden

Mr A. Chantler
Coventry Polytechnic, Priory Street, Coventry CV1 5FB, West Midlands,
United Kingdom

List of Attendees

Mr A. Chatenay
CIMSA, 10-12 Avenue de l'Europe, F-678160 Velisy, France

Mr R. Cochran
National Board of Science and Technology, Shelbourne House, Shelbourne Road, Dublin 4, Ireland

Mr M.W. Cornelious
Norsk Data Ltd, Strawberry Hill House, Bath Road, Newbury, Berkshire, United Kingdom

Mr G. Dismukes
Telesoft, 10639 Roselle Street, San Diego, CA 92121, United States

Mr V.A. Downes
Department of Computing, Imperial College, 180 Queens Gate, London SW7 2BZ, United Kingdom

Mr L. Druffel
Rational, 1501 Salado Drive, Mountain View, CA 94043, United States

Mr A.G. Duncan
GEC Corporation, Research and Development Building, K1W Room C281A, Schenectady, NY 12345, United States

Mr I. Duncan
Ferranti Plc, Ferry Road, Edinburgh EH5 2XS, United Kingdom

Mr J. Elliot
ROLM (UK) Ltd, Dorner House, Guildford Road, West End, Surrey GU24 9PW, United Kingdom

Mr A.D. Espado
Virgen de Loreto, 10-50B Alcala de Henares, Madrid, Spain

Mr J. Estdale
GEC Computers Ltd, Elstree Way, Boreham Wood, Hertfordshire, United Kingdom

Dr M. Feldman
6218 Wagner Lane, Bethesda, MD 20816, United States

Mr G. Fisher
IBM Research, Box 218 RM33-128, Yorktown Heights, NY 10598, United States

Mr B. Fougstedet
Telelogic AB, S-12386 Farsta, Sweden

Mr A. Gargaro
Computer Science Corporation, 304 W. Rte 38, Moorestown, NJ 08034, United States

Dr W.P. Gertenbach
NUCOR, c/o South African Embassy, London, United Kingdom

Mr A. Gibson
ROLM (UK) Ltd, Dorner House, Guildford Road, West End, Surrey GU24 9PW, United Kingdom

List of Attendees

Mr A. Gilbert
Systems Designers Ltd, 1, Pembroke Broadway, Camberley, Surrey GU15 3XH, United Kingdom

Mr J.G. Glynn
Secretary Ada Europe, Ferranti Computer Systems Ltd, Ty Coch Way, Cwmbran, Gwent NP44 7XX, Wales, United Kingdom

Professor S.J. Goldsack
Department of Computer Science, Imperial College, 180 Queens Gate, London SW7 2BZ, United Kingdom

Mr J.B. Goodenough
SofTech Inc., 460 Totten Pond Road, Waltham, Mass 02254 United States

Ms I Gravitis
SA1, Goodridge Drive, McLean, VA 22102, United States

Mr G. Grazia
Telettra Spa, c/o Rolm (UK), Dorner House, Guildford Road, West End, Surrey GU24 9PW, United Kingdom

Mr A. Hall
SPL International, The Charter, Abingdon, Oxford OX14 3UE, United Kingdom

Mr N.J. Hardy
Norsk Data Ltd, Strawberry Hill House, Bath Road, Newbury, Berkshire, United Kingdom

Mr M. Haug
Pixistrasse 2, D-8000 Munich 80, West Germany

Mr M. Heitz
Information International, 2 Rue Jules Vedrihes, F-31400 Toulouse, France

Mr B. Henin
Compagnies des Machines Bull, Centre de Recherche, 68 Route de Versailles, F-78430 Louveciennes, France

Mr P. Hilfinger
University of California, EECS Berkeley, CA 94720, United States

Dr A.H. Hill
CEGB, Laud House, 16 Newgate Street, London EC1A 7AX, United Kingdom

Mr A.P. Hill
Plessey Electronic Systems Ltd, Grange Road, Christchurch, Dorset BH23 4JB, United Kingdom

Dr G.S. Hodgson
NAG, Mayfield House, 256 Banbury Road, Oxford, United Kingdom

Mr M. Hodgson
GKN Technology, New Birmingham Road, Wolverhampton, United Kingdom

Mr C.F. Howard
Prospect House, The Grove, Ilkley, Yorkshire, United Kingdom

List of Attendees

Dr H. Hummel
IABG, Einsteinstrásse 20, D-8012 Ottobrunn, West Germany

Ms C. Hunt
Data General, Tour Manhattan, 5-6 Place d'Iris, F-92095 Paris, France

Mr J.R. Hunt
Plessey Electronic Systems Research Ltd, Roke Manor, Romsey, Hampshire, United Kingdom

Mr J. Itell
131/4 Hansallee, D-6000 Frankfurt am Main 1, West Germany

Mr B. Jorgensen
Telelogic AB, S-12386 Farsta Sweden

Mr L. Juuinen
Nokia Electronics, Box 780 SF-00101 Helsinki 10, Finland

Mr T. Kaer
Ericsson Radio Systems, AB Box 1001, S-73126 Moelndal, Sweden

Mr R. Kaufmann
Telesoft, 10639 Roselle Street, San Diego, CA 92122, United States

Mr R. Keyser
SPS Division, CERN, Geneva 23, Switzerland

Mr R. Kivipuro
Box 209, SF-33101 Tampere, Finland

Mr D., Klein
ROLM (UK) Ltd, Dorner House, Guildford Road, West End, Surrey GU24 9PW, United Kingdom

Mr P.A. Knoop
1476 Whispering Wood Lane, Springboro, OH 45066, United States

Mr H. Kok
PHL-TNO, Box 96864 NL-1009 YG Den Hague, The Netherlands

Mr J. Kok
Centrum voor Wiskunde en Informatica (CWI-MC), Box 4079, NL-1009 AB Amsterdam
The Netherlands

Mr J.F. Kramer
Institute for Defense Analysis, 1801 N Beauregard Street, Alexandria, VA 22311
United States

Mr B. Krieg-Brueckner
FB3 Mathematik-Informatik, Universitat Bremen, Postfach 330 440, D-2800 Bremen 33, West Germany

Dr Kronig
Dornier Gmbh ABt., D-7990 Friedrichshafen 1, West Germany

List of Attendees

Mr P. Kruchten
TELIC ALCATEL, 206 Route de Colmar, F-67023 Strasbourg Cedex, France

Mr M.G. Lamarche
ESD 55, Juani Canart, F-92214 St Cloud, France

Mr T. Lamminpaa
Nokia Electronics, Box 780 SF-00101 Helsinki 10, Finland

Mr T. Large
Telelogic AB, S-12386 Farsta, Sweden

Mr R. Leavitt
Prior Data Sciences Ltd, 39 Highway 7, Ottawa, Ontario K2H 8R2, Canada

Mr J.A.N. Lee
Virginia Tech, Department of Computer Science, Blacksburg, VA 24061, United States

Mr B. Lennartsson
Linkoping University, S-58183 Linkoping, Sweden

Dr F.W. Long
Computer Science Department, University College of Wales, Aberystwyth SY23 3BZ, Wales, United Kingdom

Mr T. Lyons
Software Sciences Ltd, Abbey House, Farnborough Road, Farnborough, Hampshire, United Kingdom

Mr M. Mac an Airchinnigh
Computer Science Department, University of Dublin, Trinity College, Dublin, Ireland

Mr R.H. Mackay
Aerospace Management Systems, Rue de Geneve 10, B-1140 Brussels, Belgium

Mr R.F. Maddock
IBM UK Laboratories, Hursley Park, Winchester SO21 2JN, United Kingdom

Mr L. Mansson
Telelogic AB, Baltzarsgat 22, S-21136 Malmo, Sweden

Mr A. Mastoras
Greek Productivity Centre, 28 Kapodistriou Street, Athens 106, Greece

Mr R. Mathis
AJPO, The Pentagon (3D139 AN), Washington DC 20301, United States

Mr M. Matsumoto
GTE Gov. Systems Corp., Box 7188-5G09, Mountain View, CA 94043, United States

Mr O. Maurel
TECSI Software, 29 Rue des Pyramides, F-75001 Paris, France

Mr D. McGlade
GEC Software Ltd, 132-135 Long Acre, London WC2E 9AM, United Kingdom

List of Attendees

Mr E. Meiling
Dansk Datamatic Centre, Lundfevej 1c, DK-2800 Lyngby, Denmark

Mr S. Mickel
237 Sierra Vista Avenue, Mountain View, CA 94043, United States

Mr A. Mikkola
Nokia Electronics, Box 780 SF-00101 Helsinki 10, Finland

Mr P. Miller
Norsk Data Ltd, Strawberry Hill House, Bath Road, Newbury, Berkshire, United Kingdom

Ms. D. Misler
ITALTEL-TELEMATICA, Laboratori IV A, Castelletto di Settimo Milanese, I-20019 Milano, Italy

Mr V. Moore
8 Avenue du Triangle, B-1420 Braine-L'Alleud, Belgium

Mr R. Moranchel
Ceselsa Division, Sistemas Radar, Apartdo 36189, Madrid, Spain

Mr E. Morel
ALSYS, Centre de la Chataigneraie, 29 Avenue de Versailles, F-78170 La Celle St Cloud, France

Mr M.R. Morron
73 Kiln Road, Reading RG4 8UF, Berkshire, United Kingdom

Mr B.S. Mossakowski
Systems Designers Ltd, 1 Pembroke Broadway, Camberley, Surrey GU15 3XH, United Kingdom

Mr M. Meunier
Electronique Serge Dassault, 55 Quai Carnot, F-92214 St Cloud, France

Mr H. Muhl-Kuhner
ROLM (UK) Ltd, Dorner House, Guildford Road, West End, Surrey GU24 9PW, United KIngdom

Mr F. Mulheim
Coutraves AG, Schaffhauser Strasse 580, CH-8052 Zurich, Switzerland

Mr K.G. Muller
SHAPE Technical Centre, Box 2501 Den Hague, The Netherlands

Mr T. Muth
Swedish Telecom Admin. Sect., Ptf Farnebogatan 81-87, S-12386 Farsta, Sweden

Mr G Myers
Naval Ocean Systems Center, Code 423, San Diego, CA 92152, United States

Mr J. Nissen
GEC Software Ltd, 132-135 Long Acre, London WC2E 9AH, United Kingdom

List of Attendees

Mr F. Norring
Danish Telecom, STT C-Mos Farvergade 17, Dk-1007 Copenhagen K, Denmark

Mr E. Nurmi
OK Softplan AB, Box 209, SF-33101 Tampere 10, Finland

Mr A. Orme
ROLM (UK), Dorner House, Guildford Road, West End, Surrey GU24 9PW,
United Kingdom

Mr O.N. Oest
Dansk Datamatic Centre, Lundtoftvej 1c, DK-2800 Lyngby, Denmark

Mr A. Patel
Eurokom, University College Dublin Computer Centre, Belfield, Dublin 4,
Ireland

Mr G. Persch
GMD, Forshungstelle Karlsruhe, Postfach 6380, Hald-und-Neu Strasse 10-14,
Karlsruhe 1, West Germany

Mr A.H. Pepperdine
Norsk Data Ltd, Strawberry Hill House, Bath Road, Newbury, Berkshire
United Kingdom

Mr M.J. Pickett
CAP Reading Ltd, Trafalgar House, Richfield Avenue, Reading, Bershire,
United Kingdom

Mr D. Pidwell
ROLM (UK) Dorner House, Guildford Road, West End, Surrey GU24 9PW,
United Kingdom

Mr E. Ploederer
c/o Tartan Laboratories, 477 Melwood Avenue, Pittsburgh PA 15213,
United States

Mr K.J. Pulford
Marconi Avionics, Airborune S/W Div., Elstree Way, Borehamwood,
Hertfordshire, United Kingdom

Professor I.C. Pile
Department of Computer Science, University of York, York YO11 5DD,
United Kingdom

Mr M. Quinones
Plaza de la Estacion, 9 Bis - 4D, Alcala de Henares, Madrid, Spain

Mr Refice
Department of Computer Science, University of Bari, Italy

Ms I.L. Bratteby-Ribbing
Philips Elektronikindustrier AB, ST Olafsgatan 9b III, S-753 Uppsala, Sweden

Mr I. Richmond
Edinburgh Regional Computing Centre, 59 Georges Square, Edinburgh EH8 9JU,
United Kingdom

List of Attendees

Mr K. Ripkin
Chairman Ada Europe, Laboratoires de Marcoussis-CGE, Route de Nozay,
F-91460 Marcoussis, France

Dr M.W. Rogers
Commission of European Communities, A25 8/12A, 200 Rue de la Loi,
B-1049 Brussels, Belgium

Mr J.K. Romanski
Systems Designers Ltd, Systems House, 1 Pembroke Broadway, Camberley,
Surrey GU15 3XH, United Kingdom

Mr J.P. Rosen
CIMS/NYU, 251 Mercer Street, New York, NY 10012, United States

Mr O. Roubine
Informatique Internationale, 20 Rue Saarinen SILIC 232, F-94578 Rungis Cedex
France

Mr W. Russell
High Integrity Sytems Ltd, 41 Bell Street, Sawbridgeworth, Hertfordshire,
United Kingdom

Mr K.L. Ryder
Marconi Radar Systems Ltd, Writtle Road, Chelmsford, Essex, United Kingdom

Mr A. Salava
Nokia Electronics, Box 780 SF-00101 Helsinki, Finland

Mr J. Sammet
IBM Federal Systems Division, 6600 Rockledge Drive, Bethesda MD 20817,
United States

Mr S. Savion
c/o ROLM (UK), Dorner House, Guildford Road, West End, Surrey GU24 9PW,
United Kingdom

Mr B. Schaar
AJPO, 3D139-400AW, The Pentagon, Washington DC 20301, United States

Dr U. Schmitt
Signal Computer Gmbh, Niebelungen Strasse 35, D-6140 Bensheim 1, West Germany

Mr E. Schonberg
NYU-CIMS, 251 Mercer Street, New York, NY 10012, United States

Dr M. Selwood
Plessey Defence Systems Ltd, Abbey Works, Titchfield, Fareham,
Hampshire PO14 4QA, United Kingdom

Dr J. Sidi
BNI, BP 105, F-78153 Le Chesnay Cedex, France

Mr W. Simonsmeir
PSI Gmbh, Heilbronner Strasse 10, D-1000 Berlin 31, West Germany

List of Attendees

Mr K. Skarvall
Telelogic, Box 1001, S-14901 Nynashamn, Sweden

Mr J. Slape
Plessey Defence Systems Ltd, Future Systems Group, Grange Road, Somerford, Christchurch, Dorset BH23 4JE, United Kingdom

Mr M. Slusarczuk
Insitute for Defense Analysis, 1801 N. Beauregard Street, Alexandria, VA 22311 United States

Ms A.M. Staugaard
NCR Systems Engineering, Copenhagen, Haslegade 16, Dk 2100, Copenhagen 0, Denmark

Mr J. Stell
University of Strathclyde, Livingstone Tower, 26 Richmond Street, Glasgow G11 XH, Scotland, United Kingdom

Mr D. Stewart
Data General Ltd, London Road, Hounslow, Middlesex, TW3 1PD, United Kingdom

Mr W. Suske
Nixdorf Computer AG, Leopoldstrasse 208, D-8000 Munich 40, West Germany

Dr G.T. Symm
National Physical Laboratory, Division of Information Technology and Computing, Teddington, Middlesex TW11 0LW, United Kingdom

Mr S. Tarkiainen
Nokia Electronics, Box 780 SF-00101 Helsinki 10, Finland

Mr M. Tasch
Bundesamt fur Wehrtechnik, FEVI 2, D-5400 Koblenz, West Germany

Mr M. Tedd
University College of Wales, Department of Computer Science, Aberystwyth, Wales, United Kingdom

Mr J. Teller
Siemens AG, DV 263, Otto Hahn Ring 6, D-8000 Munich 83, West Germany

Sq.Ldr. C. Tily
RAF Strike Command, High Wycombe, United Kingdom

Mr C. Tyndale Bisco
ROLM (UK), Dorner House, Guildford Road, West End, Surrey GU24 9PW United Kingdom

Mr E. Uthke
IABG, Einsteinstrasse 20, D-8012 Ottobrunn, West Germany

Mr C.M.A. van den Berg
ESA ESOC, Robert Borschstrasse 5, D-6100 Darmstadt, West Germany

Mr J.D. van der Eersten
Physisch Laboratory TNO, Box 9 68 64, NL-2509 JG The Hague, The Netherlands

List of Attendees

Mr I. G. van den Hanenberg
Philips CFT, Building SAQ, NL-5600 MD Eindhoven, The Netherlands

Mr C. G van der Laan
Rekencentrum RUG, Postbus 800 NL-9700 AV Landleven 1, Groningen, The Netherlands

Mr R. van Leire
Physisch Laboratorium TNO, Box 9 68 64, NL-2509 JG The Hague, The Netherlands

Dr P.J. Wallis
Department of Computer Science, University of Bath, Claverton Down,
Bath BA2 7AY, United Kingdom

Mr E. Wegner
GMD Postfach 1240, D-5205 San Augustin 1, West Germany

Mr R. P. Wehrum
Siemens AG, Department ZTI SOF2, Otto Hahn Ring 6, D-8000 Munich 83,
West Germany

Ms R.C. Weiss
Ford Aerospace Corporation, 3939 Fabian Way, MS X-21 Paolo Alto, CA 94303,
United States

Mr W. Westermann
TNO IBBC, Software Engineering Department, Lange Kleiweg 5, Rijswijk (z.h.),
Box 49, NL-2600 AA Delft, The Netherlands

Mr T.A.D White
Royal Signals and Radar Establishment, MoD (PE), St Andrews Road,
Malvern WR14 3PS, Worcestershire, United Kingdom

Mr B.A. Wichmann
National Physical Laboratory, Teddington, Middlesex TW11 0LW, United Kingdom

Mr O. Wikstroem
Ericsson Radio Stystems, H/RFK, Box 1001, S-43126 Molndal, Sweden

Mr M.C. Williams
Ericsson, Dept TN/XT/DU, S-12625, Stockholm, Sweden

Mr D.T. Winter
Centrum voor Wiskunde en Informatica, Box 4079, NL-1009 AB Amsterdam,
The Netherlands

Mr G. Winterstein
Systeam KG, AM Entenfang 10, D-7500 Karlsruhe 21, West Germany

Mr M. Woodger
10 Ottways Lane, Ashstead, Surrey KT21 2NZ, United Kingdom

Mr J. Wylie
Cossor Electronics Ltd, The Pinnacles, Harlow, Essex CM19 5BB, United Kingdom

Mr K.H. Yap
SELENIA Spa, Via Tiburtina Km 12.4, I-00131 Roma, Italy